Sociology of Health and Illness Monograph Series

Edited by Jonathan Gabe
Department of Social and Political Science
Royal Holloway
Egham
Surrey
TW20 0EX
UK

Current titles:

- **Partners in Health, Partners in Crime:**
  Exploring the boundaries of criminology and sociology of health and illness
  edited by *Stefan Timmermans and Jonathan Gabe*
- **Rationing: Constructed Realities and Professional Practices,**
  edited by *David Hughes and Donald Light*
- **Rethinking the Sociology of Mental Health (2000),**
  edited by *Joan Busfield*
- **Sociological Perspectives on the New Genetics (1999),**
  edited by *Peter Conrad and Jonathan Gabe*
- **The Sociology of Health Inequalities (1998),**
  edited by *Mel Bartley, David Blane and George Davey Smith*
- **The Sociology of Medical Science (1997),**
  edited by *Mary Ann Elston*
- **Health and the Sociology of Emotion (1996),**
  edited by *Veronica James and Jonathan Gabe*
- **Medicine, Health and Risk (1995),**
  edited by *Jonathan Gabe*

Forthcoming title:

Health and the Media
Edited by *Clive Seale*

Partners in Health, Partners in Crime

Exploring the Boundaries of
Criminology and Sociology
of Health and Illness

Edited by
Stefan Timmermans and *Jonathan Gabe*

Blackwell
Publishing

First published as Volume 24 number 5 of *Sociology of Health and Illness*

350 Main Street, Malden, MA 02148-5018, USA
108 Cowley Road, Oxford OX4 1JF, UK
550 Swanston Street, Carlton South, Melbourne, Victoria 3053, Australia
Kurfürstendamm 57, 10707 Berlin, Germany

First published 2003 by Blackwell Publishing Ltd

Library of Congress Cataloging-in-Publication Data has been applied for

ISBN 1-4051-0539-9

A catalogue record for this title is available from the British Library.

Set by Graphicraft Typesetters Limited, Hong Kong
Printed and bound in the United Kingdom
by MPG Books Ltd, Bodmin, Cornwall

For further information on
Blackwell Publishing, visit our website:
http://www.blackwellpublishing.com

Contents

Notes on Contributors

Sarah Armstrong is Lecturer in Criminology at the Centre for Law and Society, University of Edinburgh. She has a JD and is completing a PhD at the University of California, Berkeley. Her research interests are in the areas of the sociology of punishment, social history of penal reform and the privatisation of punishment. An article on the meaning and role of non-profit organisations in juvenile justice is due to be published shortly in the journal *Punishment and Society*.

David Denney is Reader in Social and Public Policy at Royal Holloway, University of London. He has published in the area of race and social policy and has recently completed a comparative study of race and the workings of the Canadian and UK criminal justice systems. He is the author of a number of books including *Racism and Antiracism in Probation* (Routledge 1992), *Social Work and Social Policy* (Oxford University Press 1998) and is currently writing a book that examines the impact of race on professional practices.

Mary Ann Elston is Senior Lecturer in Sociology at Royal Holloway, University of London and Course Director of the MSc in Medical Sociology there. Her research interests are in the history and organisation of medical work, gender in health care and in medical science and technology.

Jonathan Gabe is Reader in Sociology at Royal Holloway, University of London. His research interests include health care organisation, chronic illness and mental health. He is the author of *Going Private* (with Michael Calnan and Sarah Cant) (Open University Press 1993) and a number of edited collections including *Medicine, Health and Risk* (Blackwell 1995), *Health and the Sociology of Emotions* (with Veronica James) (Blackwell 1996), *Sociological Perspectives on the New Genetics* (with Peter Conrad) (Blackwell 1999) and *Theorising Health, Medicine and Society* (with Simon Williams and Michael Calnan) (Routledge 2000).

Emilie Gomart received her doctorate from the Ecole Nationale Superieure des Mines de Paris and is now a postdoctoral researcher in the Department of Political Science, University of Amsterdam. Her current research explores the nature of the political, following landscape designers as they attempt to define and modify the politics of spatial planning in the Netherlands.

Raymond Lee is Professor of Social Research Methods at Royal Holloway, University of London. He has written widely on a number of methodological topics including the problems and issues involved in research on 'sensitive' topics, research in dangerous environments and the impact of new technologies on the research process. He is the author of *Doing Research on Sensitive Topics* (Sage 1993), *Dangerous Fieldwork* (Sage 1995), *Computer Analysis and Qualitative Research* (with Nigel Fielding) (Sage 1998) and *Unobtrusive Methods in Social Research* (Open University Press 2000).

Nick Manning is a Professor at the University of Nottingham and non-executive director of Nottinghamshire Healthcare NHS Trust. Research interests include mental health, therapeutic communities, and Eastern Europe. Recent/forthcoming books include *Work and Welfare in the New Russia* (Ashgate 2000), *New Risks, New Welfare* (Blackwell 2000), *Poverty and Social Exclusion in the New Russia* (Ashgate 2003), *Research Evidence and Therapeutic Communities* (Jessica Kingsley 2003), and *Social Policy* (Oxford University Press 2003).

Maria O'Beirne is Research Assistant in the Department of Social and Political Science. Royal Holloway, University of London. Her research interests include social exclusion, violence against women and emotion work. She recently co-authored an article on researching professional discourses on violence in the journal *British Journal of Criminology*.

Riley Olstead is in the Department of Sociology, York University, Canada. Her work focuses on popular representations, power and health studies. Currently she is working on a project that examines women's talk about panic disorder. Recent publications include 'Race, class and gender: OJ. Revisited' in C. Reason et al. (eds) *Race, Class, Gender and Justice in the United States: A Reader* (Allyn and Bacon 2001).

Sita Reddy is a postdoctoral fellow at the University of Pennsylvania's Center for Bioethics where she is researching the ethics and politics of the genetically modified food movement. Her doctoral dissertation focused on the professionalisation of Ayurvedic medical traditions in America. Her current research interests lie at the intersections between medical sociology, science and technology studies, sociology of culture and the Asian diaspora.

Stefan Timmermans is Associate Professor of Sociology at Brandeis University. His interests include death and dying, healthcare technologies and standardisation. He is the author of *Sudden Death and the Myth of CPR* (Temple 1999) and co-author (with Marc Berg) of *The Gold Standard: A Sociological Exploration of Evidence-Based Medicine and Standardization in Health Care* (Temple, forthcoming).

Chapter 1

Introduction: connecting criminology and sociology of health and illness

Stefan Timmermans and Jonathan Gabe

A. A joint legacy of social control

Although scholars in sociology of health and illness and criminology have long been interested in questions of authority, expertise, social control, legitimacy and credibility, the two fields have developed largely independently of one another. Sociologists studying health and illness have sustained an interest in issues of social control ever since Talcott Parsons conceptualised physicians as moral gatekeepers, helping to maintain the integrative function of society. The physicians' main function consisted of normalising 'deviant' illness through the invasive treatment of the body. When physicians assigned the 'sick role' to patients, they legitimated a temporally limited state of deviance. In Parsons' theory, physicians not only treated people to retake their roles in the labour force and other institutions but they verified the legitimacy of illnesses; defining what qualifies as a bona fide reason to abandon temporarily responsibilities in society (Parsons 1951, 1975).

When functionalism lost its attraction for well-known theoretical and historical reasons, the theme of social control re-emerged in sociology of health and illness in more social constructivist perspectives, influenced by labelling theory and a critique of psychiatry as a total institution (Goffman 1961, Scull 1977, Szasz 1961). In a classic article, Irving Zola (1972) argued that medicine should be understood as an institution of social control, 'nudging aside' the traditional control institutions of law and religion. Medical social control advances through a process of medicalisation: conditions that were previously not considered to fall under the jurisdiction of health care providers, now are conceptually, interactionally and institutionally taken as illnesses, medical disorders and syndromes (Conrad and Schneider 1980). In these writings, the similarities between the prominence of the health care field and crime (or more generally deviance) in daily life is touched upon but not explored. Zola, for example, notes:

> Most analysts have tried to make a distinction between illness
> and crime on the issue of personal responsibility. The criminal is
> thought to be responsible and therefore accountable (or punishable)
> for his (sic) act, while the sick person is not. While the distinction
> does exist, it seems to be more a quantitative one rather than a
> qualitative one, with moral judgments but a pinprick below the
> surface (Zola 1972: 489).

In a review article of the medicalisation literature in 1992, Conrad noted two exceptions to the lack of developing parallels between health and crime: a study by Pastor comparing legal and medical approaches to public drunkenness and another by Melick and associates on the increased admission of males with police records to psychiatric units (Conrad 1992).

Some researchers trained in the health care field have ventured into the study of crime. Epidemiologist Kawachi and associates, for example, applied an ecological approach taken from public health to explain crime. Using data on homicide and other categories of crime they have explored the nature of the association between income distribution, mortality and a measure of social cohesion in the United States. They concluded that the violence associated with income inequality served as an indicator of the psychosocial impact of wider income differences (Wilkinson *et al.* 1998). More recently they have suggested that the crime rate reflects the quality of life in a community and have reported that crime increases when social buffers that normally exist in middle-class neighborhoods disappear (Kawachi *et al.* 1999). Catherine Ross (1993) investigated whether the fear of victimisation affects the subjective quality of life, hypothesising that the fear of crime affects the likelihood that people would engage in outdoor physical activity and generate psychological distress. Ross (2000) also found that residents of poor neighbourhoods have higher levels of depression than residents of more advantaged neighbourhoods.

In the study of crime and law enforcement the social control theme has also held centre stage (social control theory is the most frequently discussed and 'tested' theory in criminology (Stitt and Giacopassi 1992)). Social control theorists focus on the strategies and techniques leading to conformity and compliance with the rules of society, in light of temptation, peer pressure and inducement that could lead to delinquency and crime. Rather than asking why people become 'bad', social control theorists wonder why people remain 'good' most of the time. They argue that social and personal controls prevent people from committing crimes: the more committed a person is to conventional activities and attached to others, the less likely that person will violate the rules of society. Travis Hirschi (1969) remains the major social control theorist in criminology. He proposes four principal bonds that help explain the likelihood of conformity: attachment to other people; commitment through investment in education or occupation; involvement in family, school, work and extra-curricular activities; and belief in the norms and laws of the wider society. Hirschi has also provided empirical indicators for his bonds, and the theory has been extensively tested. The current consensus in criminological circles is that social control theory is weakly supported by the available evidence (Agnew 1991, Akers 2000, Greenberg 1999). One author even suggests that social control theory has mainly resonated with criminologists for its conservative ideology (Greenberg 1999).

In the 1980s and 1990s, Hirschi moved away from the classical social control theory to focus on one type of social control. In *A General Theory of Crime* Gottfredson and co-author Travis Hirschi (1990) claim that crime's attraction lies in its personal, easy and immediate gratification, rendering 'self-control' the key to understanding criminal behaviour. Criminals – including white-collar crime perpetrators – lack self-control, and tend to be 'impulsive, insensitive, physical (as opposed to mental), prone to risk-taking, short-sighted, and non-verbal' (Gottfredson and Hirschi 1990: 90). Drawing on social psychology and rational choice utilitarianism, Gottfredson and Hirschi argue that the seeds of criminal behaviour are fertilised in childhood: low self-control is established when parents provide weak direct controls for their children. When growing up, these children then lack the will to succeed in social institutions and succumb to the temptation of criminal behaviour. Again, the empirical evidence for this theory is mixed. Researchers have not been able to distinguish a strong relationship between low self-control and white-collar crime, nor specify the age-crime relationship. Yet self-control seems inversely related to general law violations and self-reported delinquency (Akers 2000, Pratt and Cullen 2000). A quantitative meta-analysis of the empirical evidence offers 'fairly impressive empirical support for the theory' (Pratt and Cullen 2000: 951), while at the same time also suggesting the importance of other theories such as social learning theory. Social control theory as specified by Hirschi and Gottfredson remains currently the most popular criminological explanation for the pervasive occurrence of criminal behaviour.

While social control theorists see themselves as asking a different kind of question (conformity instead of deviance), they are ultimately concerned with conformity in light of criminality, and not in light of health, occupational achievement, family relationships, education, religion or other possibly related topics. Social control theory remains firmly focused on the dependent variables of conventional criminology. While it would be theoretically possible to expand the insights of social control theory to accounts of medical compliance or to analyse the attraction of unproven, possibly harmful alternative medicine, such developments have not taken place.

Radical criminologists have offered a dissenting view to the liberal and conservative consensus that social control and punishment constitute a legislative enactment of public desires to punish 'harmful' and 'socially undesirable' behaviour (Cohen 1989). The basic premise of radical criminology is that crime control policy initiatives are actually aimed at social control, keeping down minorities, women and the other dispossessed. The criminal justice system and the welfare state serve the reproduction of a class-based society. Jock Young (1992) identified 'the square of crime' consisting of four elements that come together to explain the interplay of crime: victim, offender, state (formal control) and society (informal control). But, as conventional theorists point out, it remains unclear how the elements of the square might interact to generate crime, or even whether the four elements are simple, definitional terms or form an actual explanation (Akers 2000). Drawing from labelling theory and Marxism, critical researchers point out how class bias, sexism and racism are institutionalised in laws and sentencing practices, how the criminal justice system is permeated by large corporations running prisons according to business principles, and how incarceration functions to offset high unemployment rates and policy gaps due to the 'de-institutionalisation' of the mental health field (Welch 1998).

A recent development within radical criminology has been the attempt to relate crime to the growth of a competitive market economy. According to Taylor (1999) the transformation of Fordist society, with the virtual collapse in demand for unskilled work and the lack of opportunities for the development of skills within particular crafts, has produced new and heightened forms of marginality and the development of different local 'economies of crime', especially in large urban centres. Likewise the growth of transnational markets has created new opportunities for criminal activity by 'enterprising individuals' and corporations and encouraged the development of transnational institutions such as international police networks to combat such crimes. Young (1999) advanced a similar argument about the role of the market in his discussion of the development of an exclusive society. He too notes the structural changes to the labour market and the economic exclusion that has followed. But he also acknowledges the growth of social exclusion resulting from the rise of individualism and the unravelling of community, and the relationship between both these forms of exclusion and an increase in crime. Further exclusion then results from attempts to deal with such crime through incarceration and stigmatisation. For Young, increased lawlessness and economic precariousness should be confronted by a politics that embraces the excluded and seeks to devise a new form of community. Ultimately, these writings aim to generate widespread social reform.

B. Foucault

One of the few scholars active both in criminology and health was Michel Foucault. Foucault's main interest was to historicise the way in which the nexus knowledge-power operates in society and has turned human beings into subjects and modern selves. In *Madness and Civilization* he situated the emergence of the medical professional in terms of its reliance on surveillance and judgment to generate a separate science of the mind (Foucault 1965). In *The Birth of the Clinic* he analysed how the medical gaze nestled in the tissues of the corpse, turning bodies into subjects of medical knowledge (Foucault 1973). Foucault contrasted this new medical regime with medicine of the 18th century. In the earlier period, medicine was a matter of classifying symptoms, distinguishing one disease from the other, regardless of whether the conditions could actually be located in bodies. Whereas in the ancient regime death was simply the end of illness, in the era of new medical knowledge death became an analytical vantage point from which to study the pathological basis of disease in specialised clinics. The consequence was an objectification of individuals drawn from previously undifferentiated masses and the turn of medical perception towards all aspects of individual life. While such ontological changes were most apparent in medicine, they reflected a turn to individuality in Western culture. Indeed, in his accessible *Discipline and Punish* Foucault explored how deviants became objectified as individuals in the criminal justice system through a tight power-knowledge nexus (Foucault 1979). Looking at the history of penal punishment, Foucault noticed a qualitative shift in punishment: from the body to the prisoner's mind. While exploring the increasingly repressive structure of incarceration, he discusses the emergence of a new set of disciplinary techniques, new subjects and new roles in criminal justice.

For Foucauldian scholars, those three books reflect Foucault's project to discover the modern subject in history and should be viewed as explorations of the same key themes (Eribon 1992). Paul Rabinow (1984: 8), for example, notes how these works centre on the divisive practices by which people become classified and objectified in modern bureaucracies. Yet when we look at the scholarship undertaken in the name of Foucault in criminology and medical sociology, the unity Foucault intended between them seems to be lost. Not surprisingly, Foucault's legacy is marginal in 'conventional' American criminology. As the earlier, brief review of the 'social control' theorists suggests, from a Foucauldian perspective grand criminological theorising is implicated in the power-knowledge process that extracts people from the masses and creates a 'truth' about crime. In this case it distinguishes 'criminals' from the 'well-bonded-with-good-self-esteem-and-self-control' through the use of statistical profiling and calculation. Incorporating Foucault would thus necessitate an uncomfortable level of introspection and reflexivity in mainstream criminology. Except for research on penal reform that takes Foucault more as a historical source, Foucauldian theoretical contributions in criminology have largely centred on governmentality, picking up the theme of totalising procedures by which links between the state and individual are formed (Rose 1999). Critical scholars elaborate on Foucault's concern with how rationality and order are achieved from the state downwards, through all aspects of social life, with the creation of 'docile' bodies and a justice system employing ever more repressive procedures (Garland 1990). Penal policy, for example, is said to have taken a new turn, with a stronger demarcation between the socially included and excluded. Deviants are no longer just condemned but increasingly held responsible for their own fate. According to Rose (2000), there are two circuits of exclusion for managing those who fail to comply. Those who present a lower risk may be offered individualised treatment or control, with the aim of achieving ethical reconstruction through surveillance. Those for whom 're-insertion' is unrealistic, or who pose too great a threat, are quarantined in order to protect society.

In sociology of health and illness, in contrast, Foucault ranks much more prominently (for an excellent review see Armstrong 1997). Foucault's inspiration has permitted sociologists to understand the forms of power assumed by medical practices, reintroducing a more critical analysis to the study of health care. Sociologists have seized upon Foucault's writings on the medical gaze and creation of patient-bodies (Heaton 1999, Prior 1989), the spatialisation of disease (Armstrong 1993), surveillance (Nettleton 1992), and the pervasiveness of public health (Brown 2000, Bunton 1992, Petersen 1997). Of note are Bryan Turner's attempts to re-embody sociology along Foucauldian lines. According to Turner (1984), Foucault was interested in the production, regulation and representation of bodies within a context of disciplinary surveillance. Several studies elaborate on Foucault's notion of bio-power, a new power relationship aimed at fostering the life of the population and of individual bodies (Gastaldo 1997, Shim 2000). Foucault conceptualised bio-power as a displacement of judicial categories by scientific ones such as species, population and fertility. The prominence of Foucault in medicine rather than criminology might thus also be partly explained by this dislocation: the fact that public health symbolised the manifestation of new power replacing the older repressive power of the justice system. Yet even medical sociologists have not followed Foucault's lead and linked medical surveillance to surveillance in other realms.

Foucault's oeuvres highlight the lost opportunity when topics are segmented into different sub-disciplines with minimal dialogue. The result is a conceptual impoverishment and a disregard for the multiple intersections between criminal justice and medicine. For Foucault, the common denominator in the penal system and in health care is a pervasive configuration of power and knowledge that divides people up through continuous surveillance and discipline (McCallum 1997). Foucault explains the conjuncture with an example of how mental health and criminology feed into each other leading to a 'psychiatrisation of criminal danger':

> The more psychologically determined an act is found to be, the more its author can be considered legally responsible. The more the act is, so to speak, gratuitous and undetermined, the more it will tend to be excused. A paradox, then: the legal freedom of a subject is proven by the fact that his (sic) act is seen to be necessary, determined; his lack of responsibility proven by the fact that his act is seen to be unnecessary (Foucault quoted in McCallum 1997: 54).

C. The medico-legal borderland

The deep convergence of crime and health care is striking. Crimes are established along a psychiatric and psychological continuum, generating an endless proliferation of psycho-medical conditions and categories of persons. The severity of the criminal act has become dependent on the sanity of the individual as postulated by psychiatrists whose concepts and measurement techniques often lack the scientific reliability expected in court. Contemporary jurisprudence and health care intersect at a densely populated borderland and it is this overlooked borderland that forms the topic of the current special issue.

The borderland between crime and health care is populated and guarded by a number of professionals engaging in processes that contain both the criminalisation of contested medical interventions and the medicalisation of criminal danger. The medico-legal borderland has clinics, prisons, medical boards, courts, occupational and public health offices, regulatory government agencies, crisis intervention centres and street policing. The conjunction of legal and medical concerns thus occurs in specialised settings, such as the morgue of the forensic pathologist, where every action is defined in terms of a hybrid of legal and medical principles, or in places typically associated either with medicine or law enforcement such as jails or hospitals. What is typical of all these sites is that alliances are created that link medical knowledge with knowledge about criminal deviance for the purpose of social control.

As Gloria Anzaldua (1987) poetically explores in her account of inhabiting the border between a Mexican, Anglo- and native-American identity, what is at stake in the borderland is the issue of loyalty: when pressed to make a choice, whose side are you on? This question assumes a purity of two cultures, medicine and law enforcement, each with a different purpose, the eradication of disease and crime; and a license to intervene on the basis of different principles, treatment and protection from danger. The borderland might then become a site of struggle where two parties vie for hegemony in an attempt to redraw the borders to their advantage. The struggle might involve attempts to influence, occupy, colonise, or annihilate and require outside intervention (Abbott 1988, Light 2000). In the case of the medico-legal borderland, such a struggle might lead to the criminalisation of actions that were previously considered medical, or the medicalisation of issues under legal jurisdiction. Conflicts might result in the subordination of entire occupational groups, the creation of new categories of patients or offenders ('kind making' in Ian Hacking's vocabulary (Hacking 1986)), or the appropriation of procedures and terminologies. The question that emerges when medicine takes over traditionally legal domains or vice versa is how the resulting social control arrangements satisfy both the inhabitants of the borderland and those at the different centres of expertise.

Leigh Star and Donna Haraway noted that borderlands also might require a tolerance for ambiguity, for that which is not typical on either side of the frontier (Haraway 1991, Star 1991). Instead of a contentious struggle between interests, there might be a more gradual mixing of blood, land and resources. Inhabiting the borderland might involve undermining established dualisms, morphing into new kinds of social control that cannot be traced back to traditional concerns. The intersection of crime and health might thus lead to a profound questioning of values, norms and procedures that are taken for granted in the hinterland. The resulting social control contains elements from the health care field and the criminal-legal realm but cannot be reduced to either one. Or it reflects a reaction against both areas and involves a new configuration. Such third-way solutions might occur more or less spontaneously or be orchestrated from afar, but they remain notoriously precarious. The possibility that the alternative ends up reverting back to the interests of one side of the border remains distinct.

The contributors to this special issue follow Foucault's lead (but not necessarily his theories) and provide the foundations for a new sociological outpost in the borderland between health and crime. On the most general level the chapters in this volume report a *reconceptualisation* of issues that are often taken for granted in the centres of medicine and criminology. The role of health care provider becomes contested when treating people means extracting information that can be used against 'patients' in a court of law, or when patients inflict violence on health care providers instead of consenting to treatment in the subordinate 'sick role'. Similarly, what is the rehabilitative potential of a prison if offenders are diagnosed with severe mental illnesses? Health care workers practicing in a legal context are not simply faced with a new set of priorities; instead, the intersection of medicine and criminal law profoundly affects every aspect of identity and work. Similar redefinitions occur on a macro level when government agencies actively intervene in the making of knowledge to protect a population from a perceived violent threat or when popular media normalise the mentally ill as prone to violence. Even staple sociological topics such as ethnic identities receive an unexpected twist when they are incorporated in legal defence strategies.

In the borderland, often overlooked tools of health care such as drugs like methadone, or even medical records, gain importance. Marc Berg has argued that records do not merely mirror medical practice but play an active, constitutive role in current medical work (Berg 1996, Berg and Bowker 1997). The record does not simply 'copy' the staff's work but actively shapes, in a non-deterministic way, the medical encounter, forming the organisational memory of the work performed. When the same medical records are read in courts or become part of legal disputes, the legal use is not a mere addition of a new function to the record. Rather, the record makes certain criminological actions and conclusions possible and thus, in its own way, shapes the content of the medical-legal hybrid. For example, Gale Miller (1998) has noted the extent to which the routine record keeping of staff members in social work settings anticipated the possible escalation of staff-client disagreements into formal disputes. The record's prospective orientation in legal adjudication contrasted with the short-term relational demands of most client-staff relations.

Documenting medical conditions changes meaning when the records are treated as legal documents. But to what end? The ultimate question haunting the medico-legal borderland is *cui bono*, who benefits (Star 1991)? The common warrant for health care interventions is that they benefit the health of an individual or community, while the criminal justice system has a mandate to protect the public. In the borderlands, these justifications often clash, provoking fascinating debates about the rights of autonomous individuals vs. the benefits of a community. Should victims of murder be autopsied as part of a criminal investigation or should the organs of the usually young, healthy victim be removed for organ transplantation purposes? Because borderlands do not necessarily abide by the norms and values of either intersecting realm, innovative, third-way solutions are often sought and achieved. The question of *cui bono* also raises an important issue that has been left largely unaddressed in the many medicalisation studies. Medical sociologists have detailed the increased medicalisation of all areas of life (Conrad 1992), but what do we gain or lose through such medicalisation? Is the medicalisation of homosexuality 'better' than its criminalisation, or only a more insidious way of controlling it? What do we make of patient groups who actively seek out and submit to medicalisation of their conditions (Cussins 1998)? While we do not have an easy answer for the politics of social control, the borderland between crime and health is a good place to observe those politics in action because the meeting of the two realms inevitably generates friction and misalignments, often requiring translations in public ways.

D. Borderland settlements

Care providers as experts and victims of crime
The role of key informant for law enforcement positions health care providers as experts in knowledge-based societies while exposing them to potential violence (Giddens 1994, Knorr-Cetina 1999). This tension evokes questions about the nature of health care in the medico-legal borderland. Several states in the United States have 'mandatory reporting' legislation, requiring all health care providers to alert legal authorities when they encounter patients indicating or showing signs of domestic violence, child abuse, or elderly abuse. Besides the obvious privacy issues, such mandatory reporting raises a list of ambiguities, most importantly, how does one determine that abuse or maltreatment have actually taken place, and how does one overcome the resistance of victims and of relatives who might be the perpetrators (Finn and Stalans 1995, Lahoti *et al.* 2001). Such ambiguities are further exacerbated in the area of illegal drugs. Not only is illegal drug use associated with an increase in a variety of crimes and severe health problems, but the routine consumption of illegal drugs is sometimes considered a medical addiction falling under the purview of health care counsellors, sometimes a form of criminal behaviour requiring a 'stiff' prison sentence and sometimes both.

Emilie Gomart's contribution to this special issue shows that care providers can develop a third approach. Since the 1970s, policy makers in France have regarded people addicted to drugs as patients and as delinquents; they have offered them treatment under a medicalised paradigm and locked them up in prisons. In the 1990s, however, a group of critics charged that the medical and criminal approach rested on the same fallacy: the addict was viewed as a free, autonomous subject who was coerced by the drugs to behave in destructive ways. Therefore a state of complete abstinence was the only acceptable policy approach to drug addiction and a condition for treatment. Advocates of criminal and medical policies differed on whether abstinence could best be achieved in prison or in treatment programmes. The problem was, however, that the 'free subjects under influence' avoided treatment centres, thus undermining the efficacy of drug treatment programmes, and a prison sentence did not result in sustained abstinence. The critics offered an alternative based on methadone treatment: instead of trying to eradicate drug addiction, the addictive character of methadone could be used to stabilise drug dependency.

Gomart argues that methadone substitution constituted a criticism of the liberal definition of human agency. Based on extensive ethnographic observations in a clinic in a Parisian suburb and drawing on actor network theory, she details how the experimental clinic went out of its way to find users, and tailored its treatment, after a sophisticated analysis of the relationship of the user, to the drug used. Clinic staff set goals with the users and negotiated doses of different drugs with them, taking the addictive agency of the drug into consideration in order to induce and seduce the users into substitution. The clinic's approach rested on a programme of 'generous constraints'. Rather than viewing drug users as autonomous beings isolated by addiction, the staff of the experimental clinic regarded them as people acting under various constraints. Cunningly deploying these constraints offered the staff and users an opportunity to build attachments and new relationships. Gomart concludes, 'By varying constraints, staff and patients attempt a daring redefinition of the subject. Not as autonomous and free, but as an 'attachment', an entity emergent in constraining relations'.

Some professionals, such as forensic pathologists and police surgeons (Savage et al. 1997), have been working as experts for such a long time in the borderland between crime and medicine that their position seems stable. But even they might be forced to articulate their priorities when new parties question their loyalties. The forensic pathologists' main task is to make medico-legal determinations in suspicious and sudden deaths. In the US, state-appointed forensic pathologists have legal jurisdiction over corpses to determine the identity of the deceased and the cause and manner of death. While forensic pathologists have been trained in medical schools, certified by medical authorities, and employ medical procedures, their primary constituency consists of law enforcement and the legal profession. In recent decades, the equilibrium between medicine and law enforcement in the forensic realm has been disturbed by a group of health care professionals with alternative claims on the corpse. In their quest for more organs and tissues, organ-procurement organisations have been questioning the jurisdiction of forensic pathologists to autopsy corpses that also contain transplantable organs (particularly homicide and child abuse cases). Analysing this conflict from the standpoint of the professionalisation literature, the chapter by Stefan Timmermans discusses how the organ-procurement organisations have redefined their relationship with forensic experts. Procurement organisations have attempted to alter legislation, standardise collaborations with forensic pathologists and offer financial incentives. Timmermans argues that each of these strategies redefines the relationship between organ-procurement organisations and death investigators from collaborative to conflictual jurisdictional relationships, and affects forensic pathologists' abilities to investigate suspicious deaths.

Work-related violence against doctors also provides a particularly interesting context for exploring the relationship between medicalisation and criminalisation as it involves focusing on doctors as victims of criminal behaviour by those who have ostensibly sought their help for a medical problem. How do doctors interpret such deviant behaviour and how do they manage it? Are these patients seen as 'ill', as 'criminals' or as a new category altogether? And do doctors continue to treat them as patients or concentrate instead on minimising risk and trying to protect themselves from harm? Of equal interest is how these health care professionals' responses to violence are framed by state policy on work-related violence. Does such a policy advocate a more punitive approach than was the case in the past, in line with the new turn in penal policy identified by criminologists (*e.g.* Garland and Sparks 2000)? In other words, does it encourage doctors to see the individualised, medicalised management of perpetrators of violence as no longer appropriate and to be replaced by a 'zero tolerance' approach, with perpetrators being reported to the police and forfeiting their right to treatment from their existing doctor? If the answer were 'yes' then it would seem that the boundary between medical and penal jurisdiction has been redrawn.

The chapter by Elston *et al.* addresses these questions. Drawing on empirical evidence of the responses of British general practitioners to incidents of violence and those who perpetrate these acts, and an analysis of state policy as regards work-related violence against health care workers, it argues that the policy frame is consistent with the claims of criminologists that there has been a new turn in penal policy away from the needs of offenders. The doctors' accounts, on the other hand, suggest that they are not 'zero tolerant' in responding to attacks, but nor are they medical imperialists seeking to include all perpetrators within their professional jurisdiction. Instead they make contextualised judgments that are not fully captured by medical sociologists' tendency to dichotomise illness and crime.

Invoking and Controlling 'Madness'

A similar theme of freedom and coercion, treatment and imprisonment appears in the four papers on mental health in this special issue. For generations, the mentally ill were primarily patients, secluded in mental hospitals. But in the aftermath of a widespread critique of the conditions of these hospitals, and because of high cost, many of them closed, leaving their patients to be cared for in local community facilities and through medication. Yet, the mentally ill often ended up on the streets, in hospital Accident and

Emergency departments and in jail. These four chapters explore and question the explicit links made between mental health and criminal behaviour in policy and legal circles.

Sarah Armstrong offers an analysis of the juvenile justice system in Massachusetts after de-institutionalisation. In the late 1960s, the director of the Massachusetts department of youth services decided to shut down all juvenile delinquency state facilities in favour of a regional, privatised and community-based system of service providers. The state facilities' close resemblance to 'total institutions' (Goffman 1961) caused failure in their dual mission of rehabilitating the offenders and housing youths safely. Armstrong's data show that in the mid-1980s most of the new service providers came from the mental health field. She argues that the predominance of mental health providers in the realm of juvenile justice can be explained by the scientific credibility of mental health knowledge. The widespread medicalisation of deviant behaviour by psychiatrists offers the juvenile justice system a means to diagnose criminal behaviour as conduct disorders (*e.g.* oppositional defiant disorder) and offer treatment possibilities (*e.g.* cognitive behaviour therapy). Armstrong argues that the incorporation of mental health language and techniques does not constitute a retreat from rehabilitative aims as asserted by new penology theoreticians (the actuarial approach), but allows the justice system simultaneously to achieve retributive and rehabilitative aims and redefine measures of success. Success in criminal justice infused by mental health discourse and procedures is a matter of reducing risks rather than eliminating crime.

The next contribution discusses the role of the Canadian print media in the conflation of illness and criminality. Riley Olstead reports how the media fuel negative views about mental illness through linking it to ideas about violence and criminality. Based on a discursive and content analysis of mental health media depictions, Olstead describes a submerged ideological polarisation that opposes those with and without mental illnesses. The media representations achieve a view of the mentally ill as medically irrational, legally responsible and consequently socially immoral. Taken in concert, it is understood that 'They' are a danger to 'Us'. The media further portray the mentally ill as dependent and irresponsible, and their illness as something to be overcome through cultivating the 'right attitude'. Finally, Olstead draws attention to a class bias in the depictions. She argues that the almost taken-for-granted equation of mental illness with criminality resonates powerfully with politicians and the public alike, a claim taken up by Nick Manning in the next chapter.

How does a society deal with people who might be dangerous but have not committed a crime? Leaving them until an offence has been committed puts the public at risk, and incarcerating them indefinitely violates human rights treaties. Nick Manning discusses the UK government's solution to this dilemma between public and individual rights, a solution very different from the one described by Gomart but reminiscent of Rose's analysis of quarantining (Rose 2000). He notes that the perceived rise in crime on which politicians acted was not corrobated by crime statistics: violent crime had actually gone down, but – as Olstead suggested – the perception persisted that crimes committed by the mentally ill had increased. To tackle the issue of violent crime the government took an active role in the establishment of a new sub-category of personality disorder, the 'dangerous and severe personality disorder'. Personality disorders are notoriously difficult to detect since they manifest themselves through behaviours rather than through biological and psychological signs. Forensic psychiatrists and other mental health experts agreed that these disorders are marred by uncertainties in diagnosis, assessment, measurement and treatment. The government took the initiative to develop an evidence base for the disorder and to develop a new treatment service in prisons and special hospitals. The government relied on the notion of 'potential risk' to enroll people in treatment facilities, obtaining a de facto incarceration of potential offenders. Manning compares the actor network approach from sociology of science and technology with the policy network approach of policy studies to explore the government's role in justifying detention for people at risk as offenders.

Finally, Sita Reddy's chapter discusses the emergence of a new legal defence strategy modelled on established mental health categories. The 'culture defence strategy' is used by defendants in US courts to diminish responsibility for the crimes they have been accused of committing. This strategy has been employed, for example, by a Japanese woman accused of killing her children and by cuckolded Hmong and Chinese husbands. The controversial defence strategy employs 'culture' as a significant heuristic category in the criminal court, articulating an individualised perspective of immigrant culture that determined the mindset of the defendant when the 'crime' took place. In the context of the defence strategy, some cultures become mitigating pathological conditions, in the same way that an 'insanity' defence is used to diminish legal charges. Reddy argues that the culture defence strategy institutionalises a hallmark of late-modern reflexivity, the therapeutic ethic, in the criminal justice system. The defence rests on an autonomous self as the centre of moral authority; it favours the expression of feelings rather than reason or logic, an influx of psychiatric and anthropological expert testimony, a tendency to pathologise behaviour and the notion that the defendants are victims of immigrant cultural values. The criminal court thus represents a setting where connections between mental illnesses and cultural differences are fostered and re-conceptualised.

Overall, the chapters in this special issue thus reveal some of the multiple interconnections between criminology and medical sociology and the need for dialogue between them. They highlight the role of professionals in engaging in processes that involve the criminalisation of contested medical interventions, the medicalisation of criminal danger, and the generation of altogether new forms of social control. In so doing they provide the basis for questioning values, norms and procedures that are frequently taken for granted in the centres of health care and law enforcement, and place firmly on the agenda the fundamental question of *who* benefits when the health care and criminal-legal realms interact.

References

Abbott, A. (1988) *The System of Professions*. Chicago: University of Chicago Press.

Agnew, R. (1991) A longitudinal test of social control theory and delinquency, *Journal of Research in Crime and Delinquency*, 28, 126–56.

Akers, R.L. (2000) *Criminological Theories: Introduction and Evaluation* (3rd Edition). Los Angeles: Roxbury.

Anzaldua, G. (1987) *Borderlands: La Frontera the New Mestiza*. San Francisco: Aunt Lute.

Armstrong, D. (1993) Public health spaces and the fabrication of identity, *Sociology*, 27, 393–410.

Armstrong, D. (1997) Foucault and the sociology of health and illnesss: a prismatic reading. In Petersen, A. and Bunton, R. (eds), *Foucault, Health and Medicine*. London and New York: Routledge.

Berg, M. (1996) Practices of reading and writing: the constitutive role of the patient record in medical work, *Sociology of Health and Illness*, 18, 4, 499–562.

Berg, M. and Bowker, G. (1997) The multiple bodies of the medical record: toward a sociology of an artifact, *The Sociological Quarterly*, 38, 3, 513–37.

Brown, T. (2000) AIDS, risk and social governance, *Social Science and Medicine*, 50, 1273–84.

Bunton, R. (1992) More than a woolly jumper: health promotion as social regulation, *Critical Public Health*, 3, 2, 4–11.

Cohen, S. (1989) The critical discourse on 'social control': notes on the concept as a hammer, *International Journal of the Sociology of Law*, 17, 347–57.

Conrad, P. (1992) Medicalization and social control, *Annual Review of Sociology*, 18, 209–32.

Conrad, P. and Schneider, J.W. (1980) *Deviance and Medicalization: from Badness to Sickness*. St. Louis: Mosby.

Cussins, C. (1998) Ontological choreography: agency for women in an infertility clinic. In Berg, M. and Mol, A. (eds) *Differences in Medicine: Unraveling Practices, Techniques and Bodies*. Durham: Duke University Press.

Eribon, D. (1992) *Michel Foucault*. London: Faber and Faber.

Finn, M.A. and Stalans, L.J. (1995) Police referrals to shelters and mental health treatment: examining their decisions in domestic assault cases, *Crime and Delinquency*, 41, 4, 467–80.

Foucault, M. (1965) *Madness and Civilization: a History of Insanity in the Age of Reason*. New York: Pantheon.

Foucault, M. (1973) *The Birth of the Clinic*. New York: Vintage Books.

Foucault, M. (1979) *Discipline and Punish*. New York: Vintage Books.

Garland, D. (1990) *Punishment and Modern Society: a Study in Social Theory*. Chicago: University of Chicago Press.

Garland, D. and Sparks, R. (2000) Criminology, social theory and the challenge of our times, *British Journal of Criminology*, 40, 2, 189–204.

Gastaldo, D. (1997) Is health education good for you? Re-thinking health education through the concept of bio-power. In Petersen, A. and Bunton, R. (eds) *Foucault, Health and Medicine*. New York and London: Routledge.

Giddens, A. (1994) Living in a post-traditional society. In Beck, U., Giddens, A. and Lash, S. (eds) *Reflexive Modernization*. Cambridge: Polity.

Goffman, E. (1961) *Asylums*. New York: Doubleday.

Gottfredson, M.R. and Hirschi, T. (1990) *A General Theory of Crime*. Palo Alto: Stanford University Press.

Greenberg, D.F. (1999) The weak strength of social control theory, *Crime and Delinquency*, 45, 1, 66–81.

Hacking, I. (1986) Making up people. In Heller, T., Morton, S. and Wellbery, D.E. (eds) *Reconstructing Individualism*. Stanford: Stanford University Press.

Haraway, D.J. (1991) *Simians, Cyborgs, and Women: the Reinvention of Nature*. New York: Routledge.

Heaton, J. (1999) The gaze and visibility of the carer: a Foucauldian analysis of the discourse of informal care, *Sociology of Health and Illness*, 21, 6, 759–77.

Hirschi, T. (1969) *Causes of Delinquency*. Berkeley, CA: University of California Press.

Kawachi, I., Kennedy, B.P. and Wilkinson, R.G. (1999) Crime, social disorganisation and relative deprivation, *Social Science and Medicine*, 48, 719–31.

Knorr-Cetina, K. (1999) *Epistemic Cultures: how the Sciences Make Knowledge*. Cambridge: Harvard University Press.

Lahoti, S.L., McClain, N., Giardet, R., McNeese, M. and Cheung, K. (2001) Evaluating the child for sexual abuse, *American Family Physician*, 63, 5, 883–92.

Light, D. (2000) The medical profession and organizational change: from professional dominance to countervailing power. In Bird, C.E., Conrad, P. and Fremont, A.M. (eds) *Handbook of Medical Sociology* (5th Edition). New Jersey: Prentice Hall.

McCallum, D. (1997) Mental health, criminality and the human sciences. In Petersen, A. and Bunton, R. (eds) *Foucault, Health and Medicine*. London and New York: Routledge.

Miller, G. (1998) Documenting disputes: law and bureaucracy in organizational disputing, *Sociology of Crime, Law, and Deviance*, 1, 203–29.

Nettleton, S. (1992) *Power, Pain, and Dentistry*. Buckingham: Open University Press.

Parsons, T. (1951) *The Social System*. Glencoe, IL: The Free Press.

Parsons, T. (1975) The sick role and the role of the physician reconsidered, *Milbank Memorial Quarterly Fund*, 53, 3, 257–78.

Petersen, A. (1997) Risk, governance and the new public health. In Petersen, A. and Bunton, R. (eds) *Foucault, Health and Medicine*. London and New York: Routledge.

Pratt, T.C. and Cullen, F.T. (2000) The empirical status of Gottfredson and Hirschi's general theory of crime: a meta-analysis, *Criminology*, 38, 3, 931–59.

Prior, L. (1989) *The Social Organisation of Death: Medical Discourses and Social Practices in Belfast*. London: Macmillan.

Rabinow, P. (ed) (1984) *The Foucault Reader*. Pantheon Books: New York.

Rose, N. (1999) *Powers of Freedom: Reframing Political Thought*. Cambridge: Cambridge University Press.

Rose, N. (2000) Government and control, *British Journal of Criminology*, 40, 2, 321–39.

Ross, C.E. (1993) Fear of victimization and health, *Journal of Quantitative Criminology*, 9, 2, 159–75.

Ross, C.E. (2000) Neighborhood disadvantage and adult depression, *Journal of Health and Social Behavior*, 41, 177–87.

Savage, S.P., Moon, G., Kelly, K. and Bradshaw, Y. (1997) Divided loyalties? The police surgeon and criminal justice, *Policing and Society*, 7, 79–98.

Scull, A.T. (1977) *Decarceration*. Englewood Cliffs, NJ: Prentice Hall.

Shim, J.K. (2000) Bio-power and race, class, gender formation in biomedical knowledge production, *Research in the Sociology of Health Care*, 17, 173–95.

Star, S.L. (1991) Power, technologies and the phenomenology of conventions: on being allergic to onions. In Law, J. (ed) *A Sociology of Monsters: Essays on Power, Technology and Domination*. London: Routledge.

Stitt, B.G. and Giacopassi, D.J. (1992) Trends in the connectivity of theory and research in criminology, *The Criminologist*, 17, 1, 3–6.

Szasz, T. (1961) *The Myth of Mental Illness: Foundations of a Theory of Personal Conduct*. New York: Harper.

Taylor, I. (1999) *Crime in Context: a Critical Criminology of Market Societies*. Cambridge: Polity.

Turner, B.S. (1984) *The Body and Society: Explorations in Social Theory*. Oxford: Blackwell Publishers.

Welch, M. (1998) Critical criminology, social control and an alternative view of corrections. In Rosen, J.I. (ed) *Cutting the Edge: Current Perspectives in Radical/ Critical Criminology and Criminal Justice*. Westport, CO: Praeger.

Wilkinson, R., Kawachi, I. and Kennedy, B. (1998) Mortality, the social environment, crime and violence. In Bartley, M., Blane, D. and Davey Smith, G. (eds) *The Sociology of Health Inequalities*. Oxford: Blackwell Publishers.

Young, J. (1992) Ten points of realism. In Young, J. and Matthews, R. (eds) *Rethinking Criminology: the Realist Debate*. London: Sage.

Young, J. (1999) *The Exclusive Society: Social Exclusion, Crime and Difference in Late Modernity*. London: Sage.

Zola, I.K. (1972) Medicine as an institution of social control, *Sociological Review*, 20, 487–504.

Chapter 2

Towards generous constraint: freedom and coercion in a French addiction treatment

Emilie Gomart

Freedom or coercion

Is the drug addict a criminal or a patient? Is his/her pathology moral or physical? What is an acceptable response to drug addiction: coercion of or care for the user? Should the addict be thrown into jail, forced to go 'cold turkey'? Or should non-coercive, therapeutic methods be employed? Since the 1970s, the various legal and medical approaches to addiction in France have polarised and opposed these solutions of care and coercion and constructed them as irreconcilable alternatives. The French caregivers, committed to non-coercive therapy, were the sworn adversaries of law enforcement officials who argued for the benefits of the imprisonment of users.

I will show, however, that in the early 1990s a new group of actors constituted itself in the critique of *both* legal and medical actors: a similar argument was used to amalgamate and condemn the practices of both coercion and of care, which had previously been taken to be incompatible. More specifically, the critics accused both legal and medical actors of founding their respective practices on a single principle: the freedom of the subject. Just as legislators, the critics claimed, had in the law of 1970 defined the addict as depraved and incapable of exercising ordinary civil rights, so the caregivers had defined the addict as a slave to the drug. Echoing the legal goal of abstinence, the goal of treatment had been unequivocally an 'apprenticeship of freedom' (Olievenstein 1977). This unconditional love of freedom, far from curing addicts, the critics added scathingly, was precisely what had led to rates of social marginalisation and of HIV infection among French drug users in the 1980s far higher than those of other European countries (*e.g.* Courtinho *et al.* 1992, Ingold and Ingold 1989). Further, they demonstrated that not only were the specialists' abstinence treatments incapable of making users abstinent, but that the drug users had come to *avoid* their centres of care. Drug users were lost to the existing system of care. Users preferred to shoot up dope in dark passageways near Place Stalingrad, risk jail and HIV, (*e.g.* Lert and Fombonne 1989, Lebeau 1994) rather than to listen to the specialists' babble on about freedom. Strikingly, the critics rejected the basic tenet that the only morally and scientifically acceptable version of the subject was the free subject; that the only medically acceptable intervention was the one that left the individual free to chose (Morel 1997).

The specialists were caught off guard because they had sought to devise an 'ethical' approach to addiction that, in contrast to penal, coercive interventions, was not 'dogmatic'. Strongly inspired by the anti-psychiatry movement, these psychiatrists had sought to avoid 'imposing their own desires and ideology' upon the individuals they treated (Morel *et al.* 1997). For them, the smallest, lightest, least detrimental supposition was that of the free subject. When, in the late 1980s, drug users were shown how to avoid specialised centres, the specialists were accused of ignorance about the reality of the subject. Bluntly put, how could they claim to know the subject, when s/he did not even show up at their treatment centres? Through their absences and relapses, it was argued, the users themselves insisted that the specialists' definition of the subject was an illusion. Suddenly, specialists were said to have begun not with an infinitesimal but with an enormous *a priori* assumption.

The critics gave the debate on addiction treatment a crucial turn when they argued that the caregivers and legislators *shared* the same *a priori* bias in favour of freedom. Both were criticised for holding onto a liberal definition of freedom, one that might be described in Isaiah Berlin's (1958) phraseology as a '*negative* definition of freedom'. They held indeed that freedom can be measured by the autonomy of the agent's actions, that is, by the absence of exterior 'obstacles' to the implementation of an original intention or plan. Thus, critics claimed, their shared assumption is that an individual *either* acts as a full rational agent, *or* the drug acts upon him/her and s/he is coerced. The individual agent appears when s/he acts alone and vanishes the moment exterior forces express themselves upon him/her. Action, in a negative definition of freedom, is something that cannot be shared (Callon and Law 1995). Either the human acts autonomously or others act upon him/her (equally autonomously).

As I will show, throughout the 1970s and until the 1990s, this ideal of freedom was expressed most clearly in debates about methadone. The critics (ex-'specialists' and generalists allied with prominent figures of the humanitarian organisation *Medecins du Monde* as well as a new international group of statisticians investigating 'risk behaviours' among different HIV vulnerable populations) also developed an original mode of methadone treatment. Methadone had been rejected previously because it had been unthinkable that subjects might benefit from a further addiction to a medical substance. The critics of specialised treatment, however, allowed that freedom (from addiction), and the absence of constraint was not the criterion upon which to distinguish acceptable from unacceptable care. What alternative distinguishing criteria should be was precisely the topic of a pilot experimental treatment project initiated in November 1993 at the Blue Clinic, in B-, a suburb of Paris.

This chapter, then, seeks to revoke a long-reigning certainty: that freedom is *in any case* 'what we cannot not want' (Haraway 1994), that the human subject is either abstinent and active or subjugated by a drug; that a narcotic drug cannot be therapeutic, only destructive for the user. My argument is not that freedom was revealed through this debate to have been a foolish ideal all along. Rather this paper aims to describe how it progressively *became possible* in France in the mid-1990s to say that the goal of abstinence and the ideal of freedom, which much of the Western philosophical tradition constructs as desirable, were suddenly *no longer appropriate* in the case of addiction treatment. One of my aims is to record this peculiar variation for an anthology of relations between coercion and freedom, repression and care. This seems all the more important to record as the Blue Clinic experiment, and the coalition of actors backing it, were influential in convincing Ministry health officials and health practitioners, traditionally hostile to the prescription of opiates, of the usefulness of substitution products in the care of addicts. Two substitution products, methadone and Subutex, were officially designated as addiction treatments in 1995 (*i.e.* they were given an *Autorisation de mise sur le marché*). Yet, as I will suggest below, if the Blue Clinic in 1993–5 was indeed for its members an 'experiment on the usefulness of constraint' (Co-founder, interview 1995), the routines and gestures developed there could not serve as models; nor could they be transposed to generalists' consultation rooms and addiction centres all over the country without being significantly transformed. In particular, explicit reference to the theme of useful constraints, any suggestion of the non-autonomy of the subject, disappeared from official texts and practitioners' manuals (See Gomart 1999a). To allow for what they took to be an urgent generalisation of substitution treatment, the critics then had to back off (in public settings) from their most provocative claims about the freedom or coercion of the subject (Amanda, Clinic co-founder, Interview 1998). The practices described here have disappeared today, in the sense that they have become invisible: at best, they live on tacitly, inscribed in contemporary routines used throughout France for dosing and choosing between substitution products modelled on the now famous 'risk reduction' techniques of the Blue Clinic[1].

More theoretically, what is at stake here is the liberal definition of the human agent, an enterprise indelibly marked by the works of Michel Foucault. The academic reflection on whether the subject is 'found' or is constructed, and the nature of that construction has, like the addiction debate, linked discussions on the construction of the subject to assumptions about (the autonomy of) action. Is the human subject constructed, or is it what one begins with, what founds? If it is constructed, what are the building blocks of this construction: do these include narcotic drugs? To clarify my argument within this broader debate on the construction of the subject, I describe three conceptual moves inspired by ethno-methodology and Actor Network Theory, which are key to understanding the daily practice of the Blue Clinic.

Entities

The negative definition of freedom underlying the debates on addiction supposes that actors enter the scene already formed and filled to the brim with capacities, intentions and desires. 'Action' then is the expression of these inherent properties; for this manifestation to be complete, the entities must be the only actors on stage: if others act at the same time, this manifestation is corrupted. In contrast, rather than describing entities in terms of what they inherently 'are', Marc Berg and Annemarie Mol, for instance, have shifted to a description of 'networks' (Berg and Mol 1998). An entity is inseparable from the practices that reveal it (on drugs specifically, *c.f.* Becker 1963 and for a recent analysis of Becker's argument, see Gomart 2002). Thus, even the 'hardest' of entities is not given at the start but 'performed'. The individual too is the result of practices that frame, embody, localise and temporise. Echoing works on the performed autonomy of experimental facts, these works have suggested that the subject is not corrupted by the interferences of 'techniques of the self'. Instead, these techniques *grant* a self, capacities and intentions to the entity they delineate (*c.f.* the optimistic readings of Foucault (1975) and (1976) by Cussins 1998 and Gomart and Hennion 1999). The analytical focus shifts from pre-given entities to 'that which' lets them emerge: the material setting, the *'dispositif'* (Foucault 1976, Lynch 1991).

Construction
If the individual is not pre-given but 'constructed', what is the exact nature of this construction? How to describe the inter-relation between this final entity and what came before it? Do entities result from human 'interpretation' or are they 'determined' by the material world? Who *acts* in this construction, humans or objects?[2] Further, if we accept that entities are in some way the results of other's actions, are we then allowing that these entities (like the human subject) are passive entities, un-free? To avoid having to chose between humans or objects as the sources of action and to escape the simplistic dualism passive/active, free/determined in which this negative definition of freedom kept them, several authors inspired by ANT have devised a new vocabulary for describing action and construction. The term 'mediation', for instance, makes it possible to describe moments when action is not simply the autonomous expression of inherent capacities but rather is *'passed* on' from other actants (see Latour 1994b). Mediation 'exercises itself upstream as a sort of stimulant that might trigger the setting off of another's competence' (Greimas 1977: 101)[3]. Action can now be shared.

Generous constraint
Mediation further makes it possible to say that influence can be exerted upon an entity without destroying it. Much literature on the construction of the subject has focused on the oppressive force of constraints (see White 1999), to explore the alternative possibility I draw on science studies which have shown that influences from the setting (*i.e.* constraints and biases in the experimental set-up) are not to be eliminated since these are precisely what constitutes the autonomy of the phenomenon. To continue to criticise constraint in that context is to betray a nostalgia for pure science, immediate access to the phenomenon (*e.g.* Latour 1991, 1999 and Pickering 1992). It

becomes possible to say that constraints do not destroy and corrupt in all situations, some might have a 'positive' effect:

> [If you reduce] force to violence, [not only] do you not see that a force exercises itself upon another force but you deprive yourself of understanding the phenomenon of affect, that is of a force which exercises itself upon another force less to destroy it than to induce it into movement. No doubt is it a 'forced movement' [rather than a voluntary one]. . . . it is however a positive effect, which cannot be explained by destruction (Zourabichvili 1994: 41).

Thus, the task of the analyst of influences is no longer simply to eliminate constraints (*e.g.* bias in experimental settings) but to distinguish different *kinds* of forces, more specifically, to identify those that positively 'induce into movement'. Bruno Latour, for one, describes biases that actually 'give a chance' to the phenomenon in ethological experiments:

> Speaking of her new study on sheep, [Thelma Rowell] stated one of her 'biases' in the following way: '*I tried to give my sheep the opportunity to behave* like chimps, not that I believe that they would be like chimps, but because I am sure that if you take sheep for boring sheep by opposition to intelligent chimps they would not have a chance'. . . . By importing the notion of intelligent behaviour from a 'charismatic animal'. . . she might modify, subvert, elicit, in the understanding of sheep behaviour features that were until then invisible . . . It is because she artificially and willingly imposes on sheep another resource coming from elsewhere that 'they could have a chance' to behave intelligently' (Latour 2000: 372).

Forces that 'induce' and 'give a chance' could be called 'generous constraints', because, to elaborate on Latour's example, rather than obliging the sheep to behave in such a way as to confirm the age-old hypothesis of the stupidity of sheep, these generous constraints gave a chance to the sheep to behave differently and to surprise the experimenter and her colleagues. When constraints become inductions rather than obstacles to action, autonomy ceases to be the pre-condition for activity. Such new forms of influence or performativity are impossible to fit into the neat dualism of autonomy/ subjugation supposed by the liberal definition of freedom. These, however, become imaginable, as constraints become generous. Humans and things (including drugs?) can now engage in mutually constructive relations.

A note on method might be useful at this point. Three days a week I followed the practice of Blue Clinic practitioners over two periods of four months (January to April 1995, January to April 1996). I started out using methods of participant observation to collect data: in an overcrowded and under-staffed clinic my help in answering phones and guiding patients through the clinic to their appointments was at first appreciated. However, this experience soon faced me with the fact that even such minimal gestures required knowledge of and adequate performance of the *habitus* of a drug user. Indeed those usually performing these tasks were ex-drug users, capable of tactfully interacting with patients whether they were high, in withdrawal, etc . . . using words and gestures the users were familiar with. As I was unwilling to gain the necessary experience of illegal drug use myself (by using), my technique progressively switched to that of a 'silent onlooker'. Far from being an abandonment of method, this shift was for me a switch to an alternative method: rather than attempting to imitate staff or users so as to reduce the difference between me and them, participant observation forced me to become aware of their particular qualities. The philosophy of science tells us there is no un-mediated access to a phenomenon. Here, I was forced to pay attention to these mediations. I had to acknowledge that to access the phenomenon of the Clinic I too would require mediators: the staff and those patients who were most active in translation-work between staff and other patients. My hypothesis was that the skills such actors tentatively deployed at the Clinic were the 'generous constraints' (theoretical and material biases) necessary to make users speak and act in a way which successfully allowed their co-operation during treatment. It must be stressed that as I became a silent onlooker, a recorder of mediations, I did not seek to be neutral. Such a position is, to follow once more the philosophy of science, impossible. I could only search for bias other than the first ones I had deployed, more appropriate to this phenomenon. The impossibility of being neutral became a topic of controversy between staff and myself when in the summer of 1995 the Clinic suddenly doubled its number of patients (after substitution was made official) while retaining its original size and staff. As space became scarce, workloads increased and tensions in over-crowded waiting rooms rose. My presence, continually taking notes, was certainly not taken to be neutral but an additional constraint, this one not 'generous' – a disturbance of their daily activities. While attentive to suggestions about reducing the tensions my presence caused, I took these situations of controversy to be rich sources of data on what actors took to be the right constraints for substitution treatment and about the emerging difficulties caused not just by the persistence of an ethnographer but more importantly by the changing context of addiction treatment. Because of the frequency of my presence at the Clinic and their acceptance of my observation of their work in their private offices and in the main 'living room', I observed the entire range of activities of the Clinic and was engaged in countless informal exchanges with patients and staff. Outside these periods of fieldwork, I conducted annual formal interviews with each of the 12 members of the Clinic staff, as well as with five patients, between 1995 and 1998. Though less extensively, I also interviewed relevant actors in the methadone debate outside the Blue Clinic (practitioners at other centres, politically active drug users, public health officials).

In the third part of this chapter, it will become clear that the founders of the experimental substitution treatment at the Blue Clinic were searching for something just like 'generous constraints'. One of them, Amanda, the co-founder of the Clinic, a sociologist with a long practical experience in addiction treatments, describes their treatment as 'an experiment on constraint' (Amanda, Interview February 1995): rather than supposing that constraints are problematic in themselves (because they might oppress the patient), they aimed to determine the conditions under which constraints became positive. Rather than seeking to eliminate constraints, they *added and varied* constraints in the hope of hitting upon just the one that might generously 'pass' the user into action. To show the originality of this stance, I detail below the specialists and legislators' contrasting positions on drug use.

The free subject

The law of 1970[4]
The 'law of 1970' established the penal measures against drug use and traffic as well as the foundations of a specialised care system for drug addicts. The French 'law of 1970' was, in comparison with contemporary European laws, exceptionally severe. It penalised 'intimate' use of all narcotics [*stupéfiant*] (Bernat 1996: 92). The penalising of private use was recognised at the time as in contradiction with the human rights convention, in particular 'the right to do whatever does not harm others' (Cesoni 1992). Moreover, certain common law protections of individual rights (*e.g.* during police procedures) were suspended for drug-related offences. Not only had private use become a topic for legislation, legislation also turned the user into a 'hunted' individual.

During the parliamentary hearings preceding the vote on the 1970 law, the legislators explicitly justified these extraordinary measures by referring to the threat to society posed by the drug. According to them, '*la toxicomanie est un fléau*'. The drug moved on its own impetus to infect the whole of society. It was a perfectly causal object. This essentialist definition of the drug was the obligatory passage point that clinched the argument of the legislators. Thus, for example, when the text went to the Senate to be ratified, after a single objection from the audience, the *rapporteur* countered:

Ladies and gentlemen let us be serious! Either one considers that the drug is not a scourge [fleau], national or international, and the measures I have defended and you have accepted can be taken to be superfluous and, to a certain extent, to be infringing upon a number of principles dear to us, to you and to me; or we consider that it is a scourge and that it is crucial to intervene in our country before it becomes like the United States of America, and I have asked for, and you have accepted, very limited infringements, considering the health of our children and the equilibrium of an entire society (cited in Bernat 1996: 156).

The *unique* solution was to maintain the drug, and whoever came into contact with it, outside society:

> Would it be a just conception of democracy, the Republic and of liberty to let anyone do anything and not to place barriers to protect society from what threatens it so gravely . . . this is not a matter of repression, but of rescue [*sauvegarde*] (cited in Bernat 1996: 147).

Either the drug acted, and all succumbed; or the State blocked the circulation of the drug to preserve the autonomy of citizens. This definition of the drug – which fits the dualism of the liberal definition of freedom – then justified a political statement about the subject in society:

> The Commission [of the Senate] obeyed the principal concern of taking exceptional measures to protect against a plague . . . To use a quite old judicial terminology, we would say that this is a law of '*salut public*'. This definition justifies in our eyes that in a number of cases . . . we have thought it best to make the general interest come before the rights of a few individuals' (cited in Bernat 1966: 152).

The threat that the perfectly causal drug posed to the collective justified the subordination of the individual's good to that of the society as a whole.[5] Social control was a moral necessity. Furthermore, it was added, the responsibility for this repressive policy was not actually the legislators'. The addict him/herself had already 'abdicated his/her right to liberty' when s/he acquired the vice of use in a condemnable effort to reach 'artificial paradises' (cited in Bernat 1996: 153). It was the *user him/herself* who, when s/he became dependant, had demeaned him/herself and made him/herself unworthy of the protection reserved for autonomous citizens.

The specialists
The 'law of 1970' also founded the 'specialised' system of addiction treatment and installed the principles of anonymity and non-payment of treatment. The law divided the responsibilities between the judiciary and the medical sectors while identifying the former as the guarantor of the process during which, under certain conditions and at precise moments, the user might become a patient in addition to being a delinquent. Only once the court had decided to orient the user towards a 'therapeutic option' was the medical system implicated in a case (Bernat 1996: 12). The sanitary sphere was thus carefully inscribed within a judiciary process. The user was never just a patient because s/he was always also a delinquent. The 'specialists' themselves criticised this 1970 law because of the hierarchy it instituted between judiciary and care. In practice, the co-ordination between these two practices was often non-existent, but specialists never succeeded in obtaining any official separation between repression and care (Bernat 1996: 146).

The specialists' refusal to co-operate in repressive procedures against drug users structured the very identity of their profession. In the course of the 1970s, they came to define themselves by this condemnation of coercion, outside and inside treatment:

> The question of human rights is at the centre of the majority of debates among specialists in addiction treatment since the beginning of the 1970s, in the sense of the problem of the abuse of power in the therapeutic field. A majority of specialists accept today that there is no efficient treatment outside the will [*volonté*] of the subject in question [the drug user]. The crucial gap, the break between different styles of intervention is the acceptance or refusal of external constraint to help the addict . . . Thus three struggles . . . against imprisonment . . . against sects and therapeutic communities . . . against 'maintenance' treatments, of which the model is the distribution of methadone in the United States at the end of the 1960s. These treatments imply indeed the maintenance of a dependence under a very constraining form, of a nature opposed to the evolution of the subject. The specialists have therefore become the promoters of a flexible model of care, non-coercive, based permanently on the explicit request for care by the user. . . . *The goal of treatment is ideally liberty of choice. Olievenstein would say 'psychological democracy'* (Valleur 1992: 2, *emphasis mine*).

Sects, prison and methadone were counter-examples that helped define 'specialised' addiction care by designating what it was not (see also Valleur 1988: 11).

Just as it was for the legislators, the drug (heroin or methadone) was for the specialists a perfectly causal force that imposed itself on the subject. The two main techniques of care used by the specialists took for granted this definition of the drug. The first technique was the abstinence cure, which marked the beginning of all treatment (Morel 1997, Morel *et al.* 1997). The patient was required to 'withdraw' from the drug before psychological treatment might begin. The subject was 'free' (in a first sense of 'abstinent') proportionally to the distance s/he maintained from the causal drug. Treatment did not begin until the user was 'clean' and would abruptly ceased if s/he relapsed because 'one cannot speak with one's mouth full'. As in the law, the drug was either absent or deterministic.

A second tool was the 'contract of care'. Contracts sought to educate the user in relations with humans and thus to stimulate him/her to mature. In his/her relation with drugs, the user had been able to avoid the conflicts necessary for maturation because the drug brought him/her controllable, *predictable* pleasure. (The drug's action was fixed, they assumed, because it acted autonomously.) With humans, no such predictability of success could be guaranteed: the user might be rejected, his desires refused by this unruly Other. Contracts attempt to establish relations between humans (*e.g.* Castel 1981) significantly different from the relation between user and drug. Contracts do not eliminate the uncertainty of human encounters; rather they aim to construct an inter-subjective space where difficult negotiations among humans might occur:

> [With contracts], the caregiver becomes a true interlocutor . . . a subtle negotiation begins where each will try to bring the other closer to his own terrain, without breaking trust. It is a mutual adaptation which occurs in a common frame . . . It is an apprenticeship of exchange [which] will test the consistence of the other, neither lax (giving in) nor rigid (holding back). Negotiation is a process that transforms the request for care into a human tie. . . . To negotiate is to give the possibility to a patient to step away from command (the tyranny of the drug) which obsesses him . . . (Morel 1997: 224–5).

Importantly, these contracts do not 'perform' or 'construct' the free subject. For specialists, the 'construction of the subject' is an enormity since the subject was precisely what is not constructed. The notion of 'maturation' shows the specialists' very limited version of 'construction'. Subjectivity, it is assumed, is a seed present in every individual from the start. The subject develops and 'matures' as s/he *eliminates* constraints that bind him/her. The subject is either subjugated or free from constraints and thus it is impossible to conceive here that the subject might benefit from (pharmacological) constraints. The subject then is either given or already lost, there is no intermediary state of the subject where it might be in genesis, in the making. The commitment of the specialists to the eradication of coercion (abstinence from addictive drugs and freedom from penal constraints) can thus be traced to the foundation of their field in the Law of 1970 and the tenuous articulation of penal and medical powers in that law.

It has intrigued some observers that the specialists insisted on treating a delinquent, divested of basic human rights by this very Law of 1970, like a psychological patient, that is, a free subject. The addict was deemed capable of choice 'even though' the larger context was a repressive one:

> It is important to recognise that addiction is a choice, there is a search for transgression, *even though* the prohibitionist context creates a specific field for crime and that the price of the drug maintains the majority of addicts in prostitution and delinquency . . . (Valleur 1992: 15).

In the early 1990s this commitment by the specialists to the free subject was criticised for its 'excessive idealism' (*e.g.* Coppel 1994, Nadelman 1993, Reisinger 1994). Even as the specialists had attempted to distinguish themselves from the repressive interventions of the user, the critics argued, the specialists took to an extreme the very assumption which had legitimated the severity of the Law of 1970: the human subject should be autonomous and free. The specialists' critique of the law had worsened the effects of the war on drugs rather than alleviated them. Accusations proliferated. Specialists had patients unwilling or incapable of abstaining thrown onto the streets and thereby condemned them to a cycle of aggravated use-delinquency-marginalisation. Specialists severed relations with police and judges and thus cut themselves off too from just those users most 'at risk'. In the early 1980s, specialists refused to distribute leaflets, and kits (containing clean syringes, cotton and alcohol) facilitating 'clean shoots' to prevent HIV infection. Thus, like police and judges, they sacrificed the health of the users to an ideal of abstinence. The 1990s critics made an unprecedented amalgamation. They took *both* the specialists and the repressive forces to be responsible for the catastrophic state of drug users in France (*c.f.* Gomart and Martineau 1999). Whereas the specialists insisted upon their 'French originality' (Valleur 1992 and 1988), their critics took the specialists and the legislators to have shared a common theory of the subject and of the drug while widening the gap between them to the detriment of the user. If the goal was to improve the living conditions of the user, then isolating care from repression was counter-productive. The relations between these two fields, and between treatment and the use of constraint, had to be tackled anew.

The crux of the debate became just what the specialists had not questioned for over 20 years: the ideal of freedom.

What was intolerable for these specialists, carriers of the libertarian ideal, was in the nature of dependence on drugs itself: this libertarian ideal became paradoxically (because of the fascination of the caregivers for the drug users of the early 1970s) the cause of an extreme intolerance towards drugs: abstinence became the only objective of treatment . . .
　　We excluded ourselves with our patients in a superb therapeutic isolation and our ethical position of free choice became, in spite of ourselves, a selective ideology and a motto for exclusion (Hefez 1994).

Let us follow, then, a few of these actors who problematised the un-problematic.

The search for generous constraint

At the Blue Clinic, the experimenters said their goal was to 'learn how to constrain, incite, educate, inform and seduce' a user into treatment (Amanda 1989: 159[6]). But towards what end should these lures and constraints be deployed? Abstinence and autonomy were no longer the uncontested goals, so what was?

Honestly, it is not clear what the therapeutic approach to harm reduction is. We only know that it is against the one that came before [the specialists']. At the beginning, it's just a bit . . .

methadone. And we show that we give it rather than hiding it (Beatrice, Head Nurse, Fieldwork notes March 1995).

I shall begin by showing that substitution treatment started as a simple attempt to 'find' the user who had been lost to specialised treatment centres. What would come next was left open. The Clinic was located in a neighbourhood that would facilitate 'access' (near a major drug dealing centre). As the staff sought to 'go out and meet the user', the user was no longer what founds but what was found. As time went on, I will show, the ambiguity of this term 'finding' was exploited: the caregivers did not simply *locate* a missing subject, they tentatively *achieved* a specific subject. The 'subject' was an entity that afforded construction and could take on intermediary positions *between* coercion/freedom, passive/active, in some ways reminiscent of the 'mediators' described by science and technology studies (STS).

The palette of drugs
To understand how the Blue Clinic staff deployed pharmacological constraints to find and to construct the user, let us first delineate their specific definition of drugs. The substitution promoters begin with an outright rejection of the deterministic definition of drug action which had founded the legislators and specialists' approach to addiction: in the first manual this group authored, they relegate the pharmacological definition of the drug to the appendix (see Gomart 2002). The substitution promoters redefined drugs in away that emphasised the *variability*, rather that the *predictability*, of their effects (*e.g.* Zinberg 1974). Heroin and cocaine do not always have the same respective effects. Five different 'modes of use' (the concrete conditions of use, the techniques used, the company and setting of use), these actors suggest, participate in the production of different effects for the same drug (or 'cocktail' of drugs). Addiction, which had been a monolithic relation to a substance, was deployed to reveal five kinds of relation: *mode of life, functional, recreational, compulsive, and anaesthetic use.*

What exactly are these modes of use? It is clear that they are an explicit rejection not simply of the earlier (fixed, predictable, causal) definition of drug action; they are also a criticism of the specialists' psychological definition of the subject. Thus this argument serves to counter the specialists' description of 'the typical addict': 'There is no such thing as a portrait of the typical drug user' (Lowenstein *et al.* 1995: 37). Modes of use are emphatically not psychological profiles: '*The typology of the uses should not be confused with a typology of users, the use of drugs fulfilling for the same person different functions*' (Lowenstein *et al.* 1995: 41, *original emphasis*). The drug-using subject is not defined at the start. It is neither pre-given nor pre-constructed.

Further, whereas the specialists had been incapable of describing what might come in between addiction and freedom, the 'modes of use' are precisely these intermediaries. They describe different positions of the subject, *between* the psychological poles of the annulled/free subject, different modes referring to different degrees of freedom, recreational mode of use at one pole and anaesthetic use at the other. To describe these 'in-between states' it is noteworthy that the substitution promoters (with their focus on 'modes of use') shifted their attention to *practices*. The entities (drug, subject) are now coextensive with an entire network of gestures and techniques. Similar to the entities of science studies, drugs and subjects are a temporary association of actants. These entities vary in time and space and their variations can be followed as changes in the chain of elements with which the entity is coextensive. So what is the essence of that drug? Who is this user? 'All of these associations', one might answer (*e.g.* Latour 1999: 161). For example, 'functional use' defines simultaneously 'drug' and 'subject' by referring to the associations into which these enter: the user's predilection for one drug or cocktail of drugs, the regular quantities, the frequent oral use of the drug, solitary use, the users' justification of use as 'self-medication', the often unpleasant professional activities performed by the user.

Thus, the hypothesis developed by staff was not that drug effects were *in*definite, any drug possibly causing any effect. Rather, with 'modes of use', they became extremely attentive to the hundred little details of use (including the exact drugs used) (*e.g.* Gomart 2002). One sign of this attentiveness was expressed in their drive to enlarge their *palette* of substitution drugs. In the experimental stage of the Clinic's practice in 1993–5, the palette included as many as six different products (methadone, Temgesic, Antalvic, Skenan, Moscontin, Palfium), each involving a different chain of associations. Methadone, for instance, involves long-term, daily attendance to drink the substance in front of a nurse at the Clinic, weekly urinary analyses, limited protocol flexibility which made travelling with the medication difficult to negotiate; users described it as 'opiate-like' but noted after a few weeks that 'they felt nothing'. Staff and patients often identified boredom as one effect of the methadone routine (Lowenstein *et al.* 1995: 56). This palette was used towards an end significantly different from the specialists' goal of abstinence. For example, Rodrigue, a young drug user 'who still likes to use' is not required to quit injections. Rather, Temgesic is prescribed because it *matches* many elements of his current use: the Temgesic pills can be crushed and (unofficially) injected; its prescription requires only infrequent visits to the Clinic and thereby limits the pathologisation of the drug career of this young user. The Temgesic routine resembles in points the mode of use of the user and thus might seduce him/her into treatment; further, it also crucially *shifts* slightly certain associations of use: the provision of Temgesic is an encouragement to the user to 'stock up' on his now plentiful drugs, to 'plan' his use, and thereby reduce the moments of urgency and risky behaviour which cause the social and medical degradation of the user (Arielle, Social Worker, Interview March 1996).

The changes proposed by these substitution drugs tentatively shift the users towards a sixth mode of use, called 'stabilisation' (reduction of injections, abandonment of risky behaviour, distance from the subculture of drugs, ...). The drug users, too, referred to a desirable, 'less dramatic' mode of use similar to 'stabilisation' with the term 'management' (a word sometimes picked up by staff). It might be thought that both 'stabilisation' and 'management' still refer to, respectively, a 'fixing' of a passive subject by a deterministic drug and to the mastery of a liberal agent. These terms, however, point to a user's very capacity to shift from one to another 'mode of use', that is, from one to another intermediary position of the subject between the lost and the full subject. More precisely, substitution promoters did not seek directly to construct new, fuller subjects. They focused on the relations *between* user and drug, on the practices of drug use and of substitution treatment that framed the user. The palette was a series of generous constraints, occasions to slightly change use in previously un-hoped for ways.

The dose
Another series of constraints was deployed to find and construct the user during the dosage of the substitution drug. The search for the right dose shows that as the staff devised pharmacological constraints they did not abandon all concern for a moral treatment, as the specialists had feared. It shows the difference between a constraint that subjugates and the generous constraints that induce movement.

The dosage techniques, like others developed at the Clinic, were not simply imposed on users. As Amanda, founder of the Clinic explains:

The first year, the treatment went with permanent *exchanges* between the team and the drug users. Treatment had to be adapted to their cultural patterns so that the drug users could take possession of this new way of life. . . . Without these exchanges, methadone programmes would not be accepted and the product would be merely added to all other drugs without affecting any change in behaviour. The meaning of treatment must be built during interactions between users and doctors (Amanda, interview 1995a, *emphasis added*).

The users were taken to be representatives of a mode of life, who had to be not pathologised but *convinced* of the utility of substitution drugs. In order for treatment to be efficient at all, it had to begin not with a passive and compliant patient but with the staff's deference to the user's 'expertise'. In the following scene, a first dosage is evaluated with a young woman, Pascale, who had been taking Moscontin (a medication unofficially prescribed to addicts in 'risk reduction' treatments since 1993 and explicitly banned by law in 1997) for several months and, after a recent episode of intense heroin use, has been switched over to methadone. This is her second day with the new drug.

The nurse, Marie, waves through the window to a young woman, Pascale, to enter the *bocal*, the small glass room where the nurses distribute methodone. She enters. A second nurse, Charlene, more experienced at the Clinic, is sitting in a corner of the small room, next to me and the pharmacology intern.

Marie: So how is it going?

Pascale: I slept very well. I did not even want to get up to come here. With Moscontin I could not get to sleep but now I slept better than I have in months. I am still sleepy.

M: You think the metha [methadone] *knocked you out*? [. . .]

P: It had been such a long time since I had slept so well.

Charlene: Was it the excess of methadone that made you sleep, or was it the sleep you had to catch up on?

P: I had sleep to catch up on. I was exhausted.

C: When did you go to bed?

P: At eight p.m.

C: And when did you get up?

P: At eight.

C: And yesterday evening were you *out of it*?

P: No.

C: If last night, your first night, you were not out of it, then it is not the methadone. You had sleep to catch up on.

P: Yes.

C: Did you take pills [illegally used tranquillisers]?

P: No.

C: So this is what we'll do. [. . .]

Marie serves 50mg of methadone, which the patient drinks immediately. Then she takes out another bottle which she places on the counter in front of the patient.

M: We give you 50mg now and *the 10mg you take with you. It's for you to judge* (if you will need them). Maybe you'll only need 5mg, then you take 5mg (you drink half the bottle).

P: You can feel that, 5mg?

Charlene and the intern: Yes!

C: 55mg is not 60mg. Some people say, *'There's just a touch missing!'* [*Il manque un poil*]. Then we go up 5mg, and it's fine.

M: So that it's *'comfort'* as you say.

C: Or we go down 5mg, if persons have secondary effects. If they *feel out of it, if they get a headache* [*chappe de plomb*]. *Something heavy, not like an opiate effect*. (Fieldwork notes, September 1995)

The terms underlined in this discussion (withdrawal, a touch missing, out of it, comfort, opiate effect, heavy headache) belong to the vocabulary of drug users. 'You have to use the vocabulary of the user', insists the head nurse. (Fieldnotes, March 1995). This is one way to defer to the skills of the user.

I want to argue further that when they deferred to the 'expertise' of the user, it might be thought that they were producing him/her as a *fuller* subject even than the liberal agent. Instead, I suggest that this deference implied an alternative definition of patient 'activity'. One clue to this is that this expertise was not assumed to be contained within the users, but rather was afforded by certain architectural features of the Clinic. For example, the psychiatrist at the Blue Clinic describes the *lieu de vie* as a space where experienced patients talk:

> There is a strategy for negotiating doses we set up here . . . you saw that they fix their own doses, more and more? We let them dose themselves . . . For example, at the beginning of treatment, they always ask for an increase. I let them increase. Then obviously they get secondary effects. They have a 'heavy' stabilisation. So they tell me 'Something's wrong, you gotta treat that!'. For example, they have sleeping problems. You give a little . . . a useless powder [*poudre de perlimpimpin*], whatever. You give something knowing full well that it won't work. It'll work laterally. Then they realise that methadone is the problem and that they are overdosed. And they come tell me, 'So-and-so told me that I am overdosed'. So they talk about it in the *lieu de vie* and they come back to me or to the nurse . . . So I say, 'Yes I know but if I had told you that you'd said that I was trying to lower you [*te baisser*], to stop your treatment. And since so-and-so told you, it's got more value'. So we lower [the dose]. And they understand what it means to be over-dosed or at least 'stabilised'.
> (Interview DT, 1995)

With this deference to users, then, the full subject is not brought back in; rather, attention is shifted to the conditions of treatment (*i.e.* to the modes of use of substitution treatment) that perform users as competent collaborators in treatment.

> The staff of the Blue Clinic are all for harm reduction [as opposed to abstinence] and most of them are ex-users. We want to share with the users this history of harm reduction. And our patients, no matter how difficult, feel that. We are here more to help them than to judge them. We are caring for a population that is difficult. I am not making them into angels. Our work is community work [*travail communautaire*] . The nurses who give methadone do community work, without having any illusions about the users' capacity to organise themselves (Beatrice, Head Nurse, interview March 1995).

It is clear then that this 'expert' is not the liberal agent, but what is s/he? The head nurse pinpoints the type of activity which is tentatively elicited from him/her.

> When I begin a treatment I tell the guy: It's *you* [the patient] who will be the actor. It's *you* who will find the dosage. I give the limits, the frame. It's

him [sic] who will play the first card, not the doctor. [. . .] Only later [when he'll have fixed his dose] the guy will ask "And now what?" [*Et après?*] (Béatrice, Head Nurse, interview March 1995).

Beatrice says the user is an 'actor', and yet this word is followed immediately by a comment that her deference to 'his' activity is an occasion for the user to *turn back* to the caregiver and ask 'What now?'. Is the patient an actor then only insofar as s/he allows the *staff* to act again? Is s/he an (ANT) 'actant' when s/he 'passes' action? Action here is not the unhampered manifestation of an intention. The user acts, only because and when the staff act (through techniques of deference). In turn, the member of staff acts only when the user is an 'expert' who paradoxically asks, 'And now what?'. The activity of one does not preclude, but is the very occasion for the action of the other.

It might have been expected that the 'right dose' was what one calls an efficient dose, the one at which single entities are sources of action and impact upon others. But here dose efficiency is not about causation. Asked by the health authorities to define the 'efficient dose' of methadone treatment for users, Amanda offers an embarrassed answer:

Can one relate doses and stabilisation? Among the non-stabilised patients, four use heroin exclusively. The doses correspond to a request of the patients and can be considered average for two of the patients (60mg). One patient was given methadone in the course of her pregnancy and the increase was made upon her request, very progressively (from 30 to 50mg). The fourth patient had fixed for himself the goal of abstinence, obviously unrealistic, but has refused all increase of dosage. In these four cases, an increase might be useful, but is not accepted by patients at this time, either because it would require them to confront the reality of their continued use (of un-prescribed substances), and their minimisation of reality [sic], or because patients do not wish to give up their heroin use (Amanda, Annual report 1995, 8).

The health official's question about the possible correlation of high doses with increased treatment efficiency implicitly suggested that treatment depended upon the force of the drug only: the drug works better if increased, they hypothesised, the efficiency of treatment mechanically following the quantity of the drug absorbed. Amanda's answer, however, reveals a variable the administrators had overlooked: 'requests'. In practice, doses cannot be increased experimentally to test a mechanistic theory because doses are not fixed unilaterally but negotiated with patients. To increase or decrease a dose experimentally affects the relation between drug-staff-user in unacceptable ways. More radically, it seems, the dose 'works' at the very moment that the object, staff and user cannot be untangled, when the question of what should be attributed to the user or to the drug has become irrelevant. Just as in the 'chains of actants' in the sociology of technology, it is useless to ask 'who acts' because each actant acts at the same time, transforming and inducing the action of the other. To grasp this peculiar form of activity, which does not fit the liberal opposition of active-passive, free-coerced, let us contrast another tool of the Blue Clinic's with the specialists' contracts.

Mini-contracts

For the specialists, I have suggested that if a user failed to achieve the contracted goal, the patient had 'failed' in a manner typical of addicts. In contrast, when the Blue Clinic's *mini-contract* failed, the staff concluded that *they* themselves had failed to find a constraint capable of interesting this user. Their mini-contracts are exercises in the *modifications of the dispositif of treatment*, in an effort to seize the user and perhaps transform him/her. Thus, the problem for the staff was to find in each case a 'generous constraint' capable of making the user present in treatment negotiations an expert who will turn to ask 'so what?'.

Amanda explains here the difference between 'contracts' and 'mini-contracts':

> Care [at our Clinic] is an apprenticeship of management . . . The entire system of addiction treatment . . . works with contracts. It is an inheritance from psychiatrists. Before methadone, there was a contract not to get high. They [specialists] asked addicts not to be addicts! For my part, I do not like that word 'contract'. I prefer to speak of a 'process of negotiation'. I try to say 'We're going to stop injections, and then identify the obstacles to this vague goal. We'll see as time goes by whether this is our objective or not'. We do little contracts, mini-agreements as we go along. . . . I do a pedagogy of the real . . . For example, if the guy can't stop injecting and insists that he wants to stop . . . I ask how do you inject? With whom? Where?. . . . (Amanda, interview February 1995).

A mini-contract aims for a change in mode of use. Towards this end, the mini-contracts might instrumentalise elements of the users' own 'managed' mode of use (*i.e.* little tactics users have developed for themselves). A user might be advised to 'take a vacation' far away from his/her dealer who is his/her neighbour, or to change his/her work itinerary if it leads him/her by a tempting pharmacy. Treatment routines provide an additional series of constraints which can be topicalised in the same way. A user can be asked to perform a urinalysis on Fridays to help him/her stay clean during the working week (and implicitly be allowed to use at week-ends).

Let us examine one scene where a mini-contract is tentatively made. Many of these mini-contracts are drawn up and discussed in the *bocal*. Lara, a patient on Moscontin – one of the few patients on that medication asked to go to the *bocal* regularly to receive their medication – discusses with Béatrice the idea of a medical check-up. During the interview, Charlène sits behind the counter, and Béatrice stands next to her, leaning on the counter, while Lara stands facing her.

In the *bocal*, the nurse Charlene just gave Lara her Moscontin. Lara is a young, pretty and very thin gipsy, very ill with AIDS.

B comments, looking Lara in the eyes: She doesn't feel good, Lara, when she takes 'pills' [medocs, legal medication used at non-prescription doses by users, such as Rohypnol]. She is in danger. She's flipped. And she de-stabilises her Moscontin. You put into question your stabilisation with the medication, as far as you are concerned, huh, not us. So that is why we talk to you about going into hospital. But to justify this [to the hospital staff] you have to know why you want to go.

Lara: Yes.

B: You want to do a health check up or take a break? . . . Figure out where you stand as far as your AIDS is concerned, or your mother?

L nods silently.

B: Does it still seem like a valid plan today?

L: Yes.

B: Or do we programme appointments for you and go with you. That way you don't have to be hospitalised?

L: Ah.

B: If you want to take a break, it's no use going into hospital. I thought of that because last month you said to me you couldn't manage taking a break at home. But you have to know that in hospitals, there are rules. You can't leave when you want, you can't walk around corridors . . . [She turns the pages of the nurse's logbook, and takes notes during the rest of the interview]. What is your prescription for your pneumonia?

L: Augmentin, 500. Powder.

B: And should I write, 'taken by L'?

L: Y-yes.

B: At the doses prescribed?

L: Uh, no, well . . .

B [writing]:   And your use of pills, you continue, you've stopped?

L: Yes.

B: And your Moscontin, you probably fucked up, mixing it with pills?

L: Yes. I took all of it in one evening.

B: So should I write that you are now re-stabilising, as far as your drug use is concerned?

L [Hesitant, then defensive]:   . . . No!

B: Ah! But it's just a question! So for the check up, I write with
    you that way you won't have to do it again with everyone: lost
    weight, pneumonia. But also, hospitalisation not essential.
    Yet, if we can do something as an out-patient . . .

L: What's that?

B: That's when you don't go in hospital, you don't have to stay
    but you can still get tests done.

L: Ah, that's good, that thing.

B: That way you can get a precise diagnosis and proposals for
    adapted treatment. So [she writes], see if there is still room in
    the ward of [X].

L: Is it far?

B: No. It is in the department of [O]. They are nice and
    competent [with users]. We will take you by car. We know that
    otherwise it is complicated with your mother [if she has to
    take you]. So we shall organise and tell you what's planned.
    For that, you still have to make an appointment with [the
    psychiatrist at the Blue Clinic] tomorrow.

L: Yes. That's OK, I got everything! [*J'ai tout capte*]

But Lara does not come the next day, or the following week. The nurse
comments a few days later.

Charlene: She had to come for an appointment on Friday and never
    showed up. When a counsellor went to bring her her Moscontin,
    she was completely high. To make her treatment progress, she
    has to be able to make an appointment here. But every week
    end she relapses [into drug use]. Her boyfriend shows up every
    Saturday and they get high together. He demolishes
    everything we do. The perspective [sic] for her is very bad.
    [Fieldwork notes, January 1995]

The interview begins with Béatrice obliquely suggesting that Lara has used
'pills', a suggestion Lara confirms only a little later. The nurse further
deploys a variety of questions and propositions about a medical check-up.
Her writing in the logbook serves to push this reticent patient to clarify and
answer questions while retaining a tone of negotiation. This technique is a
striking mutation of the psychological 'contract' for free subjects. Here, first
of all, the goal is completely removed from abstinence. The user is not, and
does not seek (at least in the short-term) to be, autonomous and free.
Secondly, the nurse does not expect the user to be already full to the brim
of *demandes*, desires and intentions.

  The nurse's questions search and tentatively discern, as well as construct,
Lara's capacity and reticence. Unlike the specialists, the substitution promoters do not put the authenticity of the user's desire for abstinence to the
test. Rather, the nurse's questions simultaneously discover and transform
Lara's intentions. The authenticity of a subject's desires are not pre-given

but emerge in associations that already corrupt them. Béatrice sounds out the patient and proposes hypothetical desires. She, who has been married to a gypsy and is an ex-user, bounces each of her proposals off Lara, or because Lara remains mostly silent, off an imaginary user of her own. This imaginary Lara might not like being locked up in a hospital ward, might not like to have to ask her mother to accompany her, and so forth. Only twice does Lara so much as hint at an opinion she might already have about the project [Is it far?; Ah that's good, that thing]. Each variation in the description of the project is like a variation in the material constraints of an experimental apparatus or *dispositif*: Béatrice is searching for *the* constraint, the compromise that Lara will accept and which will make her participate in this project. Instead of imposing one constraint, she adjusts, switches, and replaces one element of the project with another. With her minimal project and her multiple questions, Béatrice searches for just those constraints that might make Lara accept the project of a medical check-up. If she succeeds, the staff will have more opportunities to intervene with her. They will accompany her to the hospital, check with her that all is well, discuss the results, and perhaps in the process glean enough details about her life to initiate a second project.

If staff describe this search for good constraint as an 'individualisation' of contracts, individualisation here has an unusual meaning. The individual to whom the project is adapted is not pre-given (with her 'needs' already known through the psychologist's or the social worker's evaluations, for example). The individual emerges only as the experimenter varies and adjusts her 'offer of care'. Amanda explains this tentative discovery and construction of the specificity of the user:

> We create a link and then we become capable of responding to a
> person. Via the offer of service. The person has a problem and
> realises that we help him/her . . . Our entire work is centred on the
> encounter with the person [*aller à la rencontre de*]. The person has
> to accept [*adhère*]. At first, we are very distant and the person says
> 'I don't care' and then we have to make propositions of care until we
> gain her acceptance. Already, when we get that, it's a big step. It's
> going towards the person. Listening, supporting and going towards . . .
> And then we can agree on an objective for care. Even if that's: 'We can't
> do anything about it and the only thing we can do is listen to you'
> (Amanda, interview February 1998).

The individual's specificity, like the properties of actors in science studies, emerges only *in* a certain set of constraints and *varies* with this *dispositif*. This scene shows, more radically, that there are cases when the specificity of the actant is *not* constructed-revealed. The sociology of technology has insisted upon the productivity of constraints: *dispositifs* make differences proliferate; they perform the very properties of the beings which pass through them. Properties are not contained within entities but emergent in the encounter between this being and that setting. This example however suggests that there are cases where the *dispositif* does not produce new capacities, whether interesting or not. Nothing is then constructed-revealed about an actant because the right, the generous, constraint was not found, and no resistance was therefore elicited from the actant. In this case, where the offer of care failed to interest Lara, nothing was learned about this user. The *dispositif* remained silent. Lara never did carry through the very small tasks that were required of her, even after the tentative variations of the mini-contract. The pertinence of the 'offer' is in the end tested by the user who returns or does not return to pursue the unfolding of the project. Altern- atively, the non-accomplishment of the project might be taken not just as a failure (evidence of inefficiency of treatment) but as a sign that the staff took the risk of generosity. Only generous constraints force efficiently.

The practitioners seem to be opting for a specific theory of action. Activ- ity is not conceived as the exercise of an autonomous force upon another vulnerable entity. Rather, agency here is barely visible. Human activity is the capacity to seize actions that pass. The authenticity of a subject's intentions is not pre-given but emerges in associations that already corrupt them. The agent's task is simply to 'let play in his/her favor the constraining effect in operation' (Jullien 1992: 39).

Strategy
What is crucial to the Blue Clinic's hypothesis about what it takes for sub- jects to act is that human action has nothing to do with free will. Indeed, I am not arguing that mini-contracts are 'generous' at the moment that they do *not* subjugate Lara into compliance. Another hypothesis is being tested by the staff which no longer pivots upon this opposition between consent and coercion: that the mode of use of a drug user can be significantly influenced by a deployment of new constraints. A new series of conditions are set up and tentatively affect his/her mode of action. 'Conditioning' requires both that there are external determinants to which one might abandon oneself as well as the active participation of the user in this abandonment. It weaves together passivity and activity, subjugation and free will in unexpected ways (*c.f.* Gomart 1999). The Clinic's hypothesis pivots upon a second opposi- tion: what characterises this 'conditioning' is not that it is *self*-imposed rather than *externally* constrained (*controlled rather than suffered*), a dis- tinction between forces that propose/impose, but another distinction between forces that *initiate new associations* and those that *isolate*. The ideal is no longer the liberal, autonomous agent free of constraints, but what might be called an 'attachment' which displays and shifts between several influences.

To grasp the second aspect of this hypothesis let us turn again to a scene of Clinic practice. Here, a urinalysis is requested by Florence, a methadone patient:

In the *bocal*, Florence negotiates with Marie, a nurse.

F: I would like to make an arrangement to come every two days.

M: You were to see Charlene about that.

F: Can I do a urinalysis?

M: Sure. Are you 'clean', today?

F: Yes, it has been a while. With the baby, we had said I could come every other day. But then I had messed up a bit so . . .

Beatrice, the head nurse, comes in and Marie explains the situation to her:

B: And now, do we have a series of urinalyses that are clean?

M: I don't know.

F: We'll see. [She takes out from the cupboard a pile of official urinalyses results. She searches for Florence's].

B: So, here you're got one at least [negative] from February 17th. So there's no reason to . . . if you're . . .

F: Yes, myself, I know I've been OK. Since the famous Thursday of I don't know how long ago.

B: Yeah, beginning February. One month. [She finds another urinalyses, positive this one]. Well, less than a month. This one is February 8. But it's OK you've still got others that are negative. [She finds a third and a fourth negative]. OK, there. In principle, we negotiate arrangements [at staff meetings], but for now OK, you've got your kids on vacation and you'd like to have your methadone for tomorrow and only come back Wednesday. And you have urinalyses that argue that . . . so for this week it's OK.

F: It would be nice.

B: OK. So you're back on Wednesday. [B writes on the logbook that Florence comes back Wednesday. . . . She gets her daily methadone. And M gives her two bottles of 40mg for the next day.]

Later Beatrice, very angry after having re-read the different notes in the logbook about Florence and spoken to Charlene, says:

B: Florence, there was never any question of skipping a day. It was always daily. This week, it's OK. But just this once. The official arrangements are written down and so you can check [in the logbook]. Charlene never agreed to skip a day. I played the card of 'arrangements are decided [at staff meetings]' but agreed for just this once. She's already got so much trouble moving her butt to take care of her kids, if on top of everything she didn't have to come here in the morning, [she wouldn't care for them at all] . . . (Fieldwork notes, March 1995).

The urinalyses are used by patient and staff to negotiate a temporary reduction of the frequency of attendance. They are a trick for drug 'management' (in the sense introduced above), encouraging the user to plan and reduce his/her use. Clearly, this constraint is not one that has the consent of the patient.

What differentiates this technique from discipline, the simple reduction of the actions of the user? With urinalyses, Florence is *encouraged to act* when she is required to 'argue for' the reduction by referring to these analyses. When Florence learns to argue, she also learns to (or tries to) refrain long enough from drugs to produce clean urine. She does not simply learn to verbally demonstrate her management; in the process she actually learns to perform the minimal management Amanda described. Importantly, on the occasion of this argument, the user is engaged in more negotiations. What might have been taken to be a simple 'surveillance' technique aims instead to *prompt* a rhetorically sophisticated and cunning user into 'argumentation' and associations.

The next interaction of staff with Florence further characterises what makes constraints generous.

> Beatrice advises the new nurse, Marie, in the bocal, just before Florence comes in to take her methadone. Charlene is not there that day. So Marie had to deal with her again.
>
> B: You tell her that it's too early for arrangements for two days, premature, especially in relation to the urinalyses. You stay on the surface. You say Charlene will talk to her about it more. The urinalyses, that's something you can refer to. And for the comments, she sees Charlene.
>
> Later in the *bocal*, Florence discusses with the nurse her disappointment about the arrangement being refused.
>
> F: . . . It's really hard coming here every day with the kids . . . and every day I got papers to do. If I had known methadone was so constraining . . . At least with Moscontin, you're at home. Charlene had told me just to get a few urinalyses that were OK. That it'd be fine. She knows about the children. She said, 'Try to be OK, at 80mg you are stabilised'.
>
> Marie remarks that the arrangement Florence mentioned was cancelled last time she 'screwed up'; and that since she has come everyday again, she's had at least one positive urinalysis (Fieldwork notes, March 1995).

Clearly, the user is not required passively to comply. The staff instead ask for a peculiar *concession* on the part of Florence. Florence is told to '*try to be OK, because at 80mg she is stabilised*'. Strikingly, the user is *summoned* to act when the drug acts. She *must* pass on the action passed to her by the 'right' deferential dose of the substitution drug. Is she scolded and insidiously *forced* to submit to the rules of the Clinic? Must she recognise that the medication *determines* her actions biologically? No, Florence is requested to *strategically submit* to rules and to the drug in order for them, in turn, to gain in efficiency. Like the musician slavishly practicing scales to prepare her/himself for a spontaneous and creative interpretation of a piece, like the user who carefully prepares the space of her/his shoot by, for example, closing the curtains to ensure being overcome by pleasure, the Clinic patient too must set up the conditions under which s/he might be granted action. S/he must submit to a series of preparations, routines, trainings until she is ready for action to 'arrive' (see Gomart and Hennion 1999).

> In another scene, Amanda insists to a new patient the importance of such concessions:
> Patient: If it were really efficient, methadone, how come it's not been used in years?
> A: It is a product which has finally become efficient. It is not for those [users] who want to go on getting high. For it to work, you need to get people at the very moment that they sort of do not want drugs or want to quit for a while.
> Charlene, the nurse: It is not a miracle. It gives you a possibility, but if you do nothing with it.
> The patient leaves and Amanda says to me and to the nurse:
> A: He's scared of the dependence to the drug. He's not happy. Substitution for the guys, it's dependence and dependence is the devil. One does not make a pact with the devil. He's resisting. He's scared. . . . Methadone is a card. You have to accept treatment. Once you play the card, you have to accept the game. Raoul [a charismatic user, respected by all] took six months to accept treatment (Fieldwork notes, January 1995).

For Amanda, there are specific conditions under which methadone will work. Methadone *requires* a dependent (skilled) user in order to work. The user's dependence then is a series of skills that, once slightly matched and adjusted, allow him/her to prepare for the substitution drug. Dependence on methadone and its routines is a tactic. If not a pact with the devil then at least a move in a game of cards with a force stronger than you. When the staff and user agree upon modalities of a mini-contract, the modalities of treatment do not simply oblige him to behave in a certain way (to attend the treatment daily, account for his progress, urinate in a cup, etc . . .). They list the crucial skills necessary for treatment to work, for 'stabilisation' to occur. Like Merleau-Ponty's insomniac who feigns to sleep and thus effectively falls asleep, the user who cunningly concedes, learns to espouse the contours of the drug, thus tentatively achieves stabilisation (management). The patient is not told to play *by* the rules, but to *play the rules*: use them as tricks and draw benefit from his/her cunning acceptance of constraint. The 'stabilised' patient strategically colludes with necessity.

Strategy is the register peculiar to the Clinic. This idiom distinguishes interventions at the Clinic from the register of discipline that aims to standardise and to reduce the number of possible actions, and continues to pivot upon the opposition free/determined (see Foucault 1975). The idiom of 'strategy' is by contrast characterised by a *proliferation* of tricks and tactics by both users and staff in their attempts to allow action to arrive. In the following scene, a patient has stolen medication from the *bocal*. The register of strategy tentatively opens a multitude of possible actions for the user and the staff to continue to act just when the rules have been so severely breached that both fear for a moment that the relation between user and staff is broken and that discipline is the only register left.

The counsellors (Marine and Paul) have been trying to get Tanya to admit to her theft of medication (Moscontin) in the *bocal* when the nurse's back was turned. But Tanya persists in denying everything and ups the stakes by taking their 'suspiciousness' for a sign of their lack of caring for her as a patient and friend:

Tanya: . . . You think I'd steal your Moscontin?!

M: [in a caressing voice] But of course. It's the rule of the game. You're like everybody. It's human too. You took advantage of the fact I was busy next door with the doctor. . . . Be a good player. Return the Moscontin, and tomorrow you come back and everything is like it was.

T: No! I'm going to a GP!

P: Before, I was a user; I would have done exactly the same thing.

M: It's human, Tanya. The temptation was too great. Come on, be a good player. If we wanted you to leave, imagine the number of times we could have thrown you out! We have told you enough what we think of you. [Smiles]. Come on, you give me the Moscontin and at one o'clock, we go have a beer.

T: I'd feel better with Moscontin . . . [than with methadone].

M: We'll talk about it.

T [barely audible]:   I flinched. [She returns the pills from her pocket].

M: It's human to make mistakes. When was the last time you made one? Two months ago? Well, that means now you better hold on two months before doing it again! You got two months! [Everyone laughs].

Another client enters without knocking for his methadone. Tanya leaves saying, smiling candidly:

T: They caught me with my Moscontin!

A few days later, I see the nurse again outside the Clinic. Marine sums up the event to others present:

M: She returned the Moscontin. I played the card of tenderness. What worked was when I told her 'Be a good player, you played and you lost'. She said to herself 'Yes OK, in the end I just should not have got caught' (Fieldwork notes, February 1995).

Just when every one had thought that confrontation or interruption of collective action had been inevitable, the strategic idiom creates another possible way out. This register of strategy, the tricks deployed, are ways of turning moments, when disciplining and blocking the user's action seem inevitable, into an occasion for the user to become an attachment, an actant to whom action can be passed and who will pass it again. It is the idiom of an original theory of human action.

Conclusion

To claim that humans are granted action when cunningly being made to submit to constraints is to undo the liberal theory of autonomous action. It problematises the evidence of the ideal of freedom. Freedom is not the highest good. Rather, the deployment of generous constraints is what passes humans (and drugs) into action, in a manner reminiscent of science studies where settings pass technological entities into action (see Chapter 1). The Clinic's original hypothesis rests, I have claimed, on a dualism different from the liberal domination/subjugation. It pivots upon a distinction between constraints that 'attach' and those that isolate. This new dichotomy is nowhere clearer than in Amanda's techniques of selecting patients for methadone. In these techniques themselves oppositions are embedded which contradict the liberal definition of action and offer an alternative to it. Let us listen to Amanda as she describes the patients for whom methadone works:

> The indication [of methadone] has to do with pleasure and inebriation [*défonce*].
> With methadone there is a ceiling effect [you don't get the intensity of the pleasure of heroin, and if you inject heroin after taking methadone, you won't feel it much]. Methadone doesn't make you high [*défonce*]. If the guy [sic] is not looking for inebriation [*ivresse*], then it's OK. If he's had enough, then it can be a pharmacological aid. Otherwise, it becomes an obstacle, and he'll turn to coke use. Then it's better to prescribe Moscontin so he gets a little of euphoria [*euphorie*].
> (Amanda, Interview May 1995)

Here, treatment works not for those who authentically desire to stop, but for those who are (temporarily) tired of a certain mode of use (inebriation). Those for whom methadone works might still continue to seek a mild, opiate-like pleasure, but not the un-settling rush and urgency of inebriation. Strikingly, the differentiating trait is that 'inebriation' users are less amenable to intervention.

> If there is no search for inebriation, or if the guy is looking to calm down [*calmer le jeu*], the [methadone] pharmacological response will

work. But if he wants to stick his head in the sand, not know where he is, then my goal is to reduce harm. . . . I will try to make it so that he can have his head in the sand in the least risky, the least dangerous, the most sanitary way possible. He wants to, so any way he'll do it. It's better that he does it with morphine, rather than with alcohol and pills [*benzodiazépines*]. . . . Someone under morphine, I can talk to him, you still know what you are doing. But alcohol and pills, you don't. With morphine, you don't remember everything, but still . . . The most terrifying of all is cocaine. It is a frenzied race. The control of the product is very, very difficult (Amanda, interview May 1995).

Her argument is that even if substitution drugs might not work as well for 'inebriation' users, prescribing opiates for them is not meaningless: when they use opiates, these users 'can be spoken to'. The opposition between those for whom methadone works and those for whom it will fail is strengthened here by another opposition between, on the one hand, cocaine and pill users and, on the other, opiate (heroin or substitution drugs) users. Amanda here matches cocaine with inebriation and difficult associative action; opiates with mild pleasure and a capacity to learn to manage under the influence of others (staff and substitution products).

> EG (author):   Thomas said he could not manage coke. He says he takes it all night and stops only when he can no longer withdraw money from the cash machine.
>
> A: Yes, injected coke, you can't manage it. You cannot manage ecstasy [*extase*]. Management is just not in question when you speak of ecstasy [*extase*]. The only thing you can manage is dependence. With cocaine, the only thing you can say is 'Tie me up after three days'. You can't manage the product, but you can give it limits in time. When you shoot cocaine, it's that you do not want to manage. Coke is terrifying also because of the paranoia crises and the violence, for the user and for the people around him (Amanda, interview May 1995).

Cocaine designates the *limit* of human agency in a way radically different from that of the specialists: the non-active addict is not unfree, passive, immobile, an 'empty carcass' (Vedrinne 1987, Vera Ocampo 1989). On the contrary, s/he is engaged in a frenzied race and, this is crucial – s/he is absolutely *free* of attachments, isolated, alone. The cocaine addict resembles precisely what the psychologists had aimed for, the *autonomous* liberal agent.

Equally surprising, from the perspective of liberal definitions of human action, is the characterisation of the actor as the *dependant* user. Dependence describes here not a handicap, an immaturity, an incompleteness or lack. It refers to a 'maturity', that is, the skills acquired over long-term drug use. Raoul, an older, charismatic user, echoes Amanda's assimilation of dependence and skilled action:

EG: And for you, what is methadone?

R: It's to be normal. It's the trigger, the jumpstart in the morning. I take it very early and wait for an hour for it to work and for me to feel good. I zap the TV for an hour. I am always peaked in the morning. But afterwards, I feel better, only then do I take my coffee and get ready.

EG: And heroin what was it?

R: Same thing [as methadone]. You know, after [many years of use] heroin didn't do anything to me. It was just not to feel bad [*i.e.* to soothe withdrawal], like to re-charge my batteries. Methadone is for those for whom dope has become a physical thing, to avoid feeling bad. [. . .] For those who have understood that, methadone can be that too. That's what substitution is (Raoul, fieldwork notes, March 1996).

The specialists had assumed that management and dependence were opposed; here they have become synonyms.

This hypothesis about action does not claim to be universal or ideal. The limits of this definition of management are clear: the Clinic's substitution practices do not make treatment possible and interesting for 'inebriation' users. Cocaine marks the boundary and thus the specificity of the Clinic's theory of action. Further, neither the participants of the Clinic's experiment nor I would argue the idea that human action is *under all conditions* better conceived in Amanda and Raoul's terms rather than in liberal terms. It is clear that more alternatives must yet be sought. This is the final conclusion of the Clinic's experiment. Indeed, after three years of treatment and unexpected changes in the context of care, the staff reluctantly reported that a majority of their older patients tired of substitution routines and deployed new cocktails of drugs which the staff found resistant to their intervention techniques. Users, by preferring drug use to treatment, seemed to disqualify the local definition of what it takes for human subjects to act, just as they had implicitly critiqued the specialists' definitions in the 1980s. Raoul, a symbol of the Clinic's success for both patients and staff, died of an overdose in October 1998, marking for many the end of the golden era of the Clinic (see Gomart 1999a).

In this paper, I have sought to record a striking occurrence. I was able to follow this particular event only after deploying generous theoretical and methodological constraints (adapted from ANT works on action and from medical sociology on the construction of the subject) and by following 'mediators', patients and staff capable of translating to me the specificity of the phenomenon. Between 1993 and 1997, the staff and patients of the Blue Clinic participated in an original performance of the human subject. They tried out the hypothesis that the human subject is constructed and that its building blocks might even include addictive pharmacological substances. By varying constraints (the palette of drugs, details of modes of use in mini-contracts) staff and patients attempted a daring re-definition of the subject. Not as autonomous and free, but as an *attachment*, an entity emergent in constraining relations. Human agency is tentatively and temporarily re-defined as the capacity not to act alone, but to deploy skilfully and cunningly the right conditions in order to allow action to arrive; to act because one was generously constrained.

Acknowledgements

Earlier drafts of this chapter have benefited from comments from Marc Berg, Gerard De Vries, Nicolas Dodier, Jonathan Gabe, Antoine Hennion, Bruno Latour, Isabelle Stengers, Stefan Timmermans and three anonymous reviewers. I would also like to thank the founding members of the Blue Clinic for their comments and involvement in this project. This research was made possible by a three-year grant from the French *Ministere de la Recherche* as well as by a contribution from Synthelabo's *Institut pour le Developement de la Connaissance*.

Notes

1   The very theme then of this chapter has been perceived as dangerous to the actors of the Clinic. The publication of this chapter in English further purports to avoid an extant circulation of this description among those who might recognise the Blue Clinic.

2   Antoine Hennion (1993), for instance, criticises the main figures of French sociology for allowing objects to be either screens for the projection of human representations or causes, impacting on passive humans. Bruno Latour (1994a), similarly, argues that classical philosophy offers just two options to the analyst interested in describing the inter-action between a gunman and his gun: instrumentalism (the man masterfully manipulates the gun) or determinism (the man is entirely undone by the gun which causes him to become a murderer). The action finds its source either in the object or in the subject. When one is active, one threatens the very essence of those one acts upon.

3   Mediation allows the analyst to describe entities not as what they 'are' inherently, but as particular ways of deforming and prolonging the action passed. A bridge with its height and form is not just an implementation of the designer's plan; it does more than what the designer had expected by, for example, affording certain but not other forms of circulation under the bridge. (*c.f.* Winner 1986). The *excess* of mediation is key: the object deviates from the plan in unexpected ways. This allows the analyst to speak about the *specificity* of an entity without being essentialistic, since this specificity only emerges in specific associations. The 'authentic' object then emerges at the moment that it is associated with and corrupted by others.

4   My analysis of the French law is based, unless otherwise noted, on the description of the French debates and transformations of the law by the jurist Bernat de

Celis (1996). Though following closely Bernat de Celis' description, the argument I deploy here, insisting on the definition of drug and user, is entirely mine.

5 Other reasons were given for this. First, in a system of 'social security', it was unjust that a user – though s/he only harms his/her own body – made the rest of the collective pay for the treatment s/he then required (see Bernat de Celis: 153).

6 For reasons of confidentiality, explained in note 1, the Clinic's published work must also be referred to cryptically.

References

Becker, H. (1963) *Outsiders: Studies in the Sociology of Deviance.* New York: Free Press.

Berg, M. and Mol, A. (1998) *Differences in Medicine. Unravelling Practices, Techniques and Bodies.* Durham: Duke University Press.

Berlin, I. (1958) *Two Concepts of Liberty.* Oxford: Clarendon Press.

Bernat de Celis, J. (1996) *Drogue: consommation interdite. La genese de la loi de 1970.* Paris: L'Harmattan.

Callon, M. and Law, J. (1995) Agency and the hybrid collectif. Paper presented at *Non Human Agency: a Contradiction in Terms?, Conference in Theory and Methods,* Guildford: UK.

Castel, R. (1981) *La gestion des risques: de l'antipsychiatrie a l'après-psychanalyse.* Paris: Minuit.

Cesoni, M. (1992) Droit et politiques legislatives. In Ehrenberg, A. (ed) *Penser la drogue, penser les drogues. Volume. I: Etat des Lieux.* Paris: Descartes.

Coppel, A. (1994) Pratiques de substitution en Europe et reduction des risques, *Journal de Médecine Interne,* 145: 73–5.

Courtinho, R. and Hartgers, C. (1992) AIDS and the drug abuse treatment: the value of methadone maintainance, *The Journal of Current Opinon in Psychiatry,* 5: 426–9.

Cussins, C. (1998) Ontological choreography: agency for women patients in an infertility clinic. In Berg, M. and Mol, A. (eds) *Differences in Médicine.* Durham: Duke University Press.

Foucault, M. (1975) *Surveiller et Punir: naissance de la prison.* Paris: Gallimard.

Foucault, M. (1976) *La volonté de savoir.* Paris: Gallimard.

Gomart, E. (1999) Surprised by méthadone: expériments in substitution. PhD. Thesis. Paris: Ecole Nationale Superieure des Mines de Paris.

Gomart, E. and Hennion, A. (1999) A sociology of attachment: music amateurs, drug users. In Law, J. and Hassard, J. (eds) *Actor Network Theory and After.* Oxford: Blackwell.

Gomart, E. and Martineau, H. (1999) *La politique de drogues aux Pays-Bas: expérimentations récentes,* report for the Observatoire Français des Drogues et Toxicomanies.

Gomart, E. (2002) Methadone: six effects in search of substance, *Social Studies of Science,* February, 1–49.

Greimas, A.J. (1977) Pour une théorie des modalites, *Langages,* 10: 90–106.

Haraway, D. (1994) A game of cat's cradle. Science studies, feminist theory and cultural studies, *Configurations,* 1, 59–71.

Hefez, S. (1994) Toxicomanie, la fin des libertaires, *Liberation,* 25 July.

Hennion, A. (1993) *La passion musicale.* Paris: Metailie.

Ingold, S. and Ingold, F-R. (1989) Les effets de liberation de la vente de seringues en France, *Retrovirus,* II, 78–82.

Jullien, F. (1992) *La propension des choses.* Paris: Seuil.

Latour, B. (1991) *Nous n'avons jamais été modernes. Essai d'anthropologie symmetrique.* Paris: La Decouverte.

Latour, B. (1994a) Une sociologie sans objets? Quelques remarques sur l'interobjectivité, *Sociologie du travail,* 587–607.

Latour, B. (1994b) On technical mediation: philosophy, sociology, genealogy, *Common Knowledge,* 3, 29–64.

Latour, B. (1999) *Pandora's Hope: Essays on the Reality of Science Studies.* Cambridge: Harvard University Press.

Latour, B. (2000) A well articulated primatology: reflexions of a fellow traveler. In Strum, S. and Fedigan, L. (eds) *Primate Encounters.* Chicago: Chicago University Press.

Lebeau, B. (1994) Echange de seringues: la necessaire adaptation des stratégies aux pratiques des usagers de drogues, *Transcriptase,* 30, 17–18.

Lert, F. and Fombonne, E. (1989) *La toxicomanie: vers une évaluation de ses traitements.* Paris: INSERM- La Documentation Francaise.

Lowenstein, W., Gouranier, D., Coppel, A. *et al.* (1995) *La methadone et les traitements de substitution.* Paris: Doin.

Lynch, M. (1991) Laboratory space and the technological complex: an investigation of topical contextures, *Science in Context,* 4, 51–78.

Morel, A. (1997) Les intervenants en toxicomanie et la loi de 1970, *Psychotropes,* 3, 83–91.

Morel, A., Herve, F. and Fontaine, B. (1997b) *Soigner les toxicomanes.* Paris: Dunod.

Nadelmann, E. (1993) Reflexions serieuses sur quelques alternatives a la prohibition des drogues, *Les Temps Modernes,* 49, 151–84.

Olievenstein, C. (1977) *Il n'y a pas de Drogues Heureux.* Paris: Laffont.

Pickering, A. (ed) (1992) *Science as Practice and Culture.* Chicago: Chicago University Press.

Reisinger, M. (1994) Les avantages d'une prescription détendue de méthadone. In Guffens, J.-M. (ed) *Toxicomanie, Hepatites, SIDA.* Paris: Les Empecheurs de Penser en Rond.

Valleur, M. (1988) La terre est-elle plate? La toxicomanie est-elle une maladie? *Interventions,* 15–16, 9–15.

Valleur, M. (1992) Drogue et droits du toxicomane. Paper presented at *Drogues et Droits de l'homme,* Universite Paris X, Nanterre.

Vedrinne, J. (1987) Les personalites du toxicomane, *Confrontations psychiatriques,* 28, 103–22.

Vera Ocampo, E. (1989) *L'envers de la toxicomanie: un idéal d'indépendence.* Paris: De Noel.

Winner, L. (1986) *The Whale and the Reactor. A Search for Limits in the Age of High Technology.* Chicago: University of Chicago Press.

White, S. (1999) As the world turns: ontology and politics in Judith Butler, *Polity,* 32, 2, 155–77.

Zinberg, N. (1974) *Drug, Set and Setting.* New Haven: Yale University Press.

Zourabichvili, F. (1994) *Deleuze: une philosophie de l'événement.* Paris: PUF.

Chapter 3

The cause of death vs. the gift of life: boundary maintenance and the politics of expertise in death investigation

Stefan Timmermans

The corpse as a site of jurisdiction

Several commentators on the current US death investigation system have observed that medical examiners' main strength lies in their ability to link the disparate arenas of public health and criminal justice (DiMaio and DiMaio 1989, Hanzlick 1996). Medical examiners certify suspicious deaths, and separate suicides and natural deaths (traditionally of interest to public health officials) from homicides and accidents (also of interest to law enforcement and the legal professions). Their background as scientifically-trained physicians makes them the preferred front-line investigators to gather primary public health mortality data, and positions them as independent experts to provide invaluable courtroom testimony. Other observers, however, have noted that inhabiting the borderland of health care and jurisprudence also renders medical examiners vulnerable because they are perpetually situated betwixt and between two cultures with opposing priorities (Johnson-McGrath 1995). When pressured, do the loyalties of medical examiners lie with their clinical colleagues or with their allies in law enforcement?

In the last decade this question has gained urgency because organ and tissue procurement organisations have moved aggressively onto the turf of medical examiners, requesting access to corpses for transplant purposes. The result has become a struggle about access to the corpse that pitted the transplant community's promise of 'the gift of life' against the medical examiners' mandate to determine the 'cause of death' in forensic cases. At this point, jurisdiction over the corpse is fluctuating, and different offices of medical examiners have engaged in a variety of professional arrangements to resist or accommodate the pressure of procurement organisations. The conflict between criminal justice and life-prolonging medical techniques is intertwined with a struggle over jurisdiction: to whom does the corpse belong and for what good?

Jurisdiction is usually understood as a legal term, referring to the authority given by the law to a court to try legal cases and rule on legal matters within a particular geographic area and/or over certain types of legal cases. In sociology, the concept of jurisdiction has gained currency in the analysis of professions and experts (Abbott 1988, Freidson 1994, Light 2000). Andrew Abbott, in particular, has expanded the concept to explain the historical proliferation of professions (Abbott 1988). He sees professions engaged in an ongoing competitive struggle to claim and maintain jurisdictions. A jurisdiction is defined in this case as the tie between an organisational group and its work. Professions gain jurisdiction when they control their skills through abstract knowledge and technique. In their struggle to maintain and broaden a jurisdiction, professions appeal to public opinion, attempt to sway legislation, gain advantage in the workplace, and bolster claims with scientific investigations. From a sociological perspective, the legal meaning of jurisdiction is thus only one source of authority at the disposal of a professional group. Yet, even when jurisdiction is legally solidified, professional dominance is not guaranteed; competing groups can invalidate any claim for jurisdiction. The jurisdiction of a professional group therefore needs to be situated within a system of interdependent professions, or, as Donald Light puts it, countervailing powers (Light 2000).

Struggles between countervailing powers have become more intense in late modernity because radically new technologies allow emerging occupational groups to enter the competition over jurisdiction (Drazin 1990, Giddens 1994), leading to a particular form of 'politics of expertise – that is, conflicts over the exclusionary jurisdictional domains arising out of the contested monopolization of abstract knowledge and technique' (Reed 1996: 582). According to Reed, politics of expertise centre on the knowledge base on which claims to specialised skill and technique rest, the accomplishments resulting from the application of this knowledge, the political and economic strategies followed by experts to maximise their rewards, and the institutional forms that guarantee jurisdictional security and stability (Reed 1996: 583). Benefiting from technology-based knowledge and the resulting claims of neutrality, objectivity, mobility and universality, competing groups in a tug-of-war over jurisdiction can mobilise a nexus of cognitive, technical, political and normative resources to establish expert power over contested sites (Drazin 1990). The result is that, in late modernity, expertise is marred by great flexibility and uncertainty, giving rise to new divisions of labour and organisational forms (Beck 1992, Giddens 1994).

Although Abbott and others emphasise the relationship between a professional group and its work, they mainly analyse professions and expertise on a macro-level, investigating how jurisdictions of entire professional groups vanish or expand over time under internal or external pressure. Occasionally, Abbott endows the ability to articulate jurisdictions to professional umbrella organisations, but more often agency in Abbott's theory is implied: the historical shifts in authority over subject matters become an indication of agency on a professional level. Abbott is interested in explaining the rise and fall of professions, not the daily activities of professionals. I will link Abbott's insights on a macro level to a micro-level analysis and investigate how members of a profession maintain, defend and expand their jurisdiction during their everyday activities in light of jurisdictional shifts taking place on a broader institutional level.

I start from the assumption that while much of the jurisdictional articulation work is indeed performed by professional organisations, professionals in their respective workplaces will have to describe, maintain and defend the professional control over their work on a daily basis. Professional activities are not independently defined and determined by the professionals themselves but take place within clusters of interdependent relationships. Even if a profession has achieved full jurisdiction over a subject matter, professionals still need continuously to maintain their dominance organisationally and procedurally. And if the jurisdiction is not complete or is under attack, the workplace will be an important site of contention and boundary maintenance (Gieryn 1999). The research question that I will address in this article is how do professionals maintain the boundaries of their expertise and what are the consequences of their activities for the jurisdiction they obtain? My purpose will be to articulate the resulting jurisdictional relationships when a new professional group (procurement organisations) attempts to invade the jurisdiction of an established profession (medical examiners).

Methodology

Because of the great diversity in death investigation in the United States in organisation, personnel and procedures (Pescosolido and Mendelsohn 1986), the purpose of this research is not to provide generalised findings about death investigators in the United States. Instead, my aims are mainly conceptual. In line with the premises of grounded theory (Glaser and Strauss 1967, Strauss 1987), observations and other data gathering were guided by emerging theoretical conceptualisation.

I have been observing the classification of suspicious deaths in a medical examiner's office during a three-year period. This office is responsible for the certification and classification of suspicious deaths within a geographical territory in the United States with a population of about one million residents living in an expanding urban area with adjoining suburban and rural communities. The office employs six scene investigators, three pathology assistants, four full-time forensic pathologists and a number of administrative and medicolegal staff. I observed about 220 autopsies over the course of my investigation. The estimate arises from the fact that often several autopsies occurred at the same time in adjacent bays and I would be unable to observe all of them from start to finish. After guaranteeing confidentiality and anonymity of the office, deceased, staff, and state where the research took place, I had full access to the investigative files, morning meetings and the autopsies. During the autopsies, I took notes on a clipboard and transcribed them into full field notes at the end of the day. I also conducted numerous interviews with the staff and visiting pathologists. The institutional review board of Brandeis University approved this project. To make sure that I did not even inadvertently breach confidentiality and to check for accuracy of pathological descriptions, I asked the medicolegal administrator and chief medical examiner of my research site to read over all papers before submitting them for publication.

An incident that occurred during my ethnographic research formed the main stimulus for this chapter. It became quickly apparent, however, that for a full conceptualisation of forensic jurisdiction under threat, I had to go beyond the data available in my observations and interviews. I mainly consulted three sources to complement these observations: the medical literature, the social science literature and investigative journalistic reports. I conducted a content analysis of articles published in the medical literature to determine how the conflict between medical examiners and organ procurers was construed and to evaluate the range of possible suggestions. The social science literature contained extensive scholarship on organ and tissue transplants but few studies of death investigation. Actually, the few comparable investigative death studies were conducted in the 1970s and 1980s on the coroner system of the United Kingdom (Atkinson 1978, Prior 1989). An important caveat to this study is that I analyse the jurisdictional conflict only from the perspective of medical examiners, providing a one-sided account of a jurisdictional struggle. My conceptualisation is thus limited to the effects on the established profession and does not deal symmetrically with the intentions, benefits and risks for the emerging profession.

The forensic jurisdiction of medical examiners

Since the property rights of the deceased to their bodies terminate at the moment of death, over the past century, jurisdiction over the dead body in the US has remained with the surviving relatives or with death investigators, depending on the circumstances of the death. The next-of-kin or other designated person has a:

> quasi property right to possession of the cadaver for the purposes of proper disposition. Interference with this right can give rise to a claim against anyone not releasing the body or in any other way altering it prior to release, without permission of the next of kin. This prerogative was not absolute and yielded to the public good where the demands of justice required such subordination. Until the latter part of the 1960s, the interests of the public and justice were represented by the medical examiner/coroner (Jason 1994: 193).

With the emergence of public health and the administrative interest of recording mortality statistics (Armstrong 1987), a professional death investigator on behalf of public interest received the legal mandate to investigate sudden or suspicious deaths. The origins of this legal mandate go back 600 years to the English coroner system where a 'crowner' or representative of the crown was charged with holding legal inquests over dead bodies (Fisher

1993). Initially, death investigation in the US was exclusively performed by coroners working in coroner courts. But when the Model Postmortem Examinations Act was published in 1954, some states reorganised their coroner systems to resemble the medical examiner system after reformers of the Progressive Era joined forces to clean up the widespread corruption, incompetence, and political favouritism that plagued earlier coroner offices (Johnson-McGrath 1995). With few exceptions, 'coroners' in the US have been elected lay persons who rely on available medical personnel to assist in inquests, while 'medical examiners' are usually appointed physicians and pathologists who have special training in medico-legal death investigations and forensic autopsies (I will reserve the term 'medical examiners' for forensic pathologists). The forensic pathologist became a salaried medical expert with limited medicolegal sovereignty but regulated medical investigative autonomy. The US has thus currently a mixed system of coroners and medical examiners: some states and counties rely on coroners for their death investigation while others employ medical examiners (Pescosolido and Mendelsohn 1986).

Historically, the forensic jurisdiction of death investigators has rested on three pillars: a *legal mandate* to protect the public interest, *autonomy* or independent expertness and *scientific expertise* manifested in the use of techniques grounded in medical science. First, as a public monitoring service, medical examiners work on behalf of both public health and criminal justice. They provide relatives with answers to what killed their loved one, alert public health officials to the emergence of new epidemics and natural disasters (Klinenberg 1999), and are expert witnesses in criminal trials. Second, the jurisdiction of medical examiners rests on their independence from outside influences to provide a scientifically-supported and standardised determination of the cause and manner of death. Within the legal parameters of death investigation, medical examiners have full autonomy in deciding what evidence is needed to determine a cause of death, how much ambiguity is permissible, and how to certify the death. Third, using the cultural authority of scientific medicine, medical examiners justified their violation of the body's integrity as 'pure, unbiased, and objective' (Johnson-McGrath 1995: 453). Autopsying or looking for oneself became the tool and hallmark of the scientific expertise of medical examiners. Cutting up the corpse and removing organs has been standardised into general protocols (Hanzlick 1996), aimed at increasing visibility and disease or injury discovery.

These three pillars of the medical examiners' mandate offer a unique example of a professional 'market shelter' (Freidson 1986), generating a historical moment of 'full jurisdiction' (Abbott 1988). Medical examiners have a legally-sanctioned monopoly over death investigations to determine the cause and manner of death. Put in the context of expertise in late modernity, medical examiners provide the cognitive and technical means through which technologies or surveillance and control can be mobilised in legal and medical governance (Armstrong 1987). They are part of a regime of 'biopower' anchored in social and individual bodies (Foucault 1978). Full and legally-supported forensic jurisdiction and governmental functionality, however, does not necessarily imply a position of continued dominance over a substantive task packet.

Although medical examiners have an enviable level of autonomy and job security in the narrowly defined realm of investigating suspicious deaths, they also have little means of expanding their jurisdiction, and are vulnerable to intrusions. The major weakness of the medical examiners consists of their dual role: physicians who work in the criminal justice system. As historian Johnson-McGrath has pointed out, medical examiners are not powerful in either realm (Johnson-McGrath 1995). Although medical examiners are board-certified physicians, they lack the strong professional position of most other physicians. They have the characteristics of independent professionals but they are employed in state bureaucracies (Reed 1996). Instead of charging a fee-for-service, they are salaried with relatively low reimbursement. For the central tasks of determining and certifying the cause of death, they rely on methods that were revolutionary in the 19th century, but have long been replaced in contemporary medicine (Haber 1996). In the legal arena, they are designated to be expert witnesses, meaning that they can enter an opinion and a description of the facts, while judges, juries and lawyers determine the value of their testimony. They are 'essential but obscure actors in a criminal justice system' (Johnson-McGrath 1995: 454). These weaknesses, however, have not diminished the forensic jurisdiction of medical examiners because until recently few groups have contested their authority over corpses.

Tissue and organ procurement vs. death investigation

One October weekend during my fieldwork, the following incident occurred:

> Hit in the head by a baseball bat during a shoplifting spree gone awry, 17-year-old Jonathan Pascoe lays fatally wounded on the floor of an electronics store. An ambulance transports him from the store to the local hospital's emergency department. The ER physicians attempt to stabilise him but noticing his rapidly deteriorating condition, transfer Jonathan to the university's surgical unit. Surgeons insert a pressure catheter and take a CT scan. The scan shows massive subarachnoid hemorrhage and a possible occipatar fracture. Two neurologists conduct a full neurological exam and apnea challenge. Jonathan fails the test and is declared brain dead at 8:00 pm. The attending surgeon alerts the organ bank and speaks to Jonathan's parents. They agree to organ donation and sign off on an almost full procurement: every organ besides bone marrow. Yet, before organ donation can proceed, the medical examiner needs to be notified. Because it is a Saturday evening, scene investigator Tony Best takes the call from the surgical unit. He writes down the information about the

circumstances of death and then talks to the organ and tissue procurer. The transplant coordinator explains that this is his lucky night. Tony cautions that he might not go for organ removal. He senses the disappointment and annoyance in the procurer's voice, 'But it is a full harvest'. Tony replies, 'Sure, but it's also an homicide'. He predicts that the procurer probably will only receive permission for removal of the corneas. He will talk to the doctor on call and get back to the organ procurer.

Tony calls Dr. Douglas, a forensic pathologist, and explains the situation. Dr. Douglas forbids organ procurement and restricts tissue recovery to the corneas before the autopsy, the heart valves after the external inspection, and bones and skin after the autopsy. When Tony relates this to the organ procurer, the man protests angrily but Tony ends the conversation, arguing that it is useless because he is not in charge. Around 10:00 pm the phone rings again. This time Tony is talking to Dr. Bircher, chief of organ transplantation for three neighbouring states. He demands to talk to the chief medical examiner. Dr. Cahill sticks to her decision of not letting organ procurement occur in this particular homicide. Dr. Bircher is furious and considers this arrangement unacceptable. He threatens with his political connections. He darkly predicts that on Monday the medical examiner's budget will be discussed in the state senate.

At 3:30 am Tony Best fields another call. He cannot believe his ears when it is the state governor inquiring about the homicide. Apparently, Dr. Bircher asked Jonathan's relatives to call their state representative and the press. Tony explains the office policy of not allowing organ donation in case of homicide. The governor decides not to interfere but will discuss the policy with the attorney general's office. Yet, these discussions or a budgetary review do not ensue. Jonathan tests positive for HTLV (human t-lymphotropic virus, a cause of leukaemia and lymphoma), excluding the possibility of any organ or tissue donation. The next Monday, Dr. Douglas conducts a full autopsy. The cause of death is subarachnoid hemorrhage due to laceration of left vertebral artery associated with fracture of C-1 vertebra due to blunt force trauma to head and neck. The manner of death is homicide.

This incident forms an extreme instance of a simmering conflict over jurisdiction. It is, however, not a unique occurrence in the US. In 1993, the Washington DC coroner asked for a federal inquiry in the Washington Regional Transplant Consortium after the agency removed organs from homicide victims before a death investigation could take place (Squires 1993). And in 1999, the LifeGift Organ Donation Center of Houston, Texas obtained a court order that allowed them to remove organs from a homicide victim over the objections of the local medical examiner (Stinebaker 1999).

One of the first publications on the emerging conflict between the organ transplant interests and the death investigator community warned about a potential 'moral and legal dilemma', *i.e.* medical examiners might be required to validate brain death as the new definition of death (Hauser 1969). Hauser noted that a new set of technologies – particularly the emergence of immunosuppressive drugs lowering the chance of rejection after organ transplantation (Kutner 1987) – and, with it, a new professional subspecialty could indirectly affect the work of medical examiners. Over time, the debate has shifted drastically from clarifying the idea of brain death to the access to bodies, and the level of acrimony has increased. An article in the *Journal of the American Medical Association* described the relationship between medical examiners and organ procurement organisations as 'laced with tension for years. But the stress might be mounting' (Voelker 1994). A survey of procurement organisations showed 36 per cent of respondents reporting 'bad' and 'horrible' experiences with medical examiners (Wick *et al.* 1995), while a variety of authors note persistent 'communication problems', and a blatant disregard for the essence of the work on both sides (see for example (Jason 1994, Shafer *et al.* 1999)). A forensic pathologist mentioned how the conflict was 'detrimental to medical examiners and their offices' (Sturner 1995: 215). What are the stakes behind this growing conflict?

Organ and tissue procurement pits the living against the dead and transplant surgery against criminal justice. Jonathan Pascoe's body could have been a 'gift of life' to several seriously ill people on long waiting lists, or be part of a complete death investigation that might lead to a conviction of Jonathan's alleged killer. Since medical examiners wait 24 hours following the death before conducting an autopsy (to lower the risk of infection) and routinely slice up internal organs, forensic investigations and many requests for tissue and organ procurement are mutually exclusive. The question, therefore becomes: who has primary jurisdiction over the corpse? If medical examiners cut up organs during an autopsy, procurement organisations are left with corneas and skins. If organ procurers recover body parts, medical examiners cannot conduct a full investigation and their findings are vulnerable to court challenges. Unfortunately, organ procurement organisations are interested in the cases that pose difficult medicolegal questions.

Virtually every article discussing organ transplantation offers a 'ritualistic recitation' (Joralemon 2001: 33) of similar simple statistics in the opening paragraph: in 1999 72,248 patients waited organs, the number of transplanted organs in 1999 was 21,692, and 6,125 people were removed from the waiting list because they died[1]. Of the 10,538 donors in 1999, 55 per cent were cadavers. Because coroners and medical examiners have forensic jurisdiction over about one third of the deaths in the US (Luke 1992), an organ recovery depends not only upon permission of the next-of-kin but also on coroner or medical examiner's approval. Organ and tissue procurers, therefore, depend on death investigators to increase the number of donors. Noting that a person dies every four hours waiting for an organ, the procurers offer veiled accusations of medical examiners' complicity in manslaughter when they 'deny' organ or tissue procurement. For example, 'Since an average of 3.37 organs were recovered per donor in 1992, it is *possible* that as many as 2,979 people were denied transplants in the United States from 1990 to 1992 because of medical examiner denials' (Shafer *et al.* 1994: 1612, italics in original). Or 'The paradox that exists when the investigator denies release for just one potential donor is that up to seven waiting recipients [sic] are also denied the chance for a lifesaving transplant' (Jaynes and Springer 1994: 158). Recent attempts to enlarge voluntary donors with increased public education, and a number of high profile legislative initiatives to encourage public donation, have not significantly increased the number of donors (see *e.g.* (Shafer *et al.* 1999, Spital 1997)). The organ procurement community has made organ release from medical examiners and coroners a top priority.

When medical examiners received the legal mandate to investigate suspicious dead bodies after a long history of opposition (Richardson 1996), transplant technologies had not advanced. Now that the widespread use of those technologies has resulted in an organ scarcity, every organ counts. Nancy Scheper-Hughes has noted that, 'Wherever transplant surgery moves it challenges customary laws and traditional local practices bearing on the body, death, and social relations' (2000: 194). Regardless of where a death investigation office draws a line on organ and tissue procurement, the encounter with procurement organisations has challenged the legal, moral, financial and technical ecology that allowed death investigators to conduct their inquiries. The conflict around Jonathan Pascoe's case is then a 'crystallization point' (Timmermans 1999) in a jurisdictional struggle, rendering a submerged conflict explicit and requiring a reshuffling of jurisdictional parameters to resolve it. In the remainder of this article, I will review how the procurement organisations have threatened the forensic jurisdiction of medical examiners by undermining the three foundations of its jurisdiction, creating unhealthy conflicts of interests and exploiting the relatively weak professional status of medical examiners.

Subordinated jurisdictional relationship

Jurisdictional claims tend to endure when sanctioned by legal bodies (such as legislatures, courts and administrative planning structures). In the US, the legislature has traditionally dominated the legal establishment of professional rights. Once established, legislatures and courts have been reluctant to interfere in professional life, preferring instead to leave registration and accreditation to private bodies (Abbott 1988: 61–63). Death investigators have enjoyed such legal protection of their forensic jurisdiction, but in some instances they have also lost these protections due to legislative changes initiated by the transplantation interests.

Every state and/or county has specific legislation detailing the tasks and prerogative of its death investigators. While such legal protections are durable, they are not immutable. Donald Jason argued that transplantation interests have intruded with legal means on the rights of the next-of-kin to dispose of the body, and, in some instances, also on the legal mandate of the medical examiner (Jason 1994). The 1968 Uniform Anatomical Gift Act, adopted by all states with minor variations and updated in 1987, authorised any deceased 18 years or older, and of sound mind to designate organs for transplantation premortem even if the next-of-kin objects. The 'donee' of a part must remove the part 'without unnecessary mutilation' and then relinquish custody of the body remains to the next-of-kin or other person to dispose of[2]. Current transplantation services, however, seek the permission of the next-of-kin as a practical matter and will not procure organs over their objections to avoid negative publicity or possible litigation. Yet, Jason warns, 'Since there is no legal requirement for this "custom", however, the practice may not be universal and need not be retained indefinitely' (Jason 1994: 193).

Indeed, some states have laws allowing tissue procurers to remove corneas without asking the permission from the next-of-kin (Lee et al. 1992). Investigative journalist Ralph Frammolino of the Los Angeles Times discovered that the Los Angeles coroner's office[3] abused such a 'medical examiner' state law to take corneas at autopsy if the next-of-kin offered no known objections (Frammolino 1997). This law had been passed following lobbying by California's eye banks because corneas disintegrate within 24 hours after death, and asking for permission was considered too time consuming when relatives could not be located. Tissue procurers, however, interpreted the law broadly and took it as a licence to take corneas without asking permission. Only if the next-of-kin had the insight to mention at the death scene that they did not want any organ or tissue donating would the corneas not be taken out. Routine cornea removal involved active discouragement of asking relatives whether they had any objections and disregarded protests of scene investigators and other coroner staff.

The day after the report was published in the LA Times, the coroner's office changed its procedures and required its staff to ask permission from relatives. Shortly after the policy went into place, the number of procured corneas dropped sharply, by nearly 70 per cent. A director of the Doheny Eye and Tissue Transplant Bank wrote a letter defending the donation of corneas on humanitarian grounds, and highlighted the many people who had regained their eyesight as a result of the corneas (Smith 1997). In October of 1998, the then governor of California, Pete Wilson, signed a new law into place requiring coroner offices to secure permission from relatives before removing the eye tissue for transplants. Twenty other states, including Florida and Texas, still have laws similar to the original California state law.

In the event of a suspicious death, the right to possession of the body has largely remained with the medical examiner or coroner, even if the body could be used for organ or tissue donation. This jurisdictional sequence was confirmed in § 4 (a) of the 1987 update of the Uniform Anatomical Gift Act:

The [medical examiner] may release and permit the removal of a part from a body within that official's custody, for transplantation or therapy, if: (1) the official has received a request for the part from a hospital, physician, surgeon, or procurement organization, (2) the official has made a reasonable effort (. . .) to locate and examine the decedent's medical records and inform persons listed in Section 3 (a) of their option to make, or object to making, an anatomical gift, (. . .) and (5) the removal will not interfere with any autopsy or investigation.

Local organ procurement organisations have been increasingly successful, however, in changing the medical examiner statutes. Since the early 90s, New York, Tennessee, New Jersey and Texas[4] have had laws dictating that the needs of transplantation take precedence. For example, Subdivision 1 of the New York law states that the medical examiner 'who has notice of such donation shall only perform an autopsy and/or analysis of tissue or organs in a manner and within a time period compatible with the preservation for the purposes of transplantation of said donation'[5]. The New Jersey and Texas statute requires the medical examiner to be present at the organ recovery if the medical examiner wants to withhold one or more organs. If the medical examiner denies organ donation, he or she needs to give written objections to block the procedure and explain why the organ might be involved in the cause of death. In New Jersey, 'a case occurred in which, despite the warning to the organ procurement team that more time was needed prior to release to allow further investigation, the medical examiner was forced to go to the operating room where the recovery team had already been assembled, and deny recovery' (Lantz et al. 1995: 258).

The legal attacks on the forensic jurisdiction of medical examiners imply that death investigators actively boycott organ and tissue procurement. The few available studies indicate rather that medical examiners and coroners routinely and overwhelmingly accede to the requests of procurement organisations. In 1994, The *Journal of the American Medical Association* published a retrospective study conducted by several organ procurement organisations to find out how many bodies were actually denied by medical examiners and coroners for organ and tissue donation (Shafer et al. 1994). The survey showed that in about 90 per cent of requests the medical examiner had provided the organ procurement organisation with permission to remove organs, and that between 1990 and 1992 the absolute number of donors remained the same. In addition, the rate of organ recovery from cases referred to the medical examiner was 10 times that of deaths that were not investigated. Medical examiners provided 62 per cent of all donors. The survey revealed that in 10 areas of the country no donors were denied recovery during the three years studied. The authors did not provide information on how many relatives refused organ donation after medical examiners gave permission, but other studies agree that only about 60–70 per cent of the families that are approached consent to donation (Prottas and Batten 1991).

Although the results of the survey could be interpreted as indicative of a growing collaboration between medical examiners and procurement organisations, the article instead presented a negative opinion of the work of medical examiners. Taking an advocating position on behalf of organ recipients, the authors centred their article on the observation that in the three-year period the relative number of denials had increased from 7.2 per cent to 11.4 per cent. They complained about the lack of accountability for denials by medical examiners and dismissed the argument that forensic or criminal evidence could be compromised because no defendant had been successfully acquitted using that argument. In a reply, medical examiner Randy Hanzlick disagreed with the negative interpretation of the findings and noted that even if medical examiners complied 100 per cent, the donor pool would only be marginally larger (Hanzlick 1995). Instead of the 'ignorance and contrariness' attributed to medical examiners, he argued that sound forensic and legal considerations lay behind denials. He urged the procurement community to improve the donor pool from non-medical examiner cases and to educate relatives of any donor to accede to donation.

The strongest proponent of the position that benefits of organ recovery overshadows anything medical examiners might accomplish with their forensic inquiries is Teresa J. Shafer, affiliated with the LifeGift Organ Donation Center of Fort Worth, Texas. She argues that because organ donation literally makes the difference between life and death for terminally ill people, organ procurement organisations act from an ethically superior position (Shafer et al. 1999). The claim that medical examiners are morally obligated to release organs under all circumstances because organ transplantation holds the ethical higher ground is an amazing intellectual feat, considering that ethicists and social scientists have long investigated organ procurement and transplantation as the hotbed of ethical conundrums (Fox and Swazey 1992, Hogle 1995, Joralemon 2001, Lock 2002, Scheper-Hughes 2000, Sharp 2000). But ultimately Shafer's goal is not to stake out higher ethics but to enroll ethical rhetoric to undermine the legal jurisdiction of death investigators over dead bodies:

> It is time that the issue of loss of life due to 'medical examiners/coroners' denials of organ recovery be given the same amount of attention from the government that other impediments to organ donation have been given. (. . .) Federal regulations or legislation could assist in gaining the release of more organs for transplantation. Further, states should begin earlier rather than later to move legislation through state governments similar to that passed in Texas and New Jersey (Shafer et al. 1999: 244).

Reversing the legal statute of medical examiners to conduct death investigations as they see fit alters the forensic jurisdiction of medical examiners from full to *subordinate*. This is the most radical redrawing of a jurisdictional map for an established profession, short of obliterating the profession altogether. These laws do not allow for uncertainty or ambiguity, they spell out a jurisdictional hierarchy in clear detail and reify jurisdictional relationship in absolute terms. Legally only one party can have first access to a corpse, and the statutes in the four states explicitly render the interests of medical examiners secondary to organ procurement. The legal displacement not only implies a weakening of the forensic jurisdiction of medical examiners but it also indicates a radical shift from public to private interests. What matters when a person dies is not the potential criminological or public health information gathered during a death investigation, but the condition of the organs for transplantation into individuals.

While appealing in light of the perennial organ and tissue shortage, changing legal mandates is a risky strategy for both professional groups. Medical examiners clearly lose the most when they are forced to relinquish legally-guaranteed first access to dead bodies. Procurement organisations, however, are also in a difficult situation if they do not subsume *all* the tasks of medical examiners. Forensic pathologist Michael Baden pointed out the doomsday scenario, 'If there is a "not guilty" verdict, [the procurement organizations] want to make sure it's not blamed on them. If there is just one case in which a murderer gets off because an organ wasn't there, they know people will stop giving permission' for donation (quoted in Voelker 1994: 891–892). Indeed, it is untenable to change the legal marketshelter without reconfiguring all cognitive, symbolic, technical and organisational aspects that stabilised the death investigation system, including its public health mandate and expert role in the legal system (Crompton 1990). The legal strategy to subordinate the forensic jurisdiction of medical examiners lost popularity when the National Association of Medical Examiners issued a policy statement in collaboration with major procurement organisations appealing for collaboration and case-by-base evaluation and against changing legislation (Hegert 1995).

Standardised jurisdictional relationship

Nowhere are the conflicts between procurement organisations and death investigators more intense than in the case of a child's death. In their 1994 survey of medical examiners/coroners 'denial' of organ procurement, Shafer and her associates noted that in 1992 roughly 30 per cent of the refused cases were probable child abuse cases while an additional four per cent of refusals involved sudden infant death syndrome (SIDS) cases (half of the SIDS cases were denied). Other studies also report that the most likely categories of refusals are child abuse, SIDS, and homicide (Kurachek *et al.* 1995, Wick *et al.* 1995). In order to obtain organs from those corpses, procurement organisations question the scientific and methodological basis of the death investigation and implement standardised changes under the guise of increasing collaboration, aimed at partly appropriating the forensic jurisdiction of medical examiners.

For procurement organisations the problem with having denied paediatric organs can be summed up as an issue of critical supply and too large demand. Organ procurers have few ways of gathering small organs for children in need of transplants. Relatively few children die with organs suitable for transplantation and if they do, the child is likely to have been involved in some kind of trauma, making the death a case for the medical examiner. In addition, relatives of children often agree to organ procurement with greater willingness than the families of adult patients (Morris *et al.* 1992), although relatives of paediatric patients are still more likely to refuse organ donation than medical examiners (in one study: 29 per cent versus 16 per cent (Wick *et al.* 1995).

Medical examiners are most likely to refuse organ procurement in child abuse and SIDS cases because these deaths require a careful medicolegal inquiry to exclude natural causes of death and to document the forensic evidence. Medical examiners operate under the assumption that their autopsy reports will be challenged during an adversarial court process. A challenge is unlikely in natural deaths but more common in homicides or child abuse cases where a defendant might be sentenced partly based on the testimony of the medical examiner. To compromise such an investigation might result in the death of another child at the hands of a child abuser. A medical examiner reported the case of a five-month-old baby boy brought to a hospital by the mother's boyfriend who claimed that the infant had suddenly collapsed in his arms. The procurement organisation requested tissue donation but the medical examiner refused after noting superficial injuries to the child's penis. The pathologist alerted the police who interviewed the boyfriend. He confessed to have squeezed the infant by holding him tight against his chest and was convicted of second-degree murder following a jury trial (Sturner 1995).

Whether a child's death was due to SIDS or child abuse is not known in advance but is the *outcome* of a forensic investigation. By definition, a determination of SIDS requires that the medical examiner has exhausted a full forensic investigation and did not come up with an alternative cause of death (DiMaio and DiMaio 1989, Froede 1990). Making such a case depends on a negative scene investigation *and* a negative autopsy. Signs of abuse are easy to miss without an autopsy. In a review of 184 infanticides in New York, Vincent and Dominick DiMaio found that in 10 per cent of deaths, the children showed no evidence of external injuries, while in others the external injuries were relative mild and tended to be about the head and the neck (DiMaio and DiMaio 1989: 302).

Throughout the country, different procurement organisations and medical examiners have developed protocols to facilitate organ recovery, particularly in the contested domains of child abuse and SIDS. These protocols aim to *standardise* the different jurisdictions of medical examiners and procurement coordinators in fine detail. The various protocols include:

1. Decision guides for medical examiners for the kind of cases that could be released and others that should not be released (Sturner 1995).
2. Communication protocols that delineate when a medical examiner should be notified, what kind of information should be provided, and the possible decisions a medical examiner can take with regard to organ release (Sheridan 1993). Some protocols also specify that objections should be put in writing (Duthie *et al.* 1995).
3. Attendance of the medical examiner at organ removal (Jaynes and Springer 1994).
4. Providing extra imaging tests in the hospital (full body roentgenograms, abdominal computerised tomography scans, CT scans, magnetic resonance imaging) to compensate for the lack of access to the corpse (Duthie *et al.* 1995, Zugibe *et al.* 1999). And/or providing blood and urine samples in special evidence kits (Jaynes and Springer 1996, Sheridan 1993).
5. Check-off protocols and information sheets filled in by transplant surgeons, aimed at fulfilling the basic medical-legal needs of the medical examiner (Sheridan 1993, Zugibe *et al.* 1999).
6. Making transplant surgeons available to testify in court (Jaynes and Springer 1996).
7. Videotaping the transplant procedure for medical examiners. This has only been suggested; it is unclear whether it has been implemented (Shafer *et al.* 1999).

Sturner's decision guidelines remain the closest to the traditional forensic jurisdiction of medical examiners. He distinguishes six different kinds of child deaths and evaluates whether they would qualify for organ release. In an accidental drowning of a child, for example, the medical examiner could allow organ release, but if a child is a victim of a hit-and-run accident, then organ donation should be denied because of the criminological value of the investigation.

Specifying decision-criteria in formal guidelines carries risks for professional dominance. Abbott has noted that professions thrive when they have a body of abstract knowledge that they bring to bear on the tasks they perform. Abstract knowledge provides a profession with legitimation, research and instruction. While the knowledge base of a profession cannot be too abstract that it loses all relevance to the tasks at hands, too much clarification also carries jurisdictional risks (Abbott 1988: 50–57). When the tasks of a profession are spelled out in fine detail (such as in standardised protocols and guidelines), they form an anchor point for outside interference. The worldwide turn to evidence-based medicine in the contemporary health care field forms a good example of this risk. Physician researchers have attempted to develop clinical protocols based on epidemiological research to decrease practice variation and educate their colleagues. Yet, third parties (insurance companies and government payers) have seized those guidelines to hold the profession accountable, to institute reforms, and determine financial reimbursement (Timmermans and Berg forthcoming). More generally, Reed has stressed the inherent self-defeating character of rationalisation through which expert power bases are constructed and defended:

> Rationalization of technique and practice is a central route to expert power and control, but it inevitably 'turns back' on those expert groups that have benefited the most from its implementation once they allow it to impose codified rules and programmes on their own domains of jurisdictional closure and the autonomy that it previously afforded (Reed 1996: 578).

The danger for professional jurisdiction lies not only with the standardisation format but also with the protocol content. None of the proposed protocols grants medical examiners jurisdiction over any of the procurement tasks. Instead, these protocols allow transplant surgeons to provide forensic evidence and testimony for medicolegal purposes, provide alternative procedures and techniques for forensic investigations, and set a timetable for communication and attendance at a transplant procedure out of the medical examiner's control. Such developments, although less confrontational than legislative changes, could still weaken the expertise of medical examiners. Training others to complete an external and internal forensic documentation and sign off on it could lead to a gradual decentralisation of the medical examiner's office. The range of alternatives implies a critique of the standard methodology of medical examiners: the forensic autopsy.

Pathologists know about the weakening of jurisdictional power due to methodological substitution: the hospital pathologist's authoritative position as final arbiter of clinical accuracy vanished when the hospital autopsy ceased to be the instrument of medical quality control. Autopsies used to be the moment of truth in hospitals, the ultimate touchstone to verify a surgeon's skill and physician's diagnostic acumen. For more than a century, medical understanding of the etiology and pathogenesis of disease depended on routine hospital autopsies. Due to an increased reliance on experimentation, changing accreditation standards for hospitals[6], new educational curricula, technological advances, and a lack of support from the public and physicians to use autopsies as a tool in quality assurance, autopsy rates have steadily decreased from 50 per cent of all deaths in the mid-1940s to 15 per cent in 1985 (AMA Council on Scientific Affairs 1987). In recent years, hospital pathologists have been busy interpreting submicroscopic biopsies and other tissues instead of performing autopsies (Lundberg 1996). The only place where the autopsy still flourishes is the office of the medical examiner. Bodily injuries related to trauma lend themselves easily to such investigations. The autopsy is, according to forensic pathologists, superior to any other technological innovation to track the path of a bullet through tissue or the damage caused by a knife wound (Froede 1990). When procurement organisations make advanced medical imaging technologies available for forensic work and these technologies are used in court, they might become a new legal standard of conducting death investigations. Pathologists have long claimed that imaging technologies are at best complementary to autopsies (Lundberg 1996); the reality is, however, that in hospitals such technologies have supplanted autopsies and pathologists.

These protocols are thus used to specify, subdivide, and partly appropriate the jurisdiction of medical examiners, sometimes with their active collaboration. While medical examiners keep the forensic jurisdiction over death investigation, the protocols redistribute the actual work of conducting a medicolegal investigation. They insert conditions that need to be met and processes that need to be followed before the medical examiner can deny organ and tissue recoveries. In addition, they offer substitutions for tasks central to forensic pathology and even for the forensic pathologist. From the perspective of medical examiners, a jurisdictional relationship based on standardisation remains volatile and vulnerable, continuously threatening their autonomy without changing their accountability (Light 2000). Medical examiners do not guarantee the validity of their expertise by themselves but courts and public health officials help set the standards of a 'good and complete' forensic investigation and a 'standard' methodology. The jurisdictional redistribution can only be maintained if these other groups within the forensic ecology sign on.

Commodified jurisdictional relationship

Although organs are frequently described as "gifts of life" (an expression that originates in the blood industry and that likewise is used to describe surrogacy), it is, in fact, a multi-million medical industry where clients in need pay steep fees for the procurement, preparation, transportation, and surgical replacement of body parts (Sharp 2000: 304).

Indeed, the procurement and transplantation organisations frame their work in terms of offering 'the gift of life' to people who would otherwise die, yet most of the 'donation', 'sharing', or 'recovery' in the office of the medical examiner does not relate to potentially life-saving organs but to non-vital tissue. The removal of skin, bones, heart valves, and corneas is less regulated and restrictive than organ recovery. When the Clinton administration adopted rules in 1998 that required hospitals to notify procurement agencies of all deaths, organ donations increased by less than one per cent, but the donations to tissue banks and companies increased by about 40 per cent (Razek *et al.* 2000). Unless the eyes were involved in the cause of death, the medical examiners in my study almost always permitted the harvesting of corneas. Such routine tissue recovery, however, poses threats to the third jurisdictional foundation of the medical examiner, independence, by generating conflicts of interests when tissue recovery is accompanied by financial payments.

While social scientists have written extensively about diverse kinds of body part commodification (for a review, see Sharp 2000), to my knowledge no scholar has tracked the actual money values that change hands when tissues are recovered. However, a team of investigative journalists revealed that the profit margin for tissue processing is lucrative (Katches et al. 2000). Although the National Organ Transplantation Act[7], approved by Congress in 1984, made it a federal crime to engage in interstate selling of organs, it does allow a harvesting company to charge a 'handling and processing fee'. No court has ever decided where a reasonable fee ends and where profitable marking up begins. Reviewing company records, the journalists found that the entire tissue trade has sales of about $500 million a year. Every dead body becomes a potential gold mine:

> a typical donor produces $14,000 to $34,000 in sales for the nonprofits.
> But yields can be far greater. Skin, tendons, heart valves, veins,
> and corneas are listed at about $110,000. Add bone from the same
> body, and one cadaver can be worth about $220,000 (Katches et al.
> 2000: 4).

The investigative journalists claimed that hospitals often cannot compete with the burgeoning plastic surgery industry. In particular, two major companies buy up skin: Massachusetts' Collagenesis Inc. and New Jersey's Life-cell Corp. Both companies process skin collagen for plastic surgery and reconstructive urinary surgery purposes. 'Collagenesis Inc. in Massachusetts can make $36,000 on skin from one body by turning it into a gel that is injected to smooth wrinkles and inflate lips' (Katches et al. 2000: 5). Although skin harvesters originally intended the organ for burn victims, the potential profits in cosmetic and reconstructive surgeries are 10 times larger. The result is that burn units are regularly faced with skin grafting shortages while cosmetic surgery patients do not wait. In a survey of the American Burn Association 32 per cent of burn centres reported delaying or altering treatment due to the difficulty in getting skin in the past year (Aoki 2001). Tissue procurement organisations prefer to deal with companies such as Collagenesis Inc. because the demand for skin for cosmetic surgery is steady, while burn victim units require skin sporadically, and because the cosmetic surgery suppliers pay a 'processing fee' which is four times as much as hospitals pay. The large processing fees provide a financial basis for the pressure that medical examiners experience to release bodies. With $220,000 worth of commodities in each body, the pressure for more profits closely follows the 'gift of life'. From their affluent position, organ procurement spokespeople dismiss any financial concerns for recovering organs:

> It is not acceptable public policy for a medical examiner's/coroner's
> office to deny cases, citing loss of forensic evidence, because the office
> does not have the resources to send someone to the hospital. If the issue

is resources, and not the scientific loss of evidence, then the resource issue must be addressed (Shafer *et al.* 1994: 1612).

Yet, lack of resources and compromised scientific evidence might coincide when medical examiners cannot spare the personnel to attend organ procurement, and forensic evidence is lost as a consequence. Although Jason considers the cash flow from organ procurement organisations a possible advantage for medical examiner administrative organisations (Jason 1994), the National Association of Medical Examiners takes a more prudent stance. Its policy on organ and tissue procurement states that payment for expenses incurred in the administration of an organ or tissue recovery programme should be made to the governing agency and not directly to the office of the medical examiner or coroner.

For cash-strapped county and state medical examiners' offices, the abundant flow of organ-tissue procurement money is seductive. During the cornea-harvesting episode described earlier, the budget of the LA coroner office had been slashed annually by eight per cent to 10 per cent between 1991 and 1997, dropping by six million dollars. Over the same period, the Doheny Eye and Tissue Transplant Bank paid $1.4 million to the LA coroner office, probably providing some financial relief (Frammolino 1997). Other medical examiners reported that organ and tissue procurers contributed to new facilities or leased space. Some of the pathologists I interviewed found this a clever way to deal with financial duress, while others charged that the procurement organisations bought their way into the medical examiner's office.

When medical examiners receive payments for the recovery of tissues, part of their work that previously did not depend on financial incentives becomes commercialised. Marxists have extensively documented the commodification of activities that were not pecuniary in detrimental terms (Sharp 2000). Commodification, however, does not necessarily lead to a weakening of the jurisdiction of medical examiners. Medical examiners could gather more resources and tie their work to other constituencies. But when medical examiners are in a financially weak position and depend on the monetary resources offered by procurement agencies in order to conduct their everyday activities, the financial incentives for tissue procurement invoke the image of the corrupt coroner of the beginning of the 20th century. The question is the familiar one of cui bono, who benefits? Is the access of medical examiners to corpses primarily for forensic purposes, or do medical examiners first respond to their new paymasters, the procurement organisations? Similar dilemmas are at the core of recurring proposals to provide financial incentives to potential organ donors and their kin (Joralemon 2001). From a professional perspective, financial reimbursements introduce a risky submissive component to the work of medical examiners. They maintain jurisdiction over the forensic investigation, but they run the risk of appearing to be perceived as doing the bidding of procurement organisations. Such conflation questions the independence of the death experts (Freidson 1989).

Table 1   *Conflictual jurisdictional relationship*

	Target of change	Results for daily practice	Results for knowledge base	Risks for established profession	Level of stability
Subordination	Legal mandate	Subordinated division of labour	Viewed in terms of dominant group	Loss of professional and clinical autonomy	High
Standardisation	Work practice	Rationalization	Increased codification	Loss of clinical autonomy	Volatile
Commodification	Independence	Priorities set based on renumeration	Little change, could generate more research	Loss of credibility	Volatile

Conclusion

In late modernity, the politics of expertise have become more intensely contested (Reed 1996). Where, in traditional societies, claims to expertise were based on custom and practices as the institutional repositories of collective wisdom, in contemporary expert societies expertise is invested in objective, impersonal, and codified knowledge (Giddens 1994). Medical examiners are part of a new form of governmentality; in the name of social and personal wellbeing, the individual and social body is surveilled, managed, probed and investigated as a vital resource (Foucault 1978). The corpse becomes a data bank of forensic knowledge with far-reaching legal and public health consequences (Armstrong 1987). While medical examiners are embedded in a state bureaucracy and benefit from legally-protected jurisdiction, they are not immune to challenge. New technologies and new experts generate opportunities for different rationalities, flexibility, institutionalisation, and ultimately a different relationship to the corpse, reflecting a general sense of fluidity and uncertainty about the nature of expertise.

The subordinated, standardised, and commodified relationships are all instances of *conflictual jurisdictional relationships* when an established profession is confronted with the incursions of an emerging profession on its jurisdiction, and does not prevail in the ensuing jurisdictional struggle. These three new relationships have in common that daily work activities are no longer conducted on the terms of the established profession (see a summary in Table 1).

The new relationships differ on the level of stability: the subordinated relationship is the most stable since it reifies the relationship. This reification might mean, however, that the actual practice differs from the legal prerogative;

creating new avenues for change or enforcement by legal bodies. The standardised and commodified relationships remain volatile for different reasons. Standardisation requires constant monitoring and maintenance while commodification runs the risk of unfettered greed and public disapproval. Because the jurisdiction of a profession is situated within an ecology of established constructive jurisdictional relationships, and because jurisdictional claims need to be validated by different audiences, any new configuration of jurisdictional relationships might be questioned and modified when these countervailing powers weigh in on the new arrangement. Even in a subordinated relationship, new technologies or lack of credibility might generate new divisions of labour and new organisational forms (Reed 1996).

Viewed solely from the perspective of death investigators, the encounter with procurement organisations has already changed the professional position of medical examiners. The legal, organisational, and procedural set-up that reflected the forensic autonomy of medical examiners has not only been challenged, but also in some places altered. The remaining question is how those changes in professional positioning make an impact on the actual work of a forensic death investigation and its balance between public health and criminal justice prerogatives. According to professionalisation theory, when the organisational set-up changes, the actual work content should change as well (Abbott 1988). It is difficult to isolate the effects of ongoing organisational change on the kind of causes of death medical examiners distinguish with fieldwork. But from a policy perspective, the question arises how and whether accommodating procurement demands will affect the medical examiners' record of detecting homicides, child abuse, SIDS and suicide.

Acknowledgements

I thank Peter Conrad, Jonathan Gabe and two anonymous reviewers for their comments.

Notes

1 See www.unos.org for weekly updated figures.
2 Uniform Anatomical Gift Act (1987) § 8 (a).
3 Although LA has a 'coroner's office,' the office is actually modelled on the medical examiner system.
4 Texas Health and Safety Code, Chapter 693.002.
5 New York, County Law, art 17-a, §674–1, McKinney 1991.
6 Previously, hospitals were required to meet an autopsy quota.
7 Public Law 98–507.

70   Stefan Timmermans

References

Abbott, A. (1988) *The System of Professions*. Chicago: The University of Chicago Press.

AMA Council on Scientific Affairs (1987) Autopsy: a comprehensive review of current issues, *Journal of the American Medical Association*, 285, 364–9.

Aoki, N. (2001) Healing touch, *The Boston Globe*, 25 February, F1–F4.

Armstrong, D. (1987) Silence and truth in death and dying, *Social Science and Medicine*, 24, 8, 651–7.

Atkinson, M.J. (1978) *Discovering Suicide: Studies in the Social Organization of Sudden Death*. London and Bastingstoke: The Macmillan Press Ltd.

Beck, U. (1992) *Risk Society: Towards a New Modernity*. London, Newbury Park, CA: Sage Publications.

Crompton, R. (1990) Professions in the current context, *Work, Employment, and Society*, 3, 2, 147–66.

DiMaio, D.J. and DiMaio, V.J.M. (1989) *Forensic Pathology*. New York: Elsevier.

Drazin, R. (1990) Professionals and innovation: structural-functional versus radical-structural perspectives, *Journal of Management Studies*, 27, 3, 245–64.

Duthie, S.E., Peterson, B.M., Cutler, J. and Blackbourne, B. (1995) Successful organ donation in victims of child abuse, *Clinics of Transplantation*, 9, 415–18.

Fisher, S.R. (1993) History of forensic pathology and related sciences. In Spitz, W.U. (ed) *Medicolegal Investigation of Death*, (3rd Edition), Springfield, Il: Charles C. Thomas.

Foucault, M. (1978) *The History of Sexuality: An Introduction*. New York: Vintage Books.

Fox, R.C. and Swazey, J.P. (1992) *Spare Parts: Organ Replacement in American Society*. Oxford: Oxford University Press.

Frammolino, R. (1997) Harvest of corneas at morgue questioned: corneas taken without survivor's permission are resold at huge markup by eye bank,which pays coroner's office a fee, *Los Angeles Times*, 2 November, A1.

Freidson, E. (1986) *Professional Powers: a Study of the Institutionalization of Formal Knowledge*. Chicago: Chicago University Press.

Freidson, E. (1989) *Medical Work in America: Essays in Health Care*. New Haven: Yale University Press.

Freidson, E. (1994) *Professionalism Reborn: Theory, Prophecy, and Policy*. Chicago: University of Chicago Press.

Froede, R.C. (ed) (1990) *Handbook of Forensic Pathology*: Northfield: College of American Pathologists, Ill.

Giddens, A. (1994) Living in a post-traditional society. In Beck, U., Giddens, A. and Lash, S. (eds) *Reflexive Modernization*. Cambridge: Polity.

Gieryn, T.F. (1999) *Cultural Boundaries of Science*. Chicago: University of Chicago Press.

Glaser, B. and Strauss, A. (1967) *The Discovery of Grounded Theory*. New York: Aldine de Gruyter.

Haber, S.L. (1996) Whither the Autopsy? *Archives of Pathology and Laboratory Medicine*, 120, 714–17.

Hanzlick, R. (1995) Medical examiners, coroners, and organ recovery in the United States, *Journal of the American Medical Association*, 273, 20, 1578.

Hanzlick, R. (1996) On the need for more expertise in death investigation, *Archives of Pathology and Laboratory Medicine*, 120, 329–32.

Hauser, J.E. (1969) The use of medical examiner-coroner's cases as transplant donors, *Journal of Forensic Sciences*, 14, 2, 501–6.

Hegert, T.F. (1995) Medical examiners, coroners, and organ recovery in the United States, *Journal of the American Medical Association*, 273, 20, 1578–79.

Hogle, L. (1995) Standardization across non-standard domains: the case of organ procurement, *Science, Technology, and Human Values*, 20, 4, 482–500.

Jason, D. (1994) The role of the medical examiner/coroner in organ and tissue procurement for transplantation, *The American Journal of Forensic Medicine and Pathology*, 15, 3, 192–202.

Jaynes, C.L. and Springer, J.W. (1994) Decreasing the organ donor shortage by increasing communication between coroners, medical examiners, and organ procurement organizations, *The American Journal of Forensic Medicine and Pathology*, 15, 2, 156–9.

Jaynes, C.L. and Springer, J.W. (1996) Evaluating a successful coroner protocol, *Journal of Transplant Coordination*, 6, 1, 28–31.

Johnson-McGrath, J. (1995) Speaking for the dead: forensic pathologists and criminal justice in the United States, *Science, Technology, and Human Values*, 20, 4, 438–59.

Joralemon, D. (2001) Shifting ethics: debating the incentive question in organ transplantation, *The Journal of Medical Ethics*, 27, 30–5.

Katches, M., Heisel, W. and Campbell, R. (2000) The body brokers, *The Orange County Register*, 16 April, A1.

Klinenberg, E. (1999) Denaturalizing disaster: a social autopsy of the 1995 Chicago heat wave, *Theory and Society*, 28, 2, 239–95.

Kurachek, S.C., Titus, S.L., Olesen, M. and Reaney, J. (1995) Medical examiners' attitudes toward organ procurement from child abuse/homicide victims, *The American Journal of Forensic Medicine and Pathology*, 16, 1, 1–10.

Kutner, N.G. (1987) Issues in the application of high cost medical technology: the case of organ transplantation, *Journal of Health and Social Behavior*, 28, 23–36, March.

Lantz, P.E., Jason, D. and Davis, G. (1995) Decreasing the organ donor shortage, *American Journal of Forensic Medical Pathology*, 16, 3, 257–9.

Lee, P.P., Yang, J.C., McDonell, P.J., Maumenee, A.E. and Stark, W.J. (1992) Worldwide legal requirements for obtaining corneas: 1990, *Cornea*, 11, 2, 102–7.

Light, D. (2000) The medical profession and organizational change: from professional dominance to countervailing power. In Bird, C.E., Conrad, P. and Fremont, A.M. (eds) *Handbook of Medical Sociology* (5th Edition), Upper Saddle River, New Jersey: Prentice Hall.

Lock, M. (2002) *Twice Dead: Organ Transplants and the Reinvention of Death*. Berkeley and Los Angeles, CA: University of California Press.

Luke, J.L. (1992) The shortage of organs for transplantation, *New England Journal of Medicine*, 325, 1025.

Lundberg, G.D. (1996) College of American Pathologists Conference: Restructuring autopsy practice for health care reform, *Archives of Pathology and Laboratory Medicine*, 120, 736–9.

McKinney, R. (1991) *McKinney's Consolidated Laws of New York*. St Paul Minn: West Group.

Morris, J., Wilcox, T. and Frist, W. (1992) Pediatric organ donation: the paradox of organ shortage despite the remarkable willingness of families to donate, *Pediatrics*, 89, 411–15.

Pescosolido, B.A. and Mendelsohn, R. (1986) Social causation or social construction of suicide? An investigation into the social organization of official rates, *American Sociological Review*, 51, 80–101.

Prior, L. (1989) *The Social Organisation of Death: Medical Discourses and Social Practices in Belfast*. London: MacMillan.

Prottas, J. and Batten, H. (1991) The willingness to give: the public and the supply of transplantable organs, *Journal of Health Politics, Policy, and Law*, 16, 121–34.

Razek, T., Olrhoff, K. and Reilly, P.M. (2000) Issues in potential organ donor management, *Surgical Clinics of North America*, 80, 3, 1021–32.

Reed, M.I. (1996) Expert power and control in late modernity: an empirical review and theoretical synthesis, *Organization Studies*, 17, 4, 573–97.

Richardson, R. (1996) 'Fearful symmetry: corpses for anatomy, organs for transplantation'. In Younger, S.J., Fox, R.C. and O'Connell, L.J. (eds) *Organ Transplantation: Meanings and Realities*. Madison, WI: The University of Wisconsin Press.

Scheper-Hughes, N. (2000) The global traffic in human organs, *Current Anthropology*, 41, 2, 191–224.

Shafer, T., Schkade, L.L., Warner, H.E., Eakin, M., O'Connor, K., Springer, J., Jankiewicz, T., Reitsma, W., Steele, J. and Keen-Denton, K. (1994) Impact of medical examiner/coroner practices on organ recovery in the United States, *Journal of the American Medical Association*, 272, 0, 1607–13.

Shafer, T.J., Schkade, L.L., Siminoff, L.A. and Mahoney, T.A. (1999) Ethical analysis of organ recovery denials by medical examiners, coroners, and justices of the peace, *Journal of Transplant Coordination*, 5, 4, 232–49.

Sharp, L.A. (2000) The commodification of the body and its parts, *Annual Review of Anthropology*, 29, 287–328.

Sheridan, F. (1993) Pediatric death rates and donor yield: a medical examiner's view, *The Journal of Heart and Lung Transplantation*, 12, 6, S179–86.

Smith, R. (1997) Doheny Eye Bank, *Los Angeles Times*, 10 November, B4.

Spital, A. (1997) Ethical and policy issues in altruistic living and cadaveric organ donation, *Clinics of Transplantation*, 11, 2, 77–87.

Squires, S. (1993) Two agencies in a grim battle over bodies, *The Washington Post*, 18 November.

Stinebaker, J. (1999) 'Organ harvesting sparks dispute', *The Houston Chronicle*, 10 August, A1.

Strauss, A. (1987) *Qualitative Analysis for Social Scientists*. Cambridge: Cambridge University Press.

Sturner, W.Q. (1995) Can baby organs be donated in all forensic cases? Proposed guidelines for organ donation from infants under medical examiner jurisdiction, *The American Journal of Forensic Medicine and Pathology*, 16, 3, 215–18.

Timmermans, S. (1999) Mutual tuning of multiple trajectories, *Symbolic Interaction*, 21, 4, 225–40.

Timmermans, S. and Berg, M. (forthcoming), *The Gold Standard: A Sociological Exploration of Evidence-based Medicine and Standardization in Health Care*. Philadelphia, PA: Temple University Press.

Voelker, R. (1994) Can forensic medicine and organ donation coexist for the public good? *Journal of the American Medical Association*, 271, 12, 891–2.

Wick, L., Mickell, J., Barnes, T. and Allen, J. (1995) Pediatric organ donation: impact of medical examiner refusal, *Transplantation Proceedings*, 27, 4, 2539–44.

Zugibe, F.T., Costello, J., Breithaupt, M. and Segelbacher, J. (1999) Model organ description protocols for completion by transplant surgeons using organs procured from medical examiner cases, *Journal of Transplant Coordination*, 9, 2, 73–80.

Chapter 4

Violence against doctors: a medical(ised) problem? The case of National Health Service general practitioners

Mary Ann Elston, Jonathan Gabe, David Denney, Raymond Lee and Maria O'Beirne

Introduction

For patients to swear at their doctors, threaten to harm them or punch or kick them would, according to the conventional medical sociology literature, be both exceptional and exceptionable. Such behaviours would clearly not accord with Parsons's (1951) characterisation of patients' obligations in doctor-patient relationships; nor with the prevailing ceremonial order of 'gentility' in medical consultations (Strong 1979a); nor with the norm of doctors dominating consultations reported in many studies of doctor-patient communication (*e.g.* Waitzkin 1991). In sociological terms, violence by patients towards doctors can clearly be regarded as deviance against legitimised agents of social control. But it is deviance that might be accounted for and responded to in various different ways.

For example, all the behaviours listed above might, in some circumstances, be regarded as criminal offences under English law[1], with the perpetrators processed by the criminal justice system, and the doctors regarded as 'victims' of crime, no longer expected to provide care for their assailants[2]. It is also possible for such behaviours to be given a medicalised interpretation. The literature on violence in the workplace suggests that perpetrators are disproportionately drawn from those with health-related personal 'troubles', such as substance misuse or some forms of mental illness (Chappell and Di Martino 2000, Health Services Advisory Committee 1997, Wynne *et al.* 1997). There are methodological grounds for extreme caution about causal interpretation of such statistical associations (see, for example, Dallaire *et al.* 2000, Link and Stueve 1998, Monahan 1992, Peay 1994, Rogers and Pilgrim 2001, South 1994). Nevertheless, doctors and nurses are among those occupations most at risk of threats and assaults in the workplace, according to the British Crime Survey (a bi-annual national population survey of crime victimisation) (Budd 1999). Thus at least some acts of violence against doctors are likely to be accounted for in terms of underlying clinical pathologies and/or failures in treatment and care. As such, further medical therapeutic intervention might be called for.

Consequently, studying work-related violence against doctors, specifically against general medical practitioners (GPs), primary care physicians in the

National Health Service (NHS) in England, provides a valuable opportunity to explore the boundaries between crime and illness at the turn of the 21st century. There are two parts to our empirical analysis: an examination of the framing of such violence against GPs as a policy issue; followed by analysis of individual GPs' response to violent incidents. To put these data in a sociological context, further elaboration of theorising about the relationship between illness and crime is appropriate.

The medicalisation of deviance thesis
What has become known as the 'medicalisation of deviance' thesis has been very influential in medical sociology since the 1970[3]. Put briefly, the thesis postulates that, particularly from the mid-20th century onwards, societal conceptualisations of deviance shifted from 'badness to sickness', as the subtitle of Conrad and Schneider's (1980/1992) now-classic text put it. According to Conrad,

> Medicalization consists of defining a problem in medical terms, using medical language to describe a problem, adopting a medical framework to understand a problem, or using medical intervention to treat it (Conrad 1992: 211).

Corollaries of this putative medicalising of deviance include at least partial absolution of the deviant from moral culpability for the condition and its effects on deviants' conduct; at least partial decriminalisation or conditional legitimation of continuation of deviant behaviour (conditional on deviants' willingness to accept the obligations of the sick role); a preference for therapeutic responses over solely punitive or retributive ones, and a tendency for optimism about the effectiveness of such treatment; and increased legitimacy for the medical profession's role in controlling deviance (Conrad and Schneider 1992: 246–8, Zola 1972).

In later formulations, responding to critics such as Strong (1979b), Conrad and Schneider stressed that they did not claim that the medicalisation of deviance was a universal nor necessarily a complete nor irreversible process. And they denied implying that the medical profession was an invariably victorious imperialist in an ongoing 'turf war' with the criminal justice system (Conrad and Schneider 1992: 71, 255, 277–88). Conrad (1992) also noted that medicalisation at the conceptual level (expert theories and formal policies) did not necessarily entail medicalisation at institutional and interactional levels.

These qualifications suggest that we should not assume that criminalisation and medicalisation are always and necessarily mutually exclusive modes of managing deviance. Rather, the medicalisation thesis should direct our attention to settings where medicine and the criminal justice system might meet, and to how any boundaries between 'illness' and 'badness' might be drawn. Such contexts are those in which questions of human will and moral responsibility and biomedical causation are intertwined, such as the management of substance abuse and addiction (South 1994, Strong 1980) or of the 'mentally disordered offender', a term which encapsulates the classificatory tensions that the medicalisation thesis addresses (*e.g.* Carlen 1986, Dallaire *et al.* 2000, Manning 2000, Peay 1994, Rose 1996, 1998).

We suggest that work-related violence against doctors is also such a context. Here, the deviance is directed specifically *against* social control agents with authority for managing medical problems and, often, committed *by* those seeking help for such problems. The 'victims' in this case, unlike most victims of violence, have high social and economic status and cultural authority (Levi 1994, Zedner 1994) and considerable powers of decision-making in relation to perpetrators' disposal. The medicalisation thesis predicts that, in society in general, a medical framework will be favoured in explaining the problem (*e.g.* in terms of perpetrators' mental health problems), with perpetrators seen as needing further medical treatment. However, even the most committed advocate of 'medical imperialism' (see Strong 1979b) might concede that there are likely to be limits to doctors' acceptance of violent patients as their continuing professional responsibility. The sociologically interesting questions relate to where any such limits are drawn, how the interface between medical and criminal management of violence is constructed, and how these may change over time. For, according to Conrad and Schneider, medicalisation at any level, is, or perhaps was, linked to specific historical developments.

> . . . we believe the most important [factors] for the modern medicalization of deviance were the rise of rationalism, the development of determinist theories of causation that arose in the 19th century, and the growth and success of medicine in the 20th century (1992: 261).

From the vantage point of the early 21st century, this claim prompts questions about the implications for medicalisation of those major social, economic and cultural changes that have been variously dubbed as the emergence of late- or post-modernity, post-Fordism, or the risk society (Beck 1992, Scambler 2002, Scambler and Higgs 1998) or, from a Foucauldian perspective, advanced liberalism (Rose 1996). In the context of these major social transformations, some criminologists have recently argued that societal understanding of deviance is shifting away from the assumptions that prevailed in modern(ist) criminology; assumptions which, although the term is not generally used, are clearly consonant with the concept of medicalisation. For example, Garland and Sparks (2000: 194–9) argue that modern criminology's focus on explaining individuals' criminal behaviour in terms of theories drawing on medicine, abnormal psychology and sociology is being displaced. Penal policy agendas are now being driven more directly by populist and direct political concerns about victims, risk, high crime rates, and fear of crime.

Characteristic of this putative new turn in penal policy is the reduced concern for and optimism about the value of corrective and rehabilitative measures for individual deviants. The more punitive, 'responsibilised' response to deviants is linked to the growth of a consumerist, marketised ethos in the welfare sector more generally. The socially excluded are increasingly represented as the engineers of their own misfortune (Rose 2000: 334) or assessed in terms of the risk they pose for society (see e.g. Kemshall 2002 on mental health policy). Citizenship is being reconceptualised from an entitlement based on membership of a collectivity to a set of procedural rights and duties with which individuals are exhorted to comply (Higgs 1998). According to Rose, those who fail so to comply may, if they present a relatively low risk or some prospect of reaffiliation to mainstream society, be offered individualised modes of control/treatment, often framed in terms of contract and empowerment, aiming at ethical reconstruction through surveillance. Those for whom the prospects of 're-insertion' (Rose 2000: 334) seem unrealistic, or who pose too great a risk, may be regarded as warranting sequestration or quarantine (Bauman 2000), or as forfeiting their citizenship rights (Higgs 1998). The obverse of recasting deviants in this way is recasting social control agencies' role into one of regulating levels of deviance, of assessing and managing risk, of defending society against the dangerous, the feckless and the imprudent, rather than as transforming deviant individuals (e.g. Castel 1991, Feeley and Simon 1992, Kemshall 2002, Rose 1996, Taylor 1999). Moreover, through such measures as 'zero tolerance policing', or standardised risk assessments, the scope for discretionary judgement by individual social control agents may be being circumscribed.

Thus, current criminology suggests that the medicalisation of deviance may be both in overall retreat and being transformed into risk management and surveillance. If so, we should expect emerging policies for managing violence against GPs to focus primarily on the 'victims' and on the *risks* faced by all health workers; to exhort all health care providers to become risk-conscious in their everyday practice; and to promote a relatively punitive stance towards perpetrators, with the jurisdiction of the criminal justice system emphasised. Individualised, medicalised management of the actually or potentially violent might be restricted to very low risk individuals, and made conditional on contracts with specific obligations for responsibility. In the next section we will show that, in recent policy on violence against GPs, all these features are observable. At the conceptual level, there are moves to demedicalise this form of deviance and new institutional arrangements have been set up to support this. When, however, in the following section, we examine data on the management of violence at the interactional level, it is clear that individual GPs claim to exercise extensive professional discretion in responding to incidents. Judgements are not always made in favour of punitive, criminal responses.

NHS general medical practice: a zero tolerance zone for violence?
In the United Kingdom, violence from patients and the public against NHS staff has, as a public and human resource issue, recently attracted attention

from health professional organisations (*e.g.* General Medical Services Committee (GMSC) 1995, Royal College of Nursing (RCN) 1998), and government policy makers. To understand how the issue has been framed and the policies promulgated in response, it is important for readers unfamiliar with NHS general practice, to appreciate the organisational, cultural and legal framework within which it is conducted[4].

The vast majority of NHS GPs are not NHS employees but self-employed doctors, mainly working in legally constituted practice partnerships, contracted to supply primary medical care services to NHS patients. Thus, most GPs have no line managers or employers to report to. They do have legal responsibilities as employers with respect to health and safety, for ancillary staff such as receptionists, and other health care professionals, mainly nurses. But bureaucratised risk management procedures are typically less developed in general practices than in hospitals. The public's access to NHS GPs is through ongoing registration on a doctor's 'list', and GPs are required to ensure that their patients have access to a broad range of treatment, surveillance and preventive services. Since the 1960s, vocational training for general practice has generally encouraged GPs to see patients' emotional and social troubles as falling within their professional jurisdiction (Armstrong 1979, Jefferys and Sachs 1983). They are simultaneously given a high level of clinical autonomy to meet individual patients' needs and are charged with being responsible managers of public resources, *e.g.* by acting as gatekeepers for more specialist NHS care. They also have considerable discretion as to their involvement in shared care with more specialist services, *e.g.* drug dependency treatment (Department of Health 1999b, Audit Commission 2002).

In theory, both GPs and patients have choice about whom to register/be registered with. GPs can refuse to accept or, by following the appropriate procedure, can remove patients from their lists. However, allegations that some GPs remove patients on ethically questionable grounds have made this issue a professionally sensitive one in recent years (Eaton 2002, GPC 1999, Stokes 2000). Moreover, it is the statutory right of any UK resident to be registered with an NHS GP. So GPs may be compulsorily allocated, at least on a temporary basis, patients who have been removed from another doctor's list, or even patients whom they themselves have removed, if no other doctor can be found. Total exclusion of a person from access to NHS GPs' services would require primary legislation explicitly restricting what is widely regarded as a fundamental citizenship right in the UK. As several policy makers we interviewed in the course of this study commented, this is not a measure that any British government is likely to embrace with alacrity. Nor necessarily would leaders of GPs' professional organisations, sensitive to both the public image of the profession and the spectrum of views among its members. In interviews we conducted with GP policy-makers as part of the study described below, although there was consensus that 'something' needed to be done about violence, the epithet 'fortress medicine' was sometimes used pejoratively to describe strong quarantining measures such as confining persistently violent patients to consultations in police stations[5].

In 1994, following the publication of research indicating that GPs were at relatively high levels of risk of violence (Hobbs 1991, 1994), the Department of Health and GPs' negotiating body agreed new provision for so-called 'immediate removals' if a patient caused actual violence or behaved 'in such as way that the doctor has feared for his or her safety' (General Medical Services Committee (GMSC) 1994). Once the precipitating incident has been reported to the police and the local health authority, a GP's professional responsibility for a violent patient ceases forthwith. (For normal removals, the patient is given a period of notice during which the removing GP is still responsible for care, but no reason for removal needs to be given to the patient or any third party.) The 1994 guidance advised GPs that, although they did have continuing responsibility for those patients whose violence was due to illness, in general, risk management through a vigorous punitive response should be adopted. 'To tolerate abusive or violent behaviour is to invite the perpetrator to repeat his or her actions, thus putting doctors, their staff and colleagues at risk'. Hence, removal and prosecution of offenders was strongly recommended (GMSC 1994: 72).

The late 1990s saw continued pressure for further action on violence from at least some 'grassroots' GPs and in the professional media. In 1999, the issue of violence within the NHS as a whole was placed on a new, more politicised footing. A cross-Government campaign was launched to make the NHS a zero tolerance zone (ZTZ) with respect to violence from the public (Department of Health 1999a, NHS Executive 1999, 2000). NHS organisations and staff were exhorted to adopt active preventive and zero-tolerant risk management strategies, and the inclusive definition of violence adopted by the European Commission for recording incidents:

[Work-related] 'Violence' means any incident where staff are abused, threatened or assaulted in circumstances related to their work, involving an explicit or implicit challenge to their safety, well-being or health (Wynne *et al.* 1997).

Broadening the definition of violence beyond actual physical assaults, especially if accompanied by the adoption of more systematic and comprehensive incident-reporting schemes, is likely to lead to an artefactual increase in the reported incidence rate. In this sense, the risk of violence may increasingly become a 'fact of life' for health workers, one facet of the emerging 'crime complex' (Garland and Sparks 2000). In another sense, however, health care workers are being urged not to 'normalise' violence as part of their job but to lower their tolerance thresholds when subjected to violence. 'We don't have to take it' is a recurrent slogan in the ZTZ campaign (*e.g.* NHS Executive 2000). Specific Department of Health initiatives for general practice in 2000 made new provision for persistently violent patients to forfeit the right to be registered with a GP *within their immediate locality* and called for local development schemes to deal with such patients, where needed (*e.g.* retaining security guards at designated surgeries) (Department of Health 2000). In 2001, all GP practices in England were sent a poster to display in their waiting rooms, warning that, 'Violent patients will be reported to the police and struck-off the GP's list' (NHS Executive 2001).

These policy developments reflect pressing NHS concerns about recruitment and retention of staff, including GPs (Department of Health 1999c). (The ZTZ initiative is based in the human resource section of the NHS Executive.) But, from a broader analytic perspective, the themes of the ZTZ initiative exemplify the recasting of deviants and the heightened concern for victims characteristic of the emerging punitive penal climate outlined earlier. The emphasis is on GPs and their staff as actual or potential victims of violence, and they are being exhorted to become more risk-conscious. Violent acts are represented as *bad* behaviour by 'responsibilised' perpetrators, against whom a punitive reaction on the part of the NHS and the criminal justice system is warranted. Circuits of at least partial exclusion of the violent from full citizenship rights to GP services have been established, although these are tempered by statutory citizenship entitlements and professional concerns. Normative guidance such as the ZTZ campaign encourages GPs to interpret violence in line with the punitive corollaries of the new penology. But it is only guidance, addressed, in this case, to highly autonomous professionals. In the next section of the paper, we turn to examining individual GPs' accounts of violent incidents and of those who perpetrate them, with particular reference to the extent to which they adhere to such guidance and how they define the limits to their professional medical responsibility.

Study design and methods

The data reported here were collected for a study of violence against professionals in the community, funded by the UK's Economic and Social Research Council, as part of its Violence Research Programme from 1998 to 2001 (Gabe *et al.* 2001). We conducted a postal survey of a randomly selected one in three sample of the c.3000 NHS GPs in the former South Thames NHS Region, an area of south east England, including south London and the south-east coast. A 62 per cent response rate to the survey was obtained (n=697), high for a GP survey. Respondents were representative of the population being sampled in terms of age, sex and location, although, as is common with postal surveys of UK GPs, there was a slight under-representation of single-handed GPs born outside the UK (NHS Executive 1998).

A key aim of the questionnaire was to assess the frequency of 'violence' experienced by GPs. As with any so-called 'victimisation' survey, respondents will only report those incidents which they are able and willing to identify themselves as having experienced (Zedner 1994). Because of the well-recognised variability in definitions of violence (Levi 1994, Stanko 1998) we asked separate questions about different types of transgressive behaviours, without reference to causes or consequences and within specified time periods, to minimise problems of recall (Gabe *et al.* 2001). Thus, we asked about respondents' experience of verbal abuse, threats and assaults within the past two years. We then collected contextual data, *e.g.* on perpetrators, for the most recent threat or assault experienced. We also sought information about GPs' background and practice organisation. Data were analysed using SPSS for Windows. Follow-up semi-structured interviews were conducted with a sub-sample of 26 respondents who had reported an assault or direct threat. Interviewees were purposively selected to ensure inclusion of female (nine) and ethnic minority (five) GPs. Reflecting the geographical patterning of violence found in the postal survey, most practised in south London, its suburbs or in seaside towns. The interviews covered doctors' experiences and views with respect to violence and its management in general and in relation to specific incidents (mainly, but not confined to the specific 'most recent' incidents described in the questionnaire). Interviews normally lasted between one and two hours. All were audio tape-recorded with interviewees' permission, and the tapes were fully transcribed. Atlas-TI was used to code transcripts thematically.

Findings

The incidence of violence
As Table 1 indicates, almost four-fifths of respondents reported being victims of what might be categorised as violence under the ZTZ definition, during the two years prior to the postal survey. For just over one-third of all respondents, verbal abuse was the only form of violence experienced, threats and assaults being much rarer. Of the assaults reported by 10 per cent of respondents, two-thirds were described as a 'push or shove', with no injury resulting. However, there were also eight reports of the use of weapons and

Table 1 *General practitioners' experience of 'violence' in previous two years*

Types of Behaviour	No.	%
No incidents reported	156	22
Verbal abuse	519	75
Verbal abuse only	267	38
Threat(s) – all types	261	37
Threat(s) to harm GP	153	22
Assault(s)	72	10
Total	697	

two of sexual or indecent assault, and two of the 26 interviewees' professional careers had been ended by assaults. Although 30 per cent of GPs reported verbal abuse as occurring more than 'once or twice' over two years, only four per cent (28 respondents) checked the 'lots of times' response. 'Repeat victimisation' was very rare for threats and assaults (eight and two per cent of all respondents respectively reporting more than one). So violence was not being claimed as a routine experience by GPs in our survey, although their reported annual rates of direct threats and assaults indicate that GPs are, respectively, 7.9 and 4.3 times those reported for all workers in the British Crime Survey in the 1990s (Budd 1999).

We cannot assume that respondents would necessarily have defined all the incidents of transgressive behaviour that they did report as 'violence' (any more than we can assume that all ZTZ-defined incidents of violence have been reported). Although often familiar with the inclusive ZTZ definition, interviewed GPs did not necessarily accept it. GPs sometimes distinguished between aggression and 'real' (usually physical) violence, or suggested that an abstract definition, independent of contextual factors, was of little value (Gabe *et al.* 2001). That not all reported assaults were regarded as serious or frightening (and that some incidents of verbal abuse were) was clear from the interviews.

In several respects, the social patterning of these transgressive behaviours against GPs was similar to that found in other 'violence victimisation' surveys (Stanko 1998, Zedner 1994). GPs practising in inner city and urban estates were at significantly higher risk than those in rural areas. Although there were a few adventitious attacks, *e.g.* in the street when a doctor was out on a call, the vast majority of threats and assaults occurred on practice premises, or to a lesser extent in patients' homes. Perpetrators were rarely complete strangers. Persons registered with the doctor or their relatives were involved in 95 per cent of 'most recent' threats and 78 per cent of assaults, with assaulted GPs knowing their assailant at least by sight in 63 per cent of incidents. Of course, any inferences about relative risk must recognise that GPs spend most of their working time on practice premises with patients they know. In the light of this, it is perhaps significant that 80 per cent of 'most recent' assaults were perpetrated by males. Young men were markedly over-represented among specified perpetrators, compared to the proportion they constitute of all those consulting GPs (OPCS 1995), as they are among violent offenders in general (and their victims) (Levi 1994).

Social characteristics of perpetrators of violence
Studies of discretionary decision-making in response to deviance by social control agents have generally found that characteristics of deviants are at least as salient as characteristics of the act in shaping disposal judgements (*e.g.* Bittner 1967). In the questionnaire, we asked a range of questions about characteristics of those responsible for different kinds of transgressive behaviours. Whether through open-ended questions about verbal abuse in

general or closed questions about possible factors behind specific assaults and threats, a similar picture emerged. Most violence was reportedly perpetrated by people with health-related personal troubles. For example, 72 per cent of responses relating to verbal abuse, 82 per cent for specific threats and 78 per cent for specific assaults cited drug addiction, alcohol problems or mental illness (either singly or in combination) as factors. References to frustrated or demanding consumers, without social disadvantage or personal troubles, were comparatively rare, even for verbal abuse (11 per cent of responses). However, when asked whether they regarded their assailant(s) as 'fully responsible for his/her actions during the incident', 66 per cent of GPs who had been assaulted in the past two years said that they did. Thus, perpetrators are, for the most part, typified as sufferers from the kind of problems that, according to the medicalisation thesis, will be seen as appropriate for medical management. But this does not mean that GPs necessarily exempted perpetrators from culpability in moral or legal terms, even if they had problems which might be regarded as 'illnesses'. Moreover, these problems are also characteristic of those whom criminologists have labelled as 'police property', the socially powerless whose deviance is particularly likely to be brought to police attention (Lee 1981).

The interviews provided a richer picture of doctors' typifications of perpetrators of violence and aggression and of their contextualised responses to them. For example, Dr Vickery gave a typology:

> ... if I think a patient is being loud and angry and verbally or body language threatening to me, if I think they're in pain or genuinely frightened, or at the end of their tether, I let them [get] away with a lot more, you know what I mean. If I think somebody's just being an arsehole and I think they're not in pain or sick or worried . . . // . . . , if I think it's unjustified, I'll draw the line much more quickly.
>
> Because I know what I'm like when I'm worried about the baby or my husband, I know I get on edge and unreasonable, so if I think it's situational and it's understandable, I'll, um, kind of let somebody go a lot further. Or if they have a psychiatric illness and if I think their behaviour is a direct result of their illness, then I go, I wouldn't call the police unless they needed sectioning . . . [then] I wouldn't try to deal with their illness.
>
> If somebody, with the people who are opiate addicts or any kind of drug addicts, we tend to be much stricter with them from the word go. Because, probably from other people's experience, we know, I mean, it's very judgmental [indistinct] but we know that the drug addiction makes them manipulative . . . // . . . so we don't take excuses from them at all. And we tolerate much less violence and aggression from them, because I think if you do tolerate it, it escalates and then you're in trouble.

This kind of classification of trouble-making patients with associated degrees of tolerance before terminating consultations (or subsequent sanctions) was typical (as was the implication that it was GPs who controlled the course of events). Abuse and aggression from those without any mitigating circumstances and 'who should know better' were seen as particularly illegitimate, although not necessarily dangerous. But, although patients making unjustified demands were occasionally typified as 'arrogant, busy, aggressive business people, either male or female, who expect immediate access' (Dr Fox), readiness to resort to threats and abuse when 'inappropriate' demands were not met was far more often linked by GPs to patients' social disadvantage and inadequacy than to their opposites.

Prominent in most interviewees' typifications of the violent or aggressive were Dr Vickery's next type: persons suffering from certain forms of mental disorder. For those whose aberrant behaviours were attributable to immediately stressful situations, such as sudden acute illness in very young children, or where the diagnosis of certain kinds of mental illness was relatively unambiguous, culpability for behaviour was qualified and a degree of tolerance claimed to be afforded, at least for relatively minor breaches of social order.

> We've got one or two rather eccentric patients with a history of mental illness and they can get a bit, they can be a bit obnoxious. But I think that's more their illness than anything else. Most of the staff know them, they put up with it (Dr Morley).

In practice, however, diagnoses relating to mental disorder were not always unambiguous or simple. Several doctors commented on the relatively recent conceptual reclassification of one risk group out of the category of the mentally ill into that of (untreatable) personality disorder (Kemshall 2002, Manning 2000).

> So that an awful lot of people who'd previously been locked away in a secure psychiatric unit are now out on the street and these people pose a threat to everybody (Dr George).

GPs were seen as vulnerable because they still had to provide primary care services for such people, and the division between mental illness and personality disorder was not necessarily clearcut. Dr Thorp had been assaulted attending a 'section', so there was a presumptive diagnosis of mental illness[6]. However,

> I felt it was that crossover between mad and bad . . . //. . . . I think that with young men with severe sorts of psychiatric illness and drug abuse there's always that potential for physical violence because they're so unpredictable . . . I don't know if he was mad or bad, or both. I think he's probably both actually. [Later in interview] . . . what personality he'd got by 16 would have been ruined by his illness and his drug abuse. . . . He hasn't got anything to lose really by hitting somebody.

Nor was it the case that a medical diagnosis of mental illness and involvement of the criminal justice system were necessarily regarded as incompatible by doctors. Dr Thorp and another interviewee assaulted by a paranoid schizophrenic both reported that they had been urged to prosecute by psychiatrists, to increase the chances of assailants obtaining appropriate medical treatment through court diversion (Kemshall 2002, Peay 1994). The police, however, had discouraged both GPs from further action, so no judicial proceedings had followed.

The final category in Dr Vickery's classification, those with substance dependency and addiction problems, were cited by many doctors as potential or actual perpetrators of violence. Most interviewees practised in areas with relatively high numbers of heroin addicts and usually reported that they deployed one of two circuits of control. The first was a policy of *de facto* risk reduction by semi-exclusion. By only knowingly accepting heroin addicts for general medical services, not for maintenance prescriptions (usually of methadone), the potential for conflict was reduced. The second circuit involved conditional access to maintenance prescriptions, through what were often described as 'contracts': individualised control regimes intended to achieve 'ethical reconstruction' through surveillance, very much as described by Rose (2000: 334). In the process, those for whom 're-insertion' is not realistic may be filtered out of a GP's care, either by removal or by self-selection:

> I'm very strict that they come at a certain time. I don't give it out in emergency situations. They must ring me if they're not turning up, and I have a contract with them. . . . .// . . . I mean a large part of [addicts'] problem is lack of structure in their lives and lack of any kind of discipline . . . To try and generate that in them actually does help, and it also shows that you want, not that you want respect, but that you won't tolerate . . . and it's their loss if they don't turn up when they're supposed to . . . // . . . I end up with the people who genuinely want treatment. The ones who want to mess around and are probably using as well as taking the methadone, don't come near me (Dr Quigley).

These circuits allowed GPs to emphasise, sometimes very strongly, that *their* heroin addict patients were not usually a source of trouble. However, heroin addicts in regular maintenance treatment comprise a minority of heroin users who are themselves a minority of the drug-abusing population (South 1994). Interviewees often commented that contracts were irrelevant or harder to establish for some other substance use and abuse problems, such as alcoholism, although some practices had policies of not seeing obviously intoxicated patients. GPs do not necessarily know about all their patients' substance-abuse problems, particularly those for which supply is always from illegal sources. (Dr Quigley himself had been assaulted by a patient whose cocaine habit he was unaware of.) Related to this, GPs tended to distinguish between 'victims' – dependent users – seeking medical help for their use of controlled drugs or legally available substances, and 'villains' covertly obtaining their substances through illicit supply, and not seeking re-insertion (Collison 1993: 383).

GPs rarely described actual or potential perpetrators explicitly in terms of criminalised identities. It was not that they were under any illusions as to the moral character and criminal records of some of their patients. We were often told 'war stories' (Lee 1995) about practising in areas of high ambient crime levels. But such stories were often accompanied by comments indicating that criminal convictions or known delinquencies were, in themselves, generally matters for deliberate disattention in the medical consultation. That a patient had a murder conviction was no barrier to his being, in the words of Dr Ormond, 'no problem . . . a nice chap, really'. Convicted criminals, like polydrug users or those with disordered personalities, sometimes needed the services of an NHS GP. To maintain a non-judgmental attitude and the etiquette of gentility, to keep relationships functionally specific to medical matters was portrayed as good professional practice (and occasionally as necessary for self-protection). These comments suggest that pro-active risk assessment of individuals may not fit easily into GPs' occupational culture.

Thus, the majority of those identified by GPs as perpetrators of violence were credited with serious personal troubles which, given the broadly defined scope of GPs' work, could fall within a GP's remit. GPs did make distinctions between the bad and the ill in describing perpetrators. Some were not regarded as wholly responsible for their behaviour and were accorded at least conditional tolerance because of (usually mental) illness. A few were especially blameworthy because there were no medical (or social) factors mitigating the bad behaviour. However, many perpetrators fell between these relatively clearcut poles. They were both mad and bad. Those whose problem was substance abuse were often held to be both engineers of their own misfortune and also in need of re-'responsibilisation' through enrolment in medically-controlled surveillance regimes, although there was variation in the perceived relevance of this, according to the substances involved.

Given these typifications of perpetrators, how do individual GPs respond to actual incidents of violence? In what circumstances do they invoke removal or the criminal justice system, or continue to regard the violent as their professional responsibility, seeing the violence as caused by some underlying medical problem? How far are these two courses of action, setting perpetrators on a path to criminalisation or medicalisation, mutually exclusive? Given the medicalisation thesis's emphasis on medical institutions carrying great legitimacy in deviance disposal decisions, it is relevant to consider the role of other agencies, particularly the police.

Exercising zero tolerance or professional discretion?
As might be expected from the data on GPs' typifications of the violent, GPs in our study did not generally describe themselves as following strategies of

Table 2 *General practitioners' course of action following 'most recent' incident*

Action taken	Threat %[a]	Assault %[a]
No action or only practice level report[b]	48	39
Perpetrator removed from doctor's list	32	25
Report to police	24	28
Other only	26	23
N	255	71[c]

a Percentages add up to more than 100 per cent as more than one response was permitted.
b *e.g.* discussion with colleagues, report to practice manager, entry in incident book or patient record, warning letter to patient.
c one of the 72 GPs reporting an assault in last two years did not answer these questions.

zero tolerance in response to ZTZ-defined violence. Neither patient removal nor reports to the police were reported to be automatic or even the most usual sequelae of all types of transgressive behaviour reported in the questionnaire. There was no statistically significant relationship between whether assailants were thought to be responsible for their actions and GPs' actions following assaults.

As Table 2 indicates, for almost half the threats and more than one-third of assaults, no action that went beyond the practice was taken. Self-evidently, the sanction of removal is only available where the perpetrator is actually on the practice list in the first place. This was the case for almost all threats, but only for 75 per cent (54) of assaults. So, for only one-third of the assaults perpetrated by a registered patient did removal follow. (However, interview data suggested that a few more may have 'disappeared' of their own accord after the incident.) Although GPs generally claimed to remove few patients, some claimed that their practice had firm policies of removal, or of letters warning that removal would follow a second offence, in two, often coinciding, circumstances. The first applied to addicts who breached surveillance contracts discussed above. The second was for incidents involving staff, particularly receptionists (who were believed to suffer more verbal abuse than doctors). As their employers, GPs had legal obligations to receptionists (and good ones were seen as hard to recruit and retain). And, for reasons of occupational status, experience, and professional training and responsibility, GPs implied that they themselves could and should expect to cope with or disregard some forms of trouble.

So, GPs' accounts suggest that judgements about removal following violence will be strongly situated judgements using professional discretion, especially when they themselves are the target. This was clearly illustrated in Dr Corrigan's interview. He told us about three threats of physical violence in his present practice. On two occasions he had been threatened by patients brandishing knives. In both these incidents, the doctor, although 'frightened',

defused the situation without assistance, and did not strike either patient
from his list. His explanation for not doing so was that he had contributed
to both situations by what, in retrospect, he saw as poor professional judgement, given that he was treating both patients for substance-abuse problems
before the incidents, and that the patients had both been very apologetic
afterwards. He commented,

> . . . with these two knife drawers, the relationship was rebuilt and that
> was fine, you know. In that case, an experience like that can actually be
> helpful.

> Int: How can it be helpful?

> Well, you know you've been through a crisis together basically and that's
> usually helpful if you want to achieve something later on, in that sense I
> think. You've come through a crisis, if you've come out all right and
> people often trust you better than before that. And you know you've got
> a bit of credit basically. They're a bit in debt.

This account of a shared crisis leading to enhanced trust contrasted sharply
with the third and most recent incident that Dr Corrigan described

> The only one [patient] I threw off was the chap who came through the
> window, because that really was unprovoked aggression in somebody I
> already felt very difficult, find it very hard treating him because we didn't
> seem to be on the same. . . .

Here was a physically large man, whom the doctor suspected of making
fraudulent sickness benefit claims, who burst into a consultation between his
(the patient's) partner and the GP, and threatened to beat up the GP. The GP
'felt very afraid' and called the police who arrested the man. There were no
mitigating circumstances. The doctor had no sense that he bore responsibility for the incident, which arose out of a domestic dispute and involved
unwarranted interference with another patient's care. There was no basis for
rebuilding trust. The GP removed both his assailant and the partner who
had also been abusive earlier.

We doubt that many of our respondents would, if threatened with a knife,
have given the knife-wielder the opportunity to rebuild and strengthen the
existing doctor-patient relationship. Most interviewees had rather lower
tolerance thresholds than Dr Corrigan. Indeed, several commented on the
salutary effect that the shock of removal could have on patients' subsequent
behaviour: that is, it could be therapeutically useful for a patient to have to
start afresh with a new doctor. This is the point. For the most part, decisions
to remove a patient, who had been violent to a doctor in the course of
ongoing treatment, were presented in terms of the lack of therapeutic value
of any continuing relationship. Loss of mutual trust; the doctor being too

afraid to maintain professional judgement or competence; or the patient having breached the terms of a surveillance contract: these were used to account for the removals of those with legitimate health problems. If the situation was defined as one in which there was no legitimate professional relationship or illness at issue in the incident, as in Dr Corrigan's third case, then removal was likely to follow. Dr Fox had been attacked on a home visit by one of her partner's patients, a woman with a long history of unreasonable demands and prescription drug abuse. But when the patient calmed down and apologised, this apparently rational behaviour aggravated rather than propitiated Dr Fox's annoyance and led her to seek immediate removal.

> . . . strangely enough if she hadn't come out and said she was terribly sorry, and it was a case of mistaken identity, if she'd have been away with the fairies and totally bonkers, I would have been less annoyed about it. But she was obviously in total charge of her faculties . . .

Table 2 shows that the police were involved in about one-quarter of 'most recent' threats and assaults. Interviews indicated that sometimes police involvement was purely a retrospective formality. The report required for immediate removal might be made by fax, without any expectation of extensive police investigative action, as a householder might report a minor theft for insurance purposes. More often, police had been called in the course of unfolding incidents to deter or contain situations when serious harm or disorder was feared (or had occurred). Many such incidents involved patients with acute mental disorders or suffering from substance abuse: thus the decision to involve the police in this way did not necessarily reflect a judgement that perpetrators were bad rather than sick but from the need to minimise harm. That the police were often involved in disposal decisions about the mentally ill has been noted in relation to discouraging prosecution but they were also sometimes allies of GPs against specialist services, using their legally defined powers to manage the acutely mentally ill (Rogers 1990). When one of Dr Allen's patients, with a history of psychiatric illness and alcholism, threatened to throw herself off a balcony, a psychiatrist refused to section her until she was sober: 'in the end, the police arrested her and took her to a "place of safety" '.

As these examples indicate, and as would be expected from sociological studies of police work in general (*e.g.* Reiner 1994), whether perpetrators entered the criminal justice system after the police arrived, was related to police, as well as GPs', discretionary judgements. In many cases, the police or the GP (or both) regarded the incidents as too trivial to warrant charging and seeking prosecution. Some GPs reported being criticised by police for not wishing to press charges about minor incidents. But others had apparently had police support for not doing so. The police warned Dr Naidoo that his steroid-abusing assailant was 'very, very dangerous'. But they did not demur when he said that, although he would remove the patient immediately, he would not press charges, given that the only tangible damage was to his trousers in need of dry-cleaning from a thrown cup of tea. Serious injury by perpetrators well known to the police did not always lead to prosecution being pursued. When Dr Quigley was assaulted by someone whose cocaine-using was known to police though not to the doctor, with the dispute relating to a girlfriend's rather than the assailant's treatment and with independent witnesses and significant injury sustained by the GP, prosecution and a custodial sentence did follow. Another GP, however, seriously injured in the course of a surgery burglary, attributed the police's reluctance to prosecute to his assailant's role as a local police informer.

These last two incidents were ones in which the interactional context was not a medical consultation between the doctor and the assailant, like Dr Corrigan's third threat, discussed above. As already noted, GPs might accord a degree of tolerance towards parents who became aggressive in the context of acute illness affecting their small children. Such tolerance, however, was not apparently accorded men who sought to intervene in doctors' care of their wives, or more often girlfriends, or, as in one incident, a girl-friend's grandmother. Such incidents were likely to lead to the assailants' removal from the GP's care (if they were registered with the GP) and police involvement, as were those where the primary motivation appeared to be robbery or illegitimate access to information.

In contrast, incidents that provoked no formal or only practice-level responses, were usually ones arising in the context of assailants' legitim-ate seeking of medical care, where risk of harm was thought to be low, or re-insertion into normal citizenship seemed likely. References were made to 'isolated' or 'out of character' incidents, or to giving contract-breaching addicts 'another chance' to regain responsibility for themselves. Non-removal and not involving the police did not necessarily mean no sanctions. Patients might be warned in writing or in person by doctor or practice manager. There were also many incidents which were regarded as too trivial, or as normal 'risks of the job', such that any formal response would be disproportionate, or quite simply a waste of GPs' time.

Conclusions

Our analysis of the policy framing of violence in the health workplace has shown that this policy exemplifies general trends in the management of deviance recently noted by criminologists. The emphasis is primarily on risk management and concern for victims. Perpetrators of violence against health workers are depicted in this guidance as generally responsible for their actions, and as compromising their entitlement to normal citizenship rights. As there are statutory and some professional constraints on total exclusion of the violent from GP services, circuits of semi-exclusion in the form of 'immediate removal' and, more recently, local development schemes and sequestration from local services, have been established for patients posing high risk of violence. GPs have been encouraged to be zero tolerant, not to see violence as a normal risk of the job, and to make greater use of patient removal and the criminal justice system as punitive and deterrent sanctions.

Thus, at the policy level, there is an explicit move to shift conceptualisation of the violent patient away from a medicalised approach to coping with deviant individuals towards one of making general practice safe from the violent. This shift could be described as the demedicalisation of deviance in favour of its criminalisation. But this risks obscuring the ways in which institutions and policies for the management of criminals may themselves be changing since the 1970s, away from a model that focuses on the individual deviant, except for those for whom 'ethical reconstruction' through personalised surveillance (Rose 2000) is thought realistic.

As with many sociological accounts of medicalisation, criminologists' accounts of the new turn in penal policy are mainly studies of expert theories and formal policies. They do not always examine directly the interactions between deviant and control agent or the views of individual control agents. We have presented data on GPs' reactions to incidents and of the characteristics of perpetrators of violence. Our data, qualitative and quantitative, are clearly accounts, presentations by GPs of their professional selves. We cannot regard doctors' statements as definitive descriptions of 'what really happened' in a given incident. What is of interest is the kind of account GPs presented when asked about being a victim of violence, a potentially sensitive issue for professionals accustomed to being in control (O'Beirne *et al.* 2002 forthcoming) The accounts given by GPs of perpetrators of violent incidents were often 'medicalised' in the sense that a medical framework was generally used to describe the factors that lay behind individual deviants' behaviour, and to categorise many incidents. Thus, even if the label was sometimes 'inappropriate demand', the inappropriateness relates to medical judgement about what patients should be receiving. However, even if deviants are medicalised in this way, one might ask what else might be expected in this context? The business of individual GPs is, after all, medicine: their role is to provide medical care for those who seek their services through a relatively 'open' door.

Medicine in general practice is an elastic jurisdiction, but it is not infinitely stretchable. GPs did set limits to their professional responsibilities in the face of violence. In accounting for limits, they did use distinctions between the ill and the bad in responding to incidents and perpetrators. At the poles, the difference is relatively clear. GPs were likely to regard as 'crimes' incidents which fell outside the rubric of medical consultation, for example where interference in an adult third party's confidential treatment was attempted, or where illegal drug use was not disclosed to the GP. Here, exclusion and penal sanctions were likely to be sought. Abusive language from someone whose social situation and lack of health-related problems provided no mitigating circumstances, might lead to removal. Abusive language from a demented elderly person might not (and in neither case would most GPs label the verbal abuse as 'violence'). But many incidents and perpetrators fell into the grey borderline area where criminal and medical systems meet: and where GPs' disposal decisions have to take into account other agencies' priorities and rules.

Thus the frame in which GPs set their decisions about responding to violent patients falling into this grey area was not simply one of risk management, and it was not zero tolerant. When GPs themselves were attacked, the judgement about removal was depicted as a contextual, professional one in which the wellbeing and need for care of assailant and the continuing capacity of the individual GP to provide that care may figure in the balance. The loss of professional control implied in incidents that had 'got out of hand' could be grounds for removal of those with legitimate needs for GPs' care. Those enrolled in surveillance contracts could be removed on grounds of breach of agreement if they were violent, as evidence that ethical reconstruction was failing. Involvement of the police in the course of an unfolding incident did not mean GPs were ceding responsibility to the criminal justice system, although whether subsequent judicial proceedings were pursued was as much determined by police judgement as by GPs. So understanding the perpetrator's problem in terms of a medical framework was not necessarily incompatible with apparently punitive sanctions or police involvement.

Our data suggest that calls for zero tolerance, and for removal and prosecution to be the normal response to all incidents, do not necessarily accord with GPs' construction of professional responsibility; nor do they with their pragmatism when it comes to dealing with problem patients and some other agencies. Many 'trivial' incidents of violence according to ZTZ-type definitions will not be criminalised. In this sense, GPs are similar to many other victims of violence. Victimisation surveys show that many incidents are not brought to the notice of the criminal jutice system. Where GPs differ from the victims studied in most violence research is in their legitimated role in influencing (but not always determining) disposal decisions. It is, however also clear that individual GPs' accounts gave little support to any notion of active medical imperialism on their part when it came to dealing with violent and aggressive patients, many of whom were already involved with the criminal justice system. The actual or perceived high-risk perpetrators of violent incidents were not generally popular patients; dealing with them was depicted as inevitable GP 'dirty' work (Hughes 1958: 121–2, Strong 1980), as a 'background' risk of the job. In the case of violence against GPs, drawing boundaries between crime and illness at the interactional level is more problematic than some sociological accounts of sickness and badness as mutually exclusive conceptualisations of deviance might suggest.

Acknowledgements

The research reported here was funded by the Economic and Social Research Council (Grant L135251036) as part of their Violence Research Programme. We would like to thank the editors of *Sociology of Health & Illness*, and our three anonymous reviewers for their helpful comments.

Notes

1　There are differences in the legal and health care systems of the constituent countries of the United Kingdom which make it appropriate to refer specifically to England in this paper. There is, however, no reason to think that our findings and conclusions would not be equally applicable to Scotland, Wales and Northern Ireland.

2　In general, in this paper, we use the terms 'victim' and 'perpetrator' to refer, respectively to GPs and those who allegedly have attacked them, verbally or nonverbally. We ourselves do not intend to imply that GPs always subjectively felt themselves to be (powerless) victims. Nor do we mean to imply that there are never problems of attribution of responsibility (see Walklate 1989, 1997, Zedner 1994), or that GPs are always blameless for incidents. We have only the GP's side of each story.

3　Much of the 'medicalisation' literature focuses on the medical takeover of aspects of erstwhile 'normal' life, such as childbirth, rather than on the boundaries between 'badness' and 'illness'. We are only concerned with the latter in this paper.

4　As this paper goes to press (May 2002) there are proposals for a new NHS GP contract, and and GP practices have recently been integrated into over-arching governance and monitoring frameworks known as Primary Care Trusts. But, for the foreseeable future, the description that follows is likely to remain broadly accurate.

5　The metaphor suggests parallels with the mediaeval 'fortress city', from which the undesirable could be physically excluded, an analogy made by Taylor (1999: 111) in relation to today's burgeoning 'gated communities' (upmarket residential estates) and exclusive shopping malls.

6　The term 'section' refers here to the enactment of procedures laid down in specific sections of UK mental health acts which permit compulsory detention or restriction of mentally ill persons in certain circumstances. The most commonly used section procedures require the presence of a patient's GP, a psychiatrist and a social worker, with the police usually being in attendance.

References

Armstrong, D. (1979) The emancipation of biographical medicine, *Social Science and Medicine*, 13A, 1–8.

Audit Commission (2002) *The Commissioning and Management of Community Drug Treatment*. London. Audit Commission.

Bauman, Z. (2000) Social issues of law and order, *British Journal of Criminology*, 40, 205–21.

Beck, U. (1992) *Risk Society: towards a New Modernity*. London: Sage.

Bittner, E. (1967) Police discretion in the emergency apprehension of mentally ill persons, *Social Problems*, 14, 3, 699–715.

Budd, T. (1999) *Violence at Work: Findings from the British Crime Survey*. London: Home Office.

Carlen, P. (1986) Psychiatry in prisons: promises, premises, practices and politics. In Miller, P. and Rose, N. (eds) *The Power of Psychiatry*. Cambridge: Polity.

Castel, R. (1991) From dangerousness to risk. In Burchell, G., Gordon, C. and Miller, P. (eds) *The Foucault Effect: Studies in Governmentality*. Hemel Hempstead: Harvester Wheatsheaf.

Chappell, D. and Di Martino, V. (2000) *Violence and Work*. Geneva: International Labor Office.

Collison, M. (1993) Punishing drugs: criminal justice and drug use, *British Journal of Criminology*, 33, 3, 382–99.

Conrad, P. (1992) Medicalization and social control, *Annual Review of Sociology*, 18, 209–32.

Conrad, P. and Schneider, J.W. (1980) *Deviance and Medicalization: from Badness to Sickness*. St Louis: Mosby.

Conrad, P. and Schneider, J.W. (1992) *Deviance and Medicalization: from Badness to Sickness. 2nd Edition*. Philadelphia: Temple University Press.

Dallaire, B., McCubbin, M., Morin, P. and Cohen, D. (2000) Civil commitment due to mental illness and dangerousness: the union of law and psychiatry within a treatment-control system, *Sociology of Health and Illness*, 22, 5, 679–99.

Department of Health (1999a) *Health Service Circular 99/226. Campaign to stop violence against staff working in the NHS: NHS Zero Tolerance Zone*. London: Department of Health. http://www.doh.gov.uk/coinhhtm

Department of Health (1999b) *Drug Misuse and Dependence: Guidelines on Clinical Management*. London: Stationery Office.

Department of Health (1999c) *Health Service Circular 99/229. Working Together: Securing a Quality Workforce for the NHS: Managing Violence, Accidents and Sickness Absence in the NHS*. London: Department of Health. http://www.doh.gov.uk/coinh.htm

Department of Health (2000) *Health Service Circular 2000/001. Tackling violence towards GPs and their staff. The NHS (Choice of Medical Practitioner) Amendment Regulations 1999*. London: Department of Health. http://www.doh.gov.uk/coinh.htm

Eaton, L. (2002) Ombudsman criticises GP for striking patients off without warning, *British Medical Journal*, 324, 808.

Feeley, M. and Simon, J. (1992) The new penology: notes on the emerging strategy of corrections and its implications, *Criminology*, 30, 4, 449–74.

Gabe, J., Denney, D.D., Lee, R.M., Elston, M. and O'Beirne, M. (2001) Researching professional discourses on violence, *British Journal of Criminology*, 41, 3, 460–71.

Garland, D. and Sparks, R. (2000) Criminology, social theory and the challenge of our times, *British Journal of Criminology*, 40, 189–204.

General Medical Services Committee (GMSC) (1994) *Women in General Practice*. London: GMSC/BMA.

General Medical Services Committee (1995) *Combating Violence in General Practice: Guidance for GPs.* London (GMSC/British Medical Association).

General Practitioners' Committee (GPC) of the British Medical Association (1999) *Removal of patients from GP lists* London: BMA. (www.bma.org.uk/gpc.nsf)

Health Services Advisory Committee (1997) *Violence and Aggression to Staff in Health Services: Guidance on Assessment and Management.* Sudbury: Health and Safety Commission.

Higgs, P. (1998) Risk, governmentality and the reconceptualization of citizenship. In Scambler, G. and Higgs, P. (eds) *Modernity, Medicine and Health: Medical Sociology Towards 2000.* London: Routledge.

Hobbs, F.D.R. (1991) Violence in general practice: a survey of general practitioners' views, *British Medical Journal,* 302, 329–32.

Hobbs, F.D.R. (1994) General practitioners' changes to practice due to aggression at work, *Family Practice,* 11, 75–9.

Hughes, E.C. (1958) *Men and Their Work.* Illinois: Free Press of Glencoe.

Jefferys, M. and Sachs, H. (1983) *Rethinking General Practice.* London: Tavistock.

Kemshall, H. (2002) *Risk, Social Policy and Welfare.* Buckingham: Open University Press.

Lee, J.A. (1981) Some structural aspects of police deviance in relations with minority groups. In Harlow, C. (ed) *Organisational Police Deviance.* Toronto: Butterworths.

Lee, R.M. (1995) *Dangerous Fieldwork.* Thousand Oaks and London. Sage.

Levi, M. (1994) Violent crime. In Maguire, M., Morgan, R. and Reiner, R. (eds) *The Oxford Handbook of Criminology.* Oxford: Oxford University Press.

Link, B. and Stueve, A. (1998) Editorial, *Archives of General Psychiatry,* 55, 1–3.

Manning, N. (2000) Psychiatric diagnosis under conditions of uncertainty: personality disorder, science and professional legitimacy, *Sociology of Health and Illness,* 22, 5, 621–39.

Monahan, J. (1992) Mental disorder and violent behaviour: perceptions and evidence, *American Psychologist,* 47, 4, 511–21.

NHS Executive (1998) *General and Personal Medical Services Statistics (England and Wales).* London: NHS Executive.

NHS Executive (1999) *NHS Zero Tolerance Zone. Managers' Guide – Stopping Violence against Staff Working in the NHS: We don't have to take this.* Resource Pack. Leeds: NHS Executive.

NHS Executive (2000) *NHS zero tolerance zone: primary care.* www.nhs.uk/zerotolerance/ general/criminal.htm (23/09/2000)

O'Beirne, M., Denney, D., Elston, M., Gabe, J. and Lee, R.M. (2002 forthcoming) Methodological lessons from the disclosure of violence against professionals. In Lee, R.M. and Stanko, E. (eds) *Researching Violence: Essays on Methodology and Measurement.* London: Routledge.

Office of Population Censuses and Surveys (OPCS) (1995) *Morbidity Statistics from General Practice. Fourth National Study 1991–2.* London: HMSO.

Parsons, T. (1951) *The Social System.* London: Routledge.

Peay, J. (1994) Mentally disordered offenders. In Maguire, M., Morgan, R. and Reiner, R. (eds) *The Oxford Handbook of Criminology.* Oxford: Oxford University Press.

Reiner, R. (1994) Policing and the police. In Maguire, M., Morgan, R. and Reiner, R. (eds) *The Oxford Handbook of Criminology.* Oxford: Oxford University Press.

Rogers, A. (1990) Policing mental disorder: controversies, myths and realities, *Social Policy and Administration*, 24, 3, 226–37.

Rogers, A. and Pilgrim, D. (2001) *Mental Health Policy in Britain*: 2nd Edition. Basingstoke: Palgrave.

Rose, N. (1996) Psychiatry as a political science: advanced liberalism and the administration of risk, *History of the Human Sciences*, 9, 2, 1–23.

Rose, N. (1998) Governing risky individuals: the role of psychiatry in new regimes of control, *Psychiatry, Psychology and Law*, 5, 2, 177–95.

Rose, N. (2000) Government and control, *British Journal of Criminology*, 40, 321–39.

Royal College of Nursing (1998) *Dealing with Violence against Nursing Staff: an RCN Guide for Nurses and Managers*. London: RCN.

Scambler, G. (2002) *Health and Social Change: a Critical Theory*. Buckingham: Open University Press.

Scambler, G. and Higgs, P. (1998) Introduction. In Scambler, G. and Higgs, P. (eds) *Modernity, Medicine and Health*. London: Routledge.

South, N. (1994) Drugs: control, crime and criminological studies. In Maguire, M., Morgan, R. and Reiner, R. (eds) *The Oxford Handbook of Criminology*. Oxford: Oxford University Press.

Stanko, E. (1998) *Taking Stock: What do we know about violence in the UK?*. ESRC Violence Research Programme, Royal Holloway, University of London.

Stokes, T. (2000) Removal from a GP's list, *British Medical Journal*, 320, 7247, 1447–1448. (www.bmj.com/cgi/eletters/320/7471447).

Strong, P. (1979a) *The Ceremonial Order of the Clinic: Parents, Doctors and Medical Bureaucracies*. London: Routledge.

Strong, P. (1979b) Sociological imperialism and the profession of medicine: a critical examination of the thesis of medical imperialism, *Social Science and Medicine*, 13A, 199–215.

Strong, P. (1980) Doctors and dirty work, *Sociology of Health and Illness*, 2, 1, 24–47.

Taylor, I. (1999) *Crime in Context: a Critical Criminology of Market Societies*. Cambridge: Polity.

Waitzkin, H. (1991) *The Politics of Medical Encounters*. New Haven: Yale University Press.

Walklate, S. (1989) *Victimology*. London: Unwin Hyman.

Walklate, S. (1997) Risk and criminal victimisation: a modernist dilemma?, *British Journal of Criminology*, 37, 1, 35–46.

Wynne, R., Clarkin, N., Cox, T. and Griffiths, A. (1997) *Guidance on the Prevention of Violence at Work*. Luxembourg: European Commission.

Zedner, L. (1994) Victims. In Maguire, M., Morgan, R. and Reiner, R. (eds) *The Oxford Handbook of Criminology*. Oxford: Oxford University Press.

Zola, I.K. (1972) Medicine as an institution of social control, *Sociological Review*, 20, 487–504.

Chapter 5

The emergence and implications of a mental health ethos in juvenile justice

Sarah Armstrong

Introduction

Criminology has always leaned heavily on psychology. Criminologists, however, have spent little time consciously reflecting on the nature and impact of this influence. This is not to say that criminologists entirely overlook the linkage between the realms of mental health and criminal justice: there is a substantial literature on just this topic. The research, however, rarely deviates from exploring how people subject to control in one field fall under the control of the other. The focus is on how criminals have their problems medicalised or how those with mental health needs have their problems criminalised (*e.g.* Anderson 1997, Allen 1987, Liska *et al.* 1999, respectively). This kind of work assumes that criminal justice and mental health, as arenas of social policy and control, are distinct, or else movement from one sphere to the other would not matter.

This chapter shifts its focus away from these traditional emphases to consider organisational dynamics at the system level: how do mental health and juvenile justice systems relate to and permeate each other? How and why have boundaries shifted? The neglect of system-level analysis became apparent during fieldwork I conducted as part of an ongoing project to document the aftermath of the United States' most radical experiment in juvenile decarceration – the de-institutionalisation of youth from Massachusetts' reformatories and training schools during the early 1970s. While the community-based private network of treatment that Massachusetts set up as a successor to its training schools has undergone a great deal of research attention, this has been orientated primarily towards testing the persistence of the state's commitment to non-institutional care (*e.g.* Lerner 1990). Very few evaluations attempt to characterise the approach to or style of treatment that replaced the failed rehabilitative programmes of the training schools, and none locate the Massachusetts experiment more generally in the sociology of punishment.

The privatised, community-based approach to juvenile treatment in Massachusetts has come to be permeated by what I call a mental health *ethos* – that is, providers of services targeting the juvenile delinquency population have adopted the techniques, language, and self-descriptions of mental health organisations, and mental health organisations have moved into the juvenile justice market[1]. In this chapter I first explore how decarceration has allowed this cultural interaction to occur by looking at the extent and ways that private juvenile justice vendors have become influenced by and gradually taken on mental health approaches.

I then relate the emergence of the mental health ethos to an *actuarial* theory of punishment, perhaps the most important and influential recent development in social theorising about punishment (Rigakos 1999, McAra 1997, Nelken 1994). Actuarialism in criminology posits the irrelevance of the traditional justifications of punishment – retribution, deterrence and rehabilitation – and the emergence of an entirely new paradigm, which has been captured in the concept of a 'new penology' (Feeley and Simon 1992). The new penology replaces a focus on the *individual* as a subject for moral reprobation or social training in favour of the efficient classification and management of dangerous *groups*. This new paradigm rejects ultimate outcomes such as reduced crime and moral harmony in favour of the limited notion of *containment*. It presents a nihilistic vision of criminal justice, a postmodern world view that moves beyond describing pendulum shifts from more treatment-oriented to more punitive periods by characterising contemporary punishment as an amoral, efficiency-oriented strategy of danger minimisation.

The evidence, broadly informed by Foucault's (1978, 1991) concepts of biopower and governmentality, that actuarial theorists of punishment use to support their claims, includes the increasing importance of probabilistic reasoning in evaluating dangerousness, the use of diagnostic tools to categorise types of offenders, and the pervasiveness of risk assessment in managing criminal offenders (Feeley and Simon 1992).

These practices reflect exactly the changes that I claim occurred as a result of de-institutionalisation in the Massachusetts juvenile justice system. And yet the state's development of a privatised continuum of community-based care does not appear to be driven by an overarching principle of containment; notions of personal responsibility and improvement continue to animate the post-decarceration system. I conclude the paper with an alternative explanation for the rapid and pervasive penetration of mental health techniques and treatment approaches in juvenile justice by attempting to show how they *resolve* rather than transcend the competition between the contradictory pressures on penal agents to harm and help through retributionist and rehabilitative ideologies of punishment.

Theoretical angle: a disclaimer

It should be noted that this line of argument is pursued through the particular perspective of a criminologist curious about her own (sub-)discipline's development of an actuarial perspective. It thus responds most directly to the debates and questions criminologists might have about mental health and treatment issues in the context of punishment. This is not an insignificant disclaimer, since de-institutionalisation has been a watershed development in the recent history of both mental health and crime and punishment. There is not space, however, to compare the trajectories of these respective histories, although they present important parallels and differences[2] (see e.g. Scull 1984). The main argument of this paper is not that de-institutionalisation of mental health and criminal/delinquency populations led to their merger within a unified system of social service, but that de-institutionalisation of youths from state-run facilities led to the development of mental health-influenced modes of care within the juvenile justice system. And, moreover, this influence – as it has occurred more generally in Anglo-American criminal and juvenile justice systems – has been interpreted as the rise of an actuarial ethic in punishment. I am interested in unravelling the specific ways that a mental health ethos emerged in Massachusetts juvenile justice to test the actuarial account. I hope that this project, engaging the salient debate within the sociology of punishment, will be of interest nevertheless to medical sociologists who may know as little about how criminologists make sense of the subject of their discipline as criminologists do of the ways in which medical sociology understands criminal justice and penal practice.

Criminologists have attributed to de-institutionalisation (of criminal and juvenile justice populations) the special role of marking the death of the institution-based rehabilitative ideal and initiating the emergence of community as a new treatment ideal (Cohen 1985, Allen 1981, Armstrong forthcoming). They have since discovered a more sinister element of de-institutionalisation and community treatment, arguing that the promise of alternatives to incarceration in practice has meant introducing supplements to incarceration that 'widen, deepen and strengthen' nets of social control (Austin and Krisberg 1981). The sense that reform movements in criminal justice are inevitably co-opted by agents of control has afflicted sociologists of punishment with a kind of theoretical paralysis. Any attempt to reform the justice system was assumed to be some new, more insidious form of state social control, and subsequent research inverted the traditional approach of gathering information to generate and inform analytical findings into a process of treating any new phenomenon as evidence of a foregone conclusion of net widening (see e.g. Ericson's review of the period in the preface to McMahon 1992).

Criminological adaptation of actuarialism, ironically, has allowed the sociology of punishment to transcend the broken record of net-widening claims. The turn towards actuarial theory is ironic because it finds a way out of the disillusionment with rehabilitative programmes and the cynicism about law and order politics with the essentially escapist idea that the legitimacy of the criminal justice system no longer derives from moral or social values, but from an instrumental managerialism that has as its only goal containment of the dangerous. This has set the sociology of punishment the new task of cataloguing the penal practices that look actuarial.

I use the post-de-institutionalised Massachusetts juvenile system to criticise on two levels the actuarial thesis as it has developed in criminology.

First, a mental health ethos in juvenile justice, which relies on actuarial diagnostic and assessment tools, cannot be conflated with the general emergence of actuarialism as the dominant penal value. Second, the tendency to conflate the rise of risk assessment techniques with a fundamental transformation of penal values reflects a general ignorance within the discipline about mental health and the field of sociology devoted to analysing it.

Methodology

This chapter is based on field work conducted during 2000 into the history and aftermath of de-institutionalisation of juveniles from state training schools and reformatories. The doctoral project which has generated the data on which the findings for this chapter are based is attempting both to document a recent social history of Massachusetts' juvenile justice reform and to consider the ongoing role that Massachusetts plays as a model of reform to contemporary advocates of youth. The observation of a mental health ethos in Massachusetts juvenile justice began life as a finding tangential to this larger project and thus the methodology is that of the larger project rather than one specifically tailored to a *sui generis* hypothesis about the relationship between mental health and juvenile justice generally. For this reason, the case of Massachusetts alone is presented; the findings from this research suggest, however, that this state could act as a theory-generating case and serve as a basis for testing the generalisability of these claims on a national scale.

The analysis is based on nearly 20 years' worth of data (1981–2000) on programme providers to the Massachusetts Department of Youth Services (DYS). These are contained in a number of sources including detailed annual reports produced by the DYS which provide information about juvenile population numbers, categories and placement types, as well as information about the private providers of service. Further sources are: publicly available tax records (all vendors to the DYS are public charities); corporate records on file with the state which document original and amended corporate purpose statements, name changes and merger and acquisition information; special forms required by the state's Public Charities Division (Office of the Attorney General) which document in more detail the operations of the juvenile providers, their relationships with other organisations and vendors. Then, there are sources covering miscellaneous other information; information generated by the DYS itself such as special reports, programme plans, procurement documents, planning and research documents (*e.g.* Massachusetts DYS 1998), and also including unpublished and informal information such as programme and budget analyses. Finally, there is information from private providers themselves including marketing information, mission statements, and programme plans and descriptions; and, interviews of DYS managerial and executive personnel as well as of the main private providers[3].

Information on the organisation of juvenile services in the immediate and medium-range aftermath of decarceration of the training schools and reformatories (1971–81) comes from process and evaluation studies conducted by a team led by Lloyd Ohlin (*e.g.* Ohlin *et al.* 1973, 1977, unpublished research papers archived in the Harvard Law School Library Special Collections), various evaluations conducted by later researchers (NCCD 1991, Krisberg and Austin 1993), and the memoirs and articles of key DYS managers (Miller 1991, Bakal 1998, Loughran 1988).

Juvenile de-institutionalisation in Massachusetts and the influence of mental health

The Massachusetts experiment: closure of the juvenile reformatories
Jerome Miller was appointed to lead the Massachusetts Department of Youth Services (DYS) in late 1969 and attempted to carry out de-institutionalisation in juvenile justice on a scale contemplated only by recent theorists of correctional abolitionism. After frustrations in the attempt to achieve reform among staff and programmes within state facilities, Miller made the dramatic decision to shut down the entire state system of facilities for juvenile delinquents, a system comprising about a dozen major training schools and reformatories, almost half dating from the late 19th century and including the nation's oldest reformatory, the Lyman School for Boys.

The de-institutionalisation of the Massachusetts juvenile system was a response to the perception of the state training school's endemic problems. Ohlin *et al.* (1973) singled out the failure of institutions either to reduce recidivism or to house youths safely and humanely:

A key organizing principle of traditional training schools is
punishment. . . . the institutions are basically custodial and
authoritarian. . . . Resocialization efforts are commonly reduced
to instruments for creating conformity, deference to adult authority,
and obedience to rules. Regimented marching and shaved heads and
close haircuts, omnipresent officials and punitive disciplinary measures
have been the authoritative marks of the training school, along
with the manipulation of privileges such as cigarette smoking,
TV watching, home visits, or release to reward compliance
(1973: 7).

The description of the training school regime evokes Goffman's (1968) depiction of the 'total institution' which showed how prisons and asylums work by destroying the sense of self that inmates had possessed prior to institutionalisation. The Ohlin research team, in line with Goffman's analysis, suggested that the problems observed in the large institutions were inherent rather than aberrational. The corralling of hundreds of people together necessitated population management techniques that produced order through rigid, crude systems of incentives and punishments.

Early research observations of the Massachusetts reforms identified both the general thrust of reform and its limitations. Commissioner Miller had 'a *mandate* . . . to initiate more progressive policies and treatment of delinquent youth . . . [but] the mandate was in the main broad and undefined' (Ohlin *et al.* 1973: 9, emphasis in original). The juvenile system was under pressure to change things, to do something radically different, and yet lacked guidance on exactly what that would comprise. Given the sense that the problems of the juvenile system lay not in particular lapses in practice but in the nature of large-scale institutionalisation itself, the solution could be constructed reactively out of the ashes of the old regime. This reasoning process finds the direction that reform should take in the nature of the problem itself; the vision of the future becomes a photo negative of the failed present. Thus Miller and his staff focused on three strategies: 'regionalization, privatization and community integration' (Bakal 1998: 110).

Articulating a vision of reform was one thing; coming up with a system of community-based providers to realise the strategy was another. Miller originally envisaged developing a system where the DYS would contract with numerous, perhaps even hundreds, of programme providers to provide a diverse, innovative array of services that could cater to individual needs (Miller 1991). Working with many kinds of vendors would also avoid monopolisation and bureaucratisation of juvenile services, a main weakness of the state.

The groups with whom the DYS eventually put together a loose system of privatised juvenile services might be placed into one of two categories. First, there were organisations founded mainly in response to the DYS's needs by individuals with little or no professional prior involvement in juvenile justice. The second category consisted of existing organisations with a long history of involvement in social services, charitable work and child welfare, but without much experience in residential treatment of juvenile delinquents. These included the Catholic Church's charitable services arm and YMCAs throughout the state.

These new providers to the young offenders of Massachusetts met the main criteria the DYS desired in the non-institutional system: they were smaller than the reformatories, and they were privately operated in neighbourhoods throughout the state. The vague and reactive agenda for reform thus seemed to include simply a desire not to reproduce the state-run institutional environment, by seeking out organisations filled with sympathetic and enthusiastic staff who leaned towards – rather than had systematically developed – an ethic of treatment. While the DYS was successful in dismantling an institutional system well over a century old, it lacked a specific blueprint of the successor system relying instead on a determined enthusiasm to shake up the *status quo* with a broadly conceived campaign of reform.

Development of a privatised system of juvenile placements
Regardless of the ideals of reform, following de-institutionalisation the DYS would have been confronted with the practical need to assemble quickly a number of providers to fulfil the promise of a community-based treatment continuum. Although Miller had hoped for a large number of contracting organisations to ensure diversity, innovation and responsiveness to changing youth needs, there existed real pressure to come up with a stable group of organisations which could be counted on to deal with the never-ending flow of youths committed into state care by the juvenile courts.

By 1981, the DYS contracted for 70 different juvenile programmes, residential and non-residential, run by 31 different agencies (including a minority of programmes run by the DYS itself). By 1998 there were 92 pro-grammes run by 32 agencies (again including the DYS, which by 1998 was the single biggest provider of juvenile programmes), which demonstrates a degree of concentration among providers: fewer groups were providing more and higher capacity services. And while many of the 1981 organisations survived to continue providing services to the DYS by 1998, five organisa-tions account for the lion's share of the DYS's contracting budget (Table 1).

Three agencies that dominated DYS services up to and through the 1990s were organisations either founded or re-directing their main mission in response to Jerry Miller's 1970s call to arms for a system of local community treatment providers. These were the R F Kennedy Children's Action Corps (RFKCAC), Key, and NFI. Two agencies completing the main provider group were the Old Colony Y, a YMCA programme, and Life Resources (a part of the Catholic Church charity arm). None of the organisations had experience as juvenile justice corrections agencies, although they had from the start recruited former DYS staff in both administrative and line level positions.

Four of these 'big five' developed a de facto regional dominance in Massachusetts. RFKCAC provided (and provides today) most services in the western region of the state. Key provides most services in the central part

Table 1 *Contract value of largest DYS vendors in 1998*

Organisation	Contracts value	As per cent of all DYS contracts %
JRI	$ 4,187,924	9
Key	4,211,171	9
Life Resources	2,695,504	6
NFI	2,182,921	5
Old Colony Y	7,059,720	15
RFKCAC	6,905,365	14
Total of above	$23,054,681	48
Total value of all DYS contracts	$47,812,183	

of the state. Old Colony Y dominates south-eastern Massachusetts (Life Resources also operates in this region), and NFI provides most services in the northeast. The metro region, comprising Boston and its immediate environs, was split up among Old Colony Y and Key, and a number of other organisations. During the first decade and a half of privatised juvenile care, the big five implicitly respected the regional boundaries by declining to bid on DYS procurement contracts outside their geographic regions. This handful of agencies continues to dominate the field today: the value of their contracts accounted for 42 per cent of the total 1998 DYS budget for private services (residential and non-residential). A sixth provider, JRI, Inc., dominates in a different way by monopolising the high security end of the privatised juvenile treatment field. Table 1 shows that these six organisations control nearly half the DYS's monies for contracted services.

Weak power of the DYS may have contributed to the ability of a de facto oligarchic monopoly to establish itself. This weakness followed from factors earlier identified as a lack of a strategic plan for and experience in providing desired services, and lack of experience in managing a privatised system of care. This created strong reliance of the public agency on the entrepreneurial willingness of private providers to come up with a defensible continuum of care for the state's delinquents. This may have been compounded by the recession and government social service budget cutbacks of the 1980s, during which the DYS experienced severe cuts and had little flexibility to develop its own new programmes and directions.

Movement of mental health providers into juvenile justice
Given that the same organisations that controlled the field in 1974 dominate the field a quarter of a century later, we would expect to see very little change in the providers with whom DYS contracted over the years. By 1985, however, the annual reports for the DYS began to show new organisations obtaining relatively substantial contracts that were beginning to make a dent in the control of the biggest providers of juvenile residential care.

To unravel the reasons that successful market barriers seemed to be breaking down by the mid and late 1980s, I looked at the kinds of organisations winning major DYS contracts. Among those breaking into the juvenile justice services market, one striking commonality revealed itself: a majority of the post-1985 vendors primarily or exclusively offered mental health services (Table 2). Of the 12 biggest vendors of juvenile services entering the market after 1985, seven – nearly 60 per cent of new vendors – described their main service orientation as mental health. This represents a significant shift in the service orientation of organisations contracting for DYS services before 1985. Of the 10 biggest DYS providers of residential services who were in existence by 1981, only one – 10 per cent of early providers – claimed mental health treatment as a main area of expertise.

'Mental health services' did not dominate social services jargon during the 1970s. Thus, even if many of the agencies providing services to juveniles at

Table 2 *Service orientation of largest DYS providers entering market before 1981 and after 1985*

Pre-1981 Market entry organisation	Main service type
Old Colony Y	child welfare
Massachusetts Halfway Houses	criminal justice
Dare Family Services	juv. justice, **mental health**
R. F. K. Children's Action Corps	juvenile justice
Center for Human Development	child welfare, juvenile justice
Justice Resources Institute	juvenile justice
Key Program	juvenile justice
NFI	juvenile justice
Life Resources (Catholic Church)	child welfare
Tri-County Youth Programs	juvenile justice, child welfare

Post-1985 Market entry organisation	Main service type
Accept	juvenile justice
Behavioral Health Network	**mental health**
Comcare Services	**mental health**
Corporation for Public Management	social services
CSI	child welfare
Eliot Community Human Services	**mental health**
Lynn Youth Resources Bureau	**mental health**
Mentor	**mental health**
Roxbury Youth Works	juvenile justice
Servicenet	**mental health**
Spectrum Health Systems	**mental health**
Volunteers of America of Mass.	child welfare

Main service type based on review of statement of corporate purpose and/or review of organisational literature.

that time might have offered some form of counselling, they probably would not have described such services in terms of mental health expertise. But this begs the question of why mental health has become part of the new language of dealing with troubled youngsters. In any case, the large proportion of mental health providers among newer DYS contractors cannot be attributed to changes in terminology alone, because the mental health organisations breaking into the field were not comparable to the early providers in terms of their service orientation. The organisations that came into the market in the mid-1980s and after typically had no experience in juvenile justice or child welfare services. These new vendors include Behavioral Health Network, Comcare Services, Eliot Community Human Services, Mentor Health Services, Servicenet and Spectrum Health Services, all of which began corporate life as community mental health clinics[4].

The ability of new agencies to compete successfully against the market dominators is not itself explained by the fact that many of the new bidders came from the mental health field. It may, however, suggest a partial answer. All of the new bidders from the mental health industry were well-established organisations in their own fields; most are multi-million dollar organisations. The size of these agencies thus allows them to provide real competition in bidding for high overhead contracts (setting up new residential programmes requires costly and time-consuming acquisition of property, permits and insurance for serving vulnerable people). The days in which non-professionals with little capital and experience could obtain state contracts – the climate in which the big five were able to secure their dominance – are long over. Mental health organisations seeking to expand market share, by moving into this new market, presented an altogether different level of competition.

Recasting of juvenile justice services as mental health services
The mid-1980s also marked a shift towards a more punitive, law and order, approach to criminal and juvenile justice (Garland 2001, MassINC 1996). With increasing market pressure from mental health corporations, and with DYS interest in treatment regimes clearly tied to the goals of public safety, the original vendors were under pressure to respond. No longer could these first contract providers describe their missions in a way that would risk a perception of being overly sympathetic to their youth charges, or unsophisticated about their approach to treatment. Consider the Massachusetts Halfway House, Inc. (MHHI) statement of corporate purpose from 1964, which exemplifies the idealism and informality characterising the ambience during the decarceration reform:

> to provide whatsoever professional or nonprofessional staff as the Board of Directors may decide are necessary to meet the current requirements to provide a sense of friendship, of mutual self-help, and of other elements in helping [an adult or juvenile criminal offender] adjust to the society outside. . . .

A proposal submitted by Key in pursuit of a 1998 DYS contract competition provides a strong contrast to the informal 1960s language above. In its proposal for a $549,000 service, Key states its intention to encourage:

- Strengthening the family and teaching them to take responsibility for their lives and their children;
- Greater involvement of the local communities' core institutions – schools, civic organizations, police, etc. – in rehabilitation of DYS youth;
- Interventions which promote delinquency prevention, for example – family work and collateral work with siblings;
- A behavior management system which delivers predictable responses to unacceptable behavior; and

• Adherence to DYS' four levels of supervision whereby the most serious offenders receive the highest degree of intervention.

Key notes that its commitment to these goals tracks those set out by the US Department of Justice's Office of Juvenile Justice and Delinquency Prevention (OJJDP) in its emphasis on both accountability of youth, as well as on treatment modalities with identifiable and accepted benchmarks of success. While this example shows how one of the original DYS providers has come to speak in a language approved by those demanding a strengthening of the juvenile justice system's stance against crime, it also suggests how mental health organisations might possess a 'starting gate' advantage in contract competitions.

The field of mental health provides a 'scientised' framework within which to diagnose and address the problems of juvenile delinquents, thus assuaging the chronic identity crisis of the juvenile justice system in its ambivalence towards the youth's exclusive status as either criminal or victim. As a result of the uncertainty about how to characterise its target population the juvenile court has shied away from the terminology of adult criminal courts so that young offenders are not 'sentenced' to 'penal institutions' but 'committed' as wards of the state to 'training schools'; they are not 'criminals' but 'delinquents' whose specific acts are classified through the legally, normatively and descriptively vague concepts of 'incorrigibility', 'being out of control' and 'promiscuity'.

By comparison, mental health providers come armed with non-normative and certainly less anachronistic language provided through such tools as the Diagnostic and Statistical Manual of Mental Disorders and by specialised screening instruments. Diagnosis takes 'an agglomeration of complaints and symptoms [which] may be unclear, unconnected, and mysterious', and transforms them into a coherent problem to which known solutions may be applied (Brown 1995: 39). These children, who are not quite criminals but not entirely victims either, can be subjected to a scientifically validated diagnostic process through which they might be deemed to suffer from conduct disorders (aggression, theft, dishonesty, etc.) or oppositional defiant disorder (defying adults) contained in the DSM-IV (American Psychiatric Association 1994). The diagnostic labels of mental health allow juvenile justice decision makers to stifle unease about committing youth to custody for skipping school, drinking alcohol and having sex. These borrowed labels also provide an alternative framework for describing criminal behaviour like assault, rape and theft in terms which can provide these decision makers with the political space for making treatment-orientated decisions, instead of feeling pressured to commit to punitive custody[5].

The advantage that medicalised diagnostic instruments confer to the mental health profession in winning DYS contracts was not lost on the existing juvenile programme vendors. From the period that mental health agencies began bidding for, and winning, contracts without respect for the regional boundaries in place since the 1970s, the older providers started

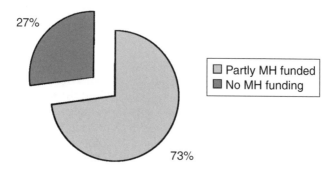

Figure 1 *DYS Providers receiving funding from mental health funding streams, 1998*

talking about their own services and mission in terms of mental health; and copies of the DSM have taken their place as standard texts on the shelves of juvenile providers. NFI, a major operator and broker of foster care services, shelter care and day care to the delinquency population, amended its corporate purpose in 1985: 'To provide and do all things necessary to providing mental health services'.

The language excerpted from Key's contract proposal distinguishes itself through terms like 'behavior management systems', 'interventions' and 'collateral work with siblings' from earlier, less medicalised rhetoric. New Perspective, Inc.'s description of its corporate purpose from 1978 shows how informally treatment was once conceived. It sought: 'to develop programs for the rehabilitation of delinquent, underprivileged, troubled, and other youth, to actually carry out said programs. . . .'.

Changes in how the original juvenile justice providers were beginning to describe their services, to encompass a mental health emphasis, reflect also the changing arena of resources for the treatment of socially troubled youth. Most of the big five have expanded their client constituency to include not just the DYS caseload of juvenile offenders, but youth who appear on the state's radar for other reasons: child abuse and neglect, developmental and other disabilities, and non-criminal anti-social behaviour. Hence, the DYS is not any longer the sole funding source supporting these agencies. Funds devoted to mental health purposes have become an increasingly dominant source of income for providers of services to delinquent youth in Massachusetts. Figure 1 shows the proportion of DYS vendors who receive some of their income from a local, state or federal mental health funding stream. As the problems of delinquency increasingly become cross-defined as issues for mental health treatment (for example, what was once the status offence of underage drinking of alcoholic beverages now also becomes a high risk indicator of the mental health problem of alcoholism), DYS providers are diversifying and increasing their contract income.

The fuzzy boundaries between contemporary mental health and juvenile justice systems among contractors to the DYS show, at the economic level,

that de-institutionalisation freed up resources formerly invested in the maintenance and operation costs associated with large state buildings: Furthermore, the organisations constituting, respectively, the mental health and
juvenile justice systems have begun consequently to move into each other's
markets. The increasing importance of assessment in juvenile programming
eases the softening of market barriers. As Brown points out, diagnostic
techniques can resolve 'boundary disputes', serving as the arena in which
service parameters are re-negotiated (1995: 45).

It does not follow, however, that, after some interpenetration between
mental health and juvenile justice systems in Massachusetts, one field can
now be reduced to the other. In particular, juvenile justice cannot be characterised as a sub-arena of the mental health system because concerns about
youth crime, public safety and justice remain distinctive and central themes
of debate (Garland 1996, 2001). That is, the *content* of the juvenile justice
system has remained intact – the concern to provide an institutionally
coherent response to the problem of juvenile offending – while the *process*
through which content decisions are made has incorporated devices deemed
by criminal justice practitioners as more politically defensible and (or,
because they are perceived as) more scientifically reliable than the more
informal reform era style.

Punishment, treatment or containment?

Certain features of the emergence of a mental health ethos in Massachusetts
juvenile justice seem to bear out a criminological theory of actuarialism in
punishment. The Massachusetts case, however, fundamentally challenges this
interpretation if we take notice of current debates among medical sociologists about the social construction of diagnosis, the limitations of cultural
risk analysis, and, at an even more basic level, the evolution of treatment
models in mental health (Clarke and Short 1993). This chapter now raises the
analysis of the case of Massachusetts to the more general stage of the sociology of punishment. It does this by reviewing how the actuarial perspective in criminology relies on some general but superficial conclusions about
the decline of a rehabilitative ideal in penal policy. From this critique of
actuarialism I conclude by posing an alternate interpretation of the role of
mental health in criminal justice, arguing that treatment models adapted
from mental health operate to sustain rather than displace the traditional
penal objectives of retribution and rehabilitation.

The decline of one rehabilitative ideal
An important turn in the sociology of punishment during the 1970s set the
agenda for criminologists of punishment to treat almost any attempt at penal
reform as a demonstration of the net-widening interest of state social control
agents. This turn was triggered by two important works in criminology,

which definitively established the conviction that criminal justice treatment programmes were failing to reduce recidivism (Martinson 1974), and, for this and other reasons, the commitment to rehabilitation as a primary aim of contemporary justice systems was in decline (Allen 1981).

Allen identified the rehabilitative ideal with the institutional setting of the prison, noting that treatment 'became an important element in . . . penological thought only when imprisonment became a principle mode of punishment' (1981: 12). While he attributes the criticisms of the rehabilitative pro-grammes of prisons to both the political left (humanitarian concern about the lack of transparency in treatment) and right (rising crime rates), that in turn created the necessary momentum to get de-institutionalisation off the ground, he does not fully appreciate the connection between the institutional setting of the prison and a *particular* model of treatment: a medicalised, individual-orientated mode. This leads him to understand the failure of support for prison-based offender programmes of the period as the *general* failure in support for *any* kind of treatment approach to criminal offending.

A social historian of psychology, however, could contextualise the disillu-sionment with medical models of treatment in prisons as a system-specific example of the decline of support for rigid behavioural modification or exclusively medical approaches to mental disorder (Rachman 1997). But no sociologist of medicine would join Allen in concluding that this moment in the evolution of mental health models marked the end of psychology's influence on the role of treatment of the criminal justice population. While Allen saw the rehabilitative ideal dying out of criminal justice, a revised view, better informed about mental health developments, would see the emergence of new therapeutic models that have come to play a role in prisoner treat-ment, specifically the increasing importance of cognitive and cognitive-behavioural strategies (Crow 2001, Hedderman and Sugg 1997).

Allen's (1981) argument, reinforced by Martinson's (1974) evidence of the failure of prison treatment programmes, encouraged widespread cynicism about penal reform. Later developments in criminal justice practice, like community corrections, offender drug treatment and diversion, came to be seen not as counter-evidence to the 'rehabilitation is dead' and 'nothing works' theses, but as support for these claims by showing how all attempts at reform were quickly undermined or co-opted by government, widening the nets of control through which to stream more people into exclusively coercive correctional institutions (Cohen 1983, 1984, 1987, Cohen and Scull 1983, Foucault 1977).

Actuarial justice and the 'new penology'
The widespread belief in the death of a rehabilitative ideal, combined with the failure of punitive law and order approaches to affect crime rates, led the sociology of punishment to a stalemate: if it has been successfully shown, conceptually and empirically, that nothing works, where does one go from here? Feeley and Simon's (1992) elaboration of a 'new penology' provided

an especially influential solution. Observing the rising use of risk assessment and risk management in criminal justice, simultaneous with the apparently ceaseless growth in prison populations, they concluded that the traditional regimes of just desserts and rehabilitation are obsolete:

> ... the New Penology has a radically different orientation. It is actuarial. It is concerned with the techniques for identifying, classifying and managing groups assorted by levels of dangerousness. It takes crime for granted. It accepts deviance as normal. It is sceptical that liberal interventionist crime control strategies do or can make a difference. Thus its aim is not to intervene in individual's lives for the purpose of ascertaining responsibility, making the guilty 'pay for their crime' or changing them. Rather it seeks to regulate groups as part of a strategy of managing danger (Feeley and Simon 1994: 173).

The new penology claims that actuarial approaches have allowed criminologists not only to make sense of their academic discipline, but also freed criminal justice decisionmakers from the impossible burden of significantly reducing crime. Actuarialism employs probabilities of risk, which by definition offer a means of managing rather than eliminating uncertainty and danger. So failures of the criminal justice system, such as when an inmate released following a risk assessment commits a heinous crime, can be reconstructed as successes by arguing that the process of screening meant that only one such re-offender was released.

The assumption of the new penology is that actuarial techniques exclusively serve political and criminal damage-minimisation functions and do not have, nor are expected to have, any impact on the rehabilitation of individuals. Diagnosis is the process of looking productive without doing anything. This represents the re-direction of the justice system from social objectives to internal process measures of efficiency. 'Thus, one finds in the correctional system today a much greater emphasis on drug testing than on drug treatment. . . . [and] testing . . . provide[s criminal justice actors] a means to document compliance with . . . internal performance requirements' (Feeley and Simon 1992: 462).

But new penology positions become as unsatisfying as the net-widening ones they have replaced, as developments in penal practice are functionally explained in terms of their role in streaming individuals into manageable groups. Indeed, actuarial techniques – statistical methods and risk assessment tools – are claimed as both the method and the value of the criminal justice system. Diagnosis and risk assessment provide the means of identifying and isolating the dangerous. These are also values of the system, as refinement of techniques and the improved collection of data and keeping of records are seen as the key to perfecting danger minimisation (Ericson and Haggerty 1997).

Some have criticised the new penologists' narrow focus on particular developments like risk assessment in criminal justice practice to develop general claims about a new post-modern paradigm of punishment (McAra 1997). There is also criticism regarding the degree to which the new penology adequately theorises and provides evidence of actuarialism. Rigakos levels the charge that the new penology 'is limited by theoretical assertions that confuse generally accepted bureaucratic practices with "apoliticism" and "neutrality" ' (1999: 146). I would add to this charge that the new penology's deep distrust of actuarialism borders on making a normative argument about the role of statistics in a justice system. It also reflects an insufficient and unsophisticated appreciation of the emergence of actuarialism to replace or complement clinical approaches in mental health.

Reinterpreting the implications of a mental health ethos in juvenile justice
The previous two sections built a critique of criminological actuarialism on the field's neglect of the study of mental health. By neglecting developments in mental health treatment, criminologists have mistaken evolution in treatment approaches for a decline of and loss of faith in treatment within penal practice. As a result, observations by criminologists of mental health tools – specifically risk assessment and diagnostic instruments – have been interpreted within this 'rehabilitation is dead' framework to construct a thesis about social containment of the marginalised. This is a thesis that categorically rejects: (1) new techniques may be intended to have an individually rehabilitative effect, or (2) new techniques can support rather than replace traditional penal values.

In this concluding section, I begin to build the positive case that the treatment strategies of a mental health ethos, as manifested in justice systems, can provide a means of allowing traditional penal values to survive the scepticism raised in writings from the 1970s. I have already discussed the legitimating function that mental health diagnostic instruments confer by 'scientising' difficult discretionary decisions. I now move from diagnosis to treatment to show how a mental health ethos can also legitimate justice system decisionmaking by reconciling the competing values of retribution and rehabiliation.

The dominant model of offender treatment, cognitive-behaviour therapy (CBT), has been adapted from the mental health field extremely successfully because its multi-modal approach accommodates both the justice system's moral interest in punishment and its practical interest in rehabilitation. CBT has become a pervasive mode of treatment in all types of offender programmes from sex offenders to petty thieves in the US and UK (Crow 2001). Popularity of the CBT model followed the development of a 'what works' literature that, mainly through meta-analysis of delinquency and offender programmes, has shown that treatment programmes with cognitive and behavioural components have had the greatest impact on recidivism (Hollin 1999, McGuire 1995, Andrews *et al.* 1990, Garrett 1985, Gendreau and Ross 1979).

CBT has brought criminal justice treatment practitioners out of a 'nothing works' stupor and placed 'offender treatment . . . firmly back on the agenda of administrators, practitioners and researchers' (Hollin 1999: 369). What I am interested to explain, however, is how the popularity of CBT can be linked to its *conceptual compatibility with the traditional aims of justice systems.*

There are two main components of a CBT approach. First, the cognitive element of programmes emphasises the gaining of insight into one's destructive behaviour as a prerequisite to reducing the undesirable conduct. Second, programmes also include behavioural strategies which encourage the modification of behaviour. For example, the proposed Key programme excerpted earlier includes in its proposed programme plan a 'behavior management system which delivers predictable responses to unacceptable behavior'.

This two-pronged approach maps onto the two traditional goals of punishment. On the one hand, the cognitive emphasis on insight and accountability parallels the *retributive* interest in defendants owning up to hurtful conduct, developing a sense of remorse and using these feelings to adjust future behaviour. On the other hand, a behavioural element marks the traditional *rehabilitative* benchmark of reducing anti-social behaviour (in the criminal justice realm measured through recidivism and crime rates). Where criminologists have been tempted to understand penal history in terms of the pendulum swinging from the more or less retributive to the more or less rehabilitative, CBT accomplishes both goals simultaneously. Holding the offender individually accountable (to use penal language) is one of the means *through* which a socially desirable goal is realised.

In addition to reconciling the conflict of competing punishment philosophies, approaches like CBT also allow the government to reduce unrealistic expectations of success. The actuarialists are right to identify the crisis of the state in failing to produce lower crime rates through rehabilitating criminals into law abiding citizens. But they have too quickly understood the acceptance by the state that it cannot significantly reduce or eliminate crime as abandonment of any interest in reducing crime through offender treatment in favour of a strategy of containing the dangerous (Garland 1996). The goals of mental health approaches like CBT do not seek guaranteed and absolute cures either. In a quite modest fashion, the mental health strategies of today aim to reduce or stem the socially dangerous conduct of delinquents, instead of seeking total cures, in terms of human redemption or elimination of crime.

The ability to understand the successful adaptation of a treatment model like CBT in criminal and juvenile justice systems requires us first to have grasped some basic information about how the treatment model is designed to work and how it has emerged out of the treatment models that preceded it. Criminologists who find actuarialism an attractive interpretive framework seem to gloss over mental health practice, perhaps hiding a lack of knowledge about this nearby field, with a normative claim of its irrelevance because of an inevitable co-optation by the state. This chapter has sought to show how both diagnosis and treatment models imported from mental health can in fact support explanations critical of the new penology thesis. These techniques lend authority to the effort of justice systems to legitimate their practices, and they additionally provide a means of responding to the chronic crises of these systems – the juvenile system's ambivalent attitude towards its charges as criminals or children in need, and the competing demands on adult and juvenile justice systems both to punish and provide helpful services to offenders. Furthermore, a specific review of Massachusetts shows how post-deinstitutionalisation market forces, and the organisational dynamics of juvenile and mental health service providers, help to explain the emergence of a mental health ethos in juvenile justice, a piece of the story missing from the new penology's tale of the political power of bureaucracy and a general state interest in containing dangerous elements.

These general claims are generated from the experience of Massachusetts in de-institutionalising its juvenile population, an experiment that is in some ways exceptional. The applicability of the evidence from Massachusetts to other states and jurisdictions remains to be shown. However, an aim closer to the heart of this chapter's interest has been to use the well-known case of Massachusetts to identify the ways in which criminology has failed to engage with sociologies of other realms, specifically mental health, and to suggest the ways that correcting this lapse would enrich and deepen theorising about punishment.

Notes

1 'Ethos' seems a better term than 'way of doing business' as I am trying to capture the sense in which mental health becomes an operational culture for juvenile justice. As more juvenile services are provided by mental health organisations, a mental health treatment approach begins to dominate the treatment programmes of all juvenile justice providers and MH diagnostic instruments have become the norm for screening juveniles adjudicated through a juvenile court into a treatment programme.

2 Perhaps the most important, and striking, difference is the comparative impact on criminal justice and mental health populations of de-institutionalisation. Mechanic and Rochefort (1990), for example, describe the significant falls in institutionalised mental health populations, with the consequent implications this has had for the development of community-based alternatives and a policy of mainstreaming. Institutionalised criminal justice populations, on the other hand, have continued to increase consistently and substantially over the past three decades.

3 Data used to support analysis contained in this article are exempt from full review by the Committee for the Protection of Human Subjects, University of California Berkeley.

4 Investigating corporate name changes proved an instructive means of illustrating how mental health organisations began to broaden their target market. From the examples given: Behavioral Health Network *fka* (was formerly known as) Community Care Mental Health Center, Comcare Services *fka* Taunton Area

Mental Health Clinic, Eliot Community Human Services *fka* Eliot Community Mental Health Center, Servicenet *fka* Hampshire Community Mental Health Center.

5   The security that diagnostic labels offer to juvenile justice system actors belies an active and critical debate about the role of diagnosis in disease and treatment (Brown 1995, Mirowsky and Ross 1989). This provides further evidence of this paper's claim that the neglect by criminal justice practitioners and criminologists of the sociology of medicine and developments in mental health have led to a stunted ability to assess the implications of reform and change in penal rehabilitative agendas.

References

Allen, F. (1981) *The Decline of the Rehabilitative Ideal*. New Haven: Yale University Press.

Allen, H. (1987) *Justice Unbalanced: Gender, Psychiatry and Judicial Decisions*. Philadelphia: Open University Press.

American Psychiatric Association (1994) *DSM-IV: Diagnostic and Statistical Manual of Mental Disorders, 4th ed.* Washington, DC: American Psychiatric Association.

Anderson, M. (1997) Mental illness and criminal behaviour: a literature review, *Journal of Psychiatric and Mental Health Nursing*, 4, 243–50.

Andrews, D.A., Zinger, I., Hodge, R.D., Bonta, J., Gendreau, P. and Cullen, F. (1990) Does correctional treatment work? A clinically relevant and psychologically informed meta-analysis, *Criminology*, 28, 369–88.

Armstrong, S. (forthcoming) Punishing not-for-profit: implications of nonprofit privatization in juvenile punishment, *Punishment and Society*.

Austin, J. and Krisberg, B. (1981) Wider, stronger, and different nets: The dialectics of criminal justice reform, *Journal of Research in Crime and Delinquency*, 18, 165–96.

Bakal, Y. (1998) Reflections: a quarter-century of reform in Massachusetts corrections, *Crime and Delinquency*, 44, 110–16.

Brown, P. (1995) Naming and framing: the social construction of diagnosis and illness, *Journal of Health and Social Behavior*, 35 Extra Issue, 34–52.

Clarke, L. and Short, J. (1993) Social organization and risk: Some current controversies, *Annual Review of Sociology*, 19, 375–99.

Cohen, S. (1983) Social control talk: telling stories about correctional change. In Garland, D. and Young, P. (eds) *The Power to Punish: Contemporary Penality and Social Analysis*. London: Heinemann Educational Books.

Cohen, S. (1985) *Visions of Social Control: Crime, Punishment and Classification*. Cambridge: Polity Press.

Cohen, S. (1987) Taking decarceration seriously: Values, visions and policies. In Lowman, J., Menzies, R. and Palys, T.S. (eds) *Transcarceration: Essays on the Sociology of Control*. Great Britain: Gower Publishing Company Limited.

Cohen, S. and Scull, A. (eds) (1983) *Social Control and the State*. New York: St. Martin's Press.

Crow, I. (2001) *The Treatment and Rehabilitation of Offenders*. London: Sage.

Ericson, R.V. and Haggerty, K. (1997) *Policing the Risk Society*. Oxford: Oxford University Press.

Feeley, M. and Simon, J. (1992). The new penology, *Criminology*, 30, 449–74.

Feeley, M. and Simon, J. (1994) Actuarial justice: The emerging new criminal law. In Nelken, D. (ed) *The Futures of Criminology*. Thousand Oaks, CA: Sage.

Foucault, M. (1977) *Discipline and Punish*. New York: Vintage Books.

Foucault, M. (1978) *The History of Sexuality, Volume I An Introduction*. New York: Random House.

Foucault, M. (1991) Governmentality. In Burchell, G., Gordon, C. and Miller, P. (eds) *The Foucault Effect: Studies in Governmentality*, Chicago: University of Chicago Press.

Garland, D. (1995) Penal modernism and post-modernism. In Blomberg, T. and Cohen, S. (eds) *Punishment and Social Control*. New York: Aldine De Gruyter.

Garland, D. (1996) The limits of the sovereign state: Strategies of crime control in contemporary society, *British Journal of Criminology*, 36, 445–71.

Garland, D. (2001) *The Culture of Control: Crime and Social Order in Contemporary Society*. Oxford: Oxford University Press.

Garrett, C.J. (1985) Effects of residential treatment on adjudicated delinquents: a meta-analysis, *Journal of Research in Crime and Delinquency*, 22, 287–308.

Gendreau, P. and Ross, R.R. (1979) Effective correctional treatment: Bibliotherapy for cynics, *Crime and Delinquency*, 25, 463–89.

Goffman, E. (1968) *Asylums: Essays on the Social Situation of Mental Patients and Other Inmates*. Harmondsworth: Penguin.

Hedderman, C. and Sugg, D. (1997) The influence of cognitive approaches: a survey of probation programmes. In *Changing Offenders Attitudes and Behaviour: What Works?* Part II, Home Office Research Study No. 171, London: Home Office.

Hollin, C.R. (1999) Treatment programs for offenders: Meta-analysis, 'what works,' and beyond, *International Journal of Law and Psychiatry*, 22, 361–72.

Krisberg, B. and Austin, J. (1993) *Reinventing Juvenile Justice*. Newbury Park, CA: Sage.

Lerner, S. (1990) *The Good News about Juvenile Justice: The Movement away from Large Institutions and toward Community-based Services*. Bolinas, CA: Common Knowledge Press.

Liska, A., Markowitz, F., Bridges, Whaley, R. and Bellair, P. (1999) Modeling the relationship between the criminal justice and mental health systems, *American Journal of Sociology*, 104, 1744–75.

Loughran, E. (1988) 'Privatization in juvenile services – competition promotes quality', *Corrections Today*, 78–83.

Martinson, R. (1974) 'What works?' – Questions and answers about prison reform, *The Public Interest*, 35, 22–54.

Massachusetts Department of Youth Services (1998) *Youth, Partnership and Public Safety – The DYS Strategic Plan*. Massachusetts: DYS.

MassINC (The Massachusetts Institute for a New Commonwealth) (1996) *Criminal Justice in Massachusetts: Putting Crime Control First*. Boston: MassINC.

McAra, L. (1997) The politics of penality: an overview of the development of penal policy in Scotland. In Duff, P. and Hutton, N. (eds) *Criminal Justice in Scotland*. Aldershot: Dartmouth Publishing Co.

McGuire, J. (ed) (1995) *What Works: Reducing Reoffending; Guidelines from Research and Practice*. Chichester: Wiley.

McMahon, M. (1992) *The Persistent Prison? Rethinking Decarceration and Penal Reform*. Toronto: University of Toronto Press.

Mechanic, D. and Rochefort, D. (1990) Deinstitutionalization: an appraisal of reform, *Annual Review of Sociology*, 16, 301–27.

Miller, J. (1991) *Last One Over the Wall: the Massachusetts Experiment in Closing Reform Schools*. Columbus: Ohio State University Press.

Mirowsky, J. and Ross, C.E. (1989) Psychiatric diagnosis as reified measurement, *Journal of Health and Social Behavior*, 30, 11–25.

National Council on Crime and Delinquency (NCCD) (1991) *Unlocking Juvenile Corrections: Evaluating the Massachusetts Department of Youth Services*. San Francisco, Calif.: NCCD.

Nelken, D. (ed) (1994) Introduction, *The Futures of Criminology*. London: Sage Publications.

Ohlin, L., Coates, R. and Miller, A. (1973) Radical correctional reform: a case study of the Massachusetts youth correctional system, typescript manuscript supported by the National Institute for Juvenile Justice and Delinquency Prevention, OJJDP, LEAA, Washington, DC: U.S. Department of Justice.

Ohlin, L., Miller, A. and Coates, R. (1977) *Juvenile Correctional Reform in Massachusetts: a Preliminary Report of the Center for Criminal Justice of the Harvard Law School*, Washington, DC: National Institute for Juvenile Justice and Delinquency Prevention, OJJDP, LEAA, Washington, DC: U.S. Department of Justice.

Rachman, S. (1997) The evolution of cognitive behaviour therapy. In Clark, D.M. and Fairburn, C.G. (eds) *The Science and Practice of Cognitive Behaviour Therapy*. Oxford: Oxford University Press.

Rigakos, G. (1999) Risk society and actuarial criminology: Prospects for a critical discourse, *Canadian Journal of Criminology*, 137–50.

Scull, A. (1984) *Decarceration: Community Treatment and the Deviant – a Radical View*, 2nd Edition. Cambridge: Polity Press.

Chapter 6

Contesting the text: Canadian media depictions of the conflation of mental illness and criminality

Riley Olstead

Introduction

How the popular media use language to represent the social world has much to do with how that world is understood. Portrayals of mental illness, for instance, can be understood as expressions of 'myths about the world, the ideas that we project on to it and that shape our understanding of the realities we experience' (Gilman 1988: 37). Thus, the process of experiencing the world is highly charged by the qualities ascribed to illness, in part through popular imagery and representation. Studies of media representations of mental illness are important in assessing how social tropes are created and maintained by media depictions, particularly where those depictions have negative social consequences. In particular, one of the central themes running though media depictions of mental illness is the association between mental illness and criminal behaviour. Such textual inaccuracies play a significant role in reproducing harmful misconceptions, which have serious implications for how mentally ill people are treated (Wahl 1995, 1992, Wahl and Roth 1982). Notable however, is that most research to date has focused on revealing *what* the media say about mental illness as opposed to investigating *how* it is constituted in text. In doing so, previous studies have failed to make the connection between strategies of reporting and power.

This chapter examines the techniques of power that sustain the ideological reproduction of 'mental illness' in the popular media. It is argued that mental illness and thus, those who are defined as mentally ill, are constituted through particular organised discourses. This work explores *how* exactly the press is involved in the continuity of the system of power around mental illness and the ways in which it is linked to ideas about criminality. Where most previous research has utilised content analysis (Nunnally 1961, Wahl and Roth 1982, Fruth and Padderud 1985, Day and Page 1986, Mathieu 1993, Wahl 1995), this study employs both a content and discourse analysis to examine the detailed textual structures and strategies that are utilised in talk about mental illness. Furthermore, while extensive research has been conducted on the conflation of mental illness with depictions of violence and criminality (Nunnally 1961, Fleming and Manvell 1985, Wahl and Roth 1982, Wahl 1995, Mathieu 1993, Fruth and Padderud 1985), very few studies have demonstrated the relevance that other kinds of media portrayals have in informing meaning around the mentally ill criminal depiction. For instance, meaning around criminality may not only come from articles specifically referencing the subject of criminality, but may also be found in articles about mentally ill people as passive, obedient and docile. Thus, I examine media portrayals of mental illness with an interest in assessing polarised talk within, and interplay between, different types of mentally ill representations.

There are several assumptions driving this research. There is the belief by the author that the portrayals of mental illness are not only highly inaccurate, but also harmful to mentally ill people. While this is not an unusual position taken by researchers in this area (Nunnally 1961, Day and Page 1986, Wahl 1982, 1995, Wahl and Roth 1982, Mathieu 1993, Fruth and Padderud 1985), some have suggested otherwise. For instance, Howlett's (1998) analysis of data gathered in a 1997 Market and Opinion Research International (MORI) national survey suggests that, while perhaps inaccurate, depictions of mentally ill people as violent have generated public support for funding of programmes to enable them to live in community settings. Further, Morrall (2000) has argued that, in Britain, reports portraying mentally ill people as violent have been couched in a critique of a disorganised and poorly managed mental health system (2000: 164). Consequently, violent depictions may in fact be the basis for restructuring health services in a way that improves access and quality of treatment for the mentally ill.

Nonetheless, the position taken in this chapter is that, despite the possibility that violent imagery may achieve some positive goals, these accomplishments are merely temporary and do not fundamentally alter the social arrangements that keep mentally ill people in subordinate social positions. Furthermore, it seems reasonable to assume that funding born out of the notion that the mentally ill are inherently violent would be used in ways to preserve the safety of a public presumably at risk, as opposed to filling a gap in psychiatric services. In our current climate in which substantial negative media imagery coincides with dramatic cuts to health care funding (Deber 2000), there is no evidence of a link between portrayals of violence and gains by the mental health community.

The idea that media imagery may have an impact on government policy raises the question of the degree to which media discourse affects audiences, in general. Reception theory has been the subject of much work in the area of media studies (Philo 1998, 1996, Kitzinger 1998, 1994, Davis 1985) and has generated ample debate around the ways in which audience members interpret/receive media messages (Miller and Philo 1998, Lull 1988, Morley 1986). Much of this debate has centred on the tensions arising from theories emphasising the agency of audiences to interpret, and therefore reject media messages and theories that see the media as directly creating audience beliefs (Miller and Philo 1998). This study sees both as possible.

My research assumes the media to be but one of many influences in defining/generating meaning around mental illness, but also sees audiences as actively engaged in the interpretive process. Philo (1998) takes a similar position arguing that media influence is always part of a matrix of other social relationships, which affect the development and transfer of values

(1998: 52). Consequently, meanings are not simply received by a readership, they are mediated in relation to meanings generated and sustained by families and peer groups, and through personal experience. Thus, while 'the media can exert great influence over audiences . . . people are not simply blank slates on which its messages are written' (Philo 1996: 103).

One such instance where the media have been found to exert 'great influence' is around reports about violence and mental illness, and public perceptions (Philo 1996). The extent to which these images impact upon the public imagination has been attributed to the degree to which such images draw upon anxieties about security, safety and the unknown (Philo 1996, Colombo 1997). While images of violence and mental illness seem to have influence on audience interpretations, there is never a predetermined acceptance of a message. Such is the case, for instance, where personal experience is able to contradict media content (Philo 1996: 103–4). Viewers/readers, therefore, may operationalise resistant readings and may, in some cases, offer alternative interpretations to particular media messages. Yet, in the case of imagery of violence and mental illness, those tools of resistance seem not to be significantly employed.

An additional assumption driving this research is that mental illness is socially constructed. This is an important claim to make as it flags some of the political underpinnings of the discourse analysis that follows. A constructionist lens allows for a view of 'mental illness' as connected to the production of meaning, a body of knowledge that is systematically informed by the assembly of discourse. It is in this way that mental illness is 'created', 'shifted', 'bent', 'formed' and 'produced'. Approaching media representations from this perspective enables us to challenge the interpretations that reify scientific and legal categories. For instance, it unhinges the authority of the medical model throwing into question the legitimacy of mental illness as an individual, biological phenomenon. This enables the possibility of viewing mental illness in other ways. Some theorists have suggested that mental illness is a form of residual rule breaking (Scheff 1966), a product of social strain and disorganisation (Durkheim 1964), or simply problems of living (Szasz 1973). This research leans towards seeing mental illness not as illness at all, but rather as a form of suffering related to social, economic or political circumstances.

Viewing mental illness as socially constructed shows that the meanings produced in the media about mental illness are not 'actual', or 'real' representations, but formulations of meaning that are attributed to mental illness as a category. Throughout this analysis, it is hoped that these meanings are rendered visible such that the mechanisms of power, instrumental in 'creating' mental illness, are problematised, refuted and disengaged from the circularity of meaning that shapes mental illness. One of the objectives of this research, therefore, has been to subvert the practices of power that legitimise inequality between those who speak about mental illness and those being spoken about.

Assessing the literature

The negative portrayal of mental illness is perhaps the most common finding among researchers interested in media depictions of mental illness (Day and Page 1986, Wahl 1995, Wahl and Roth 1982, Mathieu 1993, Fruth and Padderud 1985). Indeed, the very first concentrated study regarding media portrayals of mental illness looked at television, newspapers, magazines and radio between 1954 and 1955 and found that there existed a 'negative' depiction of the mentally ill in the media that played a part in informing public perceptions (Nunnally 1961). Negative portrayals include those that see the mentally ill as 'evil', 'different', 'violent', 'deviant' and 'helpless' (Wahl and Roth 1982, Wahl 1995, Fleming and Manvell 1985). Most commonly reported, however, is the association between mental illness and 'violence' (Nunnally 1961, Fleming and Manvell 1985, Wahl and Roth 1982, Wahl 1995, Mathieu 1993, Fruth and Padderud 1985).

It has been found that portrayals of the mentally ill as violent are most apparent in the context of 'horror' and 'sin' (Nunnally 1961: 235) which typically presents the mentally ill as 'dangerous' and 'unpredictable' (1961: 76). Research focusing on feature films has also found that the mentally ill are portrayed as 'evil' as well as 'sadistic', 'menacing' and as 'villains' (Fleming and Manvell 1985). In fact, some researchers have identified the portrayal of 'evil' in relation to mental illness couched in representations of mentally ill people as 'devils' and 'demons', who are 'depraved' and 'insatiable' (Fleming and Manvell 1985: 57–68).

Yet, of all of the techniques of negative representation, perhaps most implicit are those that depict mentally ill people as lacking in markers of social identity (Day and Page 1986, Wahl and Roth 1982). The portrayal of one-dimensional characters supports the depiction of a 'subhuman' group, within which individual distinctions are difficult to ascertain. Day and Page (1986) provide evidence that saying almost nothing at all about mentally ill people operates as a more subtle means to talk negatively than simply associating mental illness with 'violence' or 'evil'. This has also been substantiated by Wahl and Roth (1982) who argue that mentally ill characters are most commonly portrayed as having no specified occupation, no specific age, no family connections, unspecified marital status and therefore, no social identity. Thus, the mentally ill are portrayed as not part of the usual fabric of society. As suggested by the authors, such portrayals can only add to the public's tendency to view mentally ill people as 'different' and unlike most 'real' people.

In these depictions, mental illness becomes the master status for the person being represented or talked about. In some cases, this master status is conflated with portrayals of other stigmatised groups, which serves to underline that mentally ill people are fundamentally different from others (Wahl 1995). Several studies, for instance, have shown that mental illness is commonly portrayed through talk about homelessness (Mathieu 1993, Wahl

1995). It is argued that media reports that focus on homelessness often associate or infer that homeless people are mentally ill (Wahl 1995, Mathieu 1993) and imply that, as a consequence, they are violent (Wahl 1995, Mathieu 1993). Likewise, the association of mental illness with homelessness supports the idea that mentally ill people are economically dependent on the 'rest' of society (Day and Page 1986).

Viewing power/knowledge and ideology in text

Power plays a central role in managing how meaning is constituted in text and how particular forms of knowledge acquire authority in the formation of ideology (Foucault 1972). Ideology is defined as the formulation of rules, which prescribe certain ways of talking about topics while excluding other forms of talk. Ideology governs what is 'sayable' or 'thinkable' about a topic (Hall 1997: 45). More specifically, power and knowledge find their articulation in the form of ideology, and it is through ideology that knowledge linked to power assumes the authority of 'the truth' (Hall 1997: 49). Suppositions of 'truth' and what is constituted as knowledge are generally enacted in text through ideology (Foucault 1972, 1980). However, the production of ideology is not always successful. There exist slippages – power is never unidirectional (Foucault 1980). Consequently, there are opportunities, such as that undertaken here, where power may be produced in a way that works against ideological representations. Accordingly, I will attend to an analysis of ideological talk in the print media to determine the ways in which mental illness is depicted through specific and repeated ways of reporting. This will include assessing the techniques for presenting various 'truth' claims about mental illness, the strategies utilised to legitimise certain forms of knowledge around mental illness and the ways in which the media carefully manage presentations of mental illness, allowing certain depictions to exist, while simultaneously suppressing others.

It is difficult to see how power is produced in a systemic way if, methodologically, each article is simply read in isolation. Instead, I will utilise Foucault's (1972) notion of the épistème in order to view power as it is produced not only across all the articles selected for this study, but in the context of all representations of mental illness, whether they be medical, juridical, lay or other forms of discourse. Thus, the assessment of media representations undertaken here is done with the intention of acknowledging that mental illness as a more unified discourse is sustained not just by media representations but also by multiple other sources of discursive production. In this way, nothing is outside discourse (Foucault 1972).

By approaching the media in this way, there exists an ability to view the individual fields of constitution (such as the ways in which a particular story represents mental illness) as well as the successive rules of use (how newspapers 'talk' about mental illness in general) in the formulation of power and ideology. Ideological power has the social function of serving certain interests. Yet, in order to accomplish this goal, ideologies must represent the basic principles that govern judgment (van Dijk 1998: 25). That is, ideologies must reflect what group members think is right or wrong, true or false. It has been noted that media representations of mental illness go some way in influencing, supporting or subverting group beliefs, most notably in opposition to the interests of those considered mentally ill (Wahl 1995, 1992, Wahl and Roth 1982, Philo 1996). Researchers have already achieved some understanding of how group interests are preserved or denounced in media talk about mental illness. However, we have yet to have a clear sense of the ways in which such ideologies are strategically expressed in text (van Dijk 1998: 25). It has been proposed that the typical structure and content of ideologies include the representation of Self and Other. As van Dijk (1998) argues, 'many [ideologies] therefore seem to be polarized "We are Good and They are Bad" especially when conflicting interests are involved' (1998: 25). This is not to imply that ideologies are uniform but may be seen as having some consistent relationship to the basic interests of a particular group. Ideologies, therefore, 'reflect the basic criteria that constitute the social identity and define the interests of a group' (van Dijk 1998: 25).

Considering that ideologies are the basic 'axioms' of socially shared representations of groups (van Dijk 1998: 62), an assessment of ideologies gets at the question of how the media constitute the social identity of being mentally ill. In doing so, the media also constitute the social identity of *not* being mentally ill. That is, how the media talk about mental illness through ideological categories prescribes who belongs in a certain group (Us), as well as who does not (Them). Such basic propositions of positive self-presentation and negative other-presentation reflect the ways in which discourse is produced and produces power and knowledge regardless of whether or not what is being reported is indeed 'true'. Thus, an assessment of ideology shows the play of power within the text and the linkages that power has with certain co-ordinates of knowledge.

Through attention paid to how power is produced in text, it is possible to see not only how mental illness is represented in popular media, but also how these portrayals may benefit/harm certain groups. By assessing the ideological, polarised talk that constitutes distinctions between Us and Them, I propose to reveal how newspaper discourse is not just about 'what the media say' about mental illness, but what are the relations of power being sustained or contested through discourse.

The study

For this research, an analysis was carried out on 195 articles taken from two Canadian newspapers, the *Globe and Mail* and the *Toronto Star*, over the past decade (Jan. 1990–Nov. 1999). The breakdown consisted of 83 articles from the *Globe and Mail* and 112 from the *Toronto Star*. The *Globe and Mail* and the *Toronto Star* were considered suitable for this project based on the extent of the readership and influence that each has locally[1]. The Canadian Business and Current Affairs Index was utilised as a primary database for recovering the articles, which were generated out of a quick search of the term 'mental illness'. These articles included background and feature articles, columns and editorials as well as several letters to the editor.

The articles were coded for a number of standard properties such as the name of the paper, date, page number, minority or majority actors (and whether these were quoted or not) and overall subject matter (such as homicide investigation, amendment to law or report on a study). The articles were also sorted according to the most recent, to least recent publication date, along with what was identified as 'interesting' elements discovered in the text. What was considered interesting was broadly defined as anything that stood out, appeared to be important, was repeated, unclear, explicit or implicit or absent. Further, I looked for the presupposed and implied talk about groups, power relations, conflicts, positive and negative opinions about the mentally ill or other groups represented in the text as well as the formal structures that (de)emphasise polarised group representations. At this point, certain regularities within the corpus were more readily seen and patterns of ideological talk about mental illness became more visible.

Several key textual strategies have been indicated to operationalise ideological talk in newspaper articles (van Dijk 1998: 57). For the purposes of this exercise, however, I looked for any references to a major overall strategy that proposed positive self-presentation and negative 'other' presentation (van Dijk 1998: 61). This overarching strategy can be made observable in text through a methodological model called the 'ideological square' (van Dijk 1998). The ideological square has four key principles. In the first move, the text emphasises Our good properties/actions. Second, the emphasis is placed on Their bad properties/actions. Third, the text attempts to mitigate Our bad properties/actions and finally, Their good properties/actions are mitigated.

In order to view the articulation of ideology in the corpus, I have divided the findings into two primary sections. In the first section, I focus on the basic talk that establishes the polarisation between Us versus Them. Throughout the analysis We are defined as an ambiguous, undifferentiated group whose primary identifying feature is that we are not mentally ill. On the other hand, the mentally ill are constituted as an outgroup who represent a valueless subclass portrayed as bad, violent and criminal. In the second section, I look at the various forms of otherness that are articulated by the media in the form of a hierarchy of mental illness. Thus, I expand on the Us versus Them framework to show that They are represented as having 'degrees' of difference that radiate from what is constituted as the core, 'normal'. In this discussion I focus on the techniques whereby the media create distinctions between different kinds of mentally ill people, and different kinds of mental illness.

Where three primary 'types' of depiction were isolated in the course of the analysis, including the Passive Patient, the Class Based Illness and the Mentally Ill Criminal, it is notable that the most common portrayal evidenced in text was of the Mentally Ill Criminal. It should be noted that of the 195 articles constituting the corpus, 50 (26 per cent) did not contain any reference to the discursive categories established for this study. Furthermore, 32 of the 195 articles, or 16 per cent, indicated more than one discursive category. Accordingly, the Mentally Ill Criminal portrayal existed within 57 per cent of the 195 articles reviewed, the Class Based Illness category was evident in 30 per cent and the Passive Patient portrayal was featured in 12 per cent.

In both sections, I utilise a convention for referencing articles in order to maintain some clarity. More specifically, I use 'illness' (single scare quotes) to indicate that I wish to emphasise or problematise a word, as well as directly to quote from text other than newspaper articles used in the corpus. However, I use *'illness'* (single scare quotes in italics), to indicate that a word or phrase has been taken from the corpus.

Us versus Them: ideological polarisation

The press reports about mentally ill people were explicit in their articulation of a polarised ideological framework that supported a division between Us (the world) and Them (the mentally ill). The fundamental distinction between Us and Them rested upon the determination that They are mentally ill and We are not. Thus, despite the attempt to organise the articles in a way that emphasised Our desire to uphold humanitarian values (safety, equality and fairness), these values lost much of their validity because the humanitarian content was organised within the structure of a dominant discriminatory narrative[2]. In this structure, demonstration of Our humanitarian ethos was not necessarily apparent in the form of empirical evidence, but rather was evidenced in an implied inhumanity and contempt that the mentally ill have toward social values, morality and life itself. This attempt to polarise Us in opposition to Them is the legitimising framework for the ideological conflation of mental illness with criminality.

Example 1.0
Psychopaths hunt the available, vulnerable
Captives' panic arouses killer's sexual appetite.
   He was the perfect gentleman, handsome, debonair and very tender –
right up to the moment he strangled her to death. They had just made
love, but as she was getting ready to leave something inside him snapped,
his hatred for women took control and he struck, killing another victim.
(Pron, N. (1992) Psychopaths hunt the available, vulnerable, *Toronto Star*,
3 April, A4).

Illustration of this technique is evidenced in the above Example 1.0, which provides clear demonstration of negative – 'other' presentation. In the headline, as well as in the rest of the text, the main attention is on '*Psychopaths*'. The negative evaluation of psychopaths is explicitly expressed in the use of the terms '*hunt*' and '*vulnerable*'; the first predicate being associated with stalking with intent to kill, and the second with the weakness or helplessness of the victim. Both predicates are intended in the sensationalist sense, and express the shared belief that the mentally ill are powerful and that their 'prey' are weak.

Media analysts have noted that when reporting on mental illness, the media often present subjects as simultaneously rational and irrational (Philo 1996), which emphasises that psychopaths who organise their '*hunt*' specifically to target the '*available*' and '*vulnerable*' have intent. This is also supported by the claim that the current story is about one of several acts of killing ('killing another victim') and therefore, cannot be interpreted as coincidental or accidental but plainly purposeful. However, the article also alludes to the idea that the '*Psychopath*' was behaving in what was a stimulus response ('*snapped*') to '*his hatred for women*'. Without negating the possibility of either claim, this portrayal of mental illness includes elements of both rationality and irrationality, the consequence of which suggests that the mentally ill are not only 'mad' but 'bad'.

The relevant ideological structure expressed in the example appears first in the lexical style, in words such as '*strangled*', '*death*', '*snapped*', '*hatred*', '*struck*', '*killing*', '*arouses*', '*appetite*', and '*victim*', meant as a generic description that fits all psychopaths. The evaluation becomes obvious in the choice of '*snapped*', which categorises psychopaths not only as mentally ill or even violent, but also as unpredictably violent. This follows the ideological principle that Their bad behaviour is emphasised (van Dijk 1998: 33).

Another ideological sequence continuing the idea of the pathological killer is the use of '*hatred*', which implies that psychopaths kill because they hate. However, this emotion is presented as having no context. That is, there is no reason offered as to why psychopaths have hatred toward others. In this absence, the fact that they are mentally deficient becomes an important explanatory proposition: Perhaps they hate because they are 'insane'.

Polarisation also expresses itself through the juxtaposition between the victim and the assailant. The victim is shown to be naïve and innocent as she '*makes love*' to the man that will eventually '*strangle her*'. It is implied that the '*victim*' has been fooled into trusting what appears to be a '*perfect gentleman*'. While the victim is never explicitly described in terms of her personal values or moral character, she is eventually strangled, and is therefore positioned in opposition to the psychopath. This framing context interpolates our participation in the role of the victim such that her '*vulnerability*' and '*availability*' is also Our own. In this way, the battle between Us and Them is one of good versus evil.

In explanatory contexts, acts may be variously attributed to actors and explained in terms of their properties (van Dijk 1998: 43). Agency, responsibility and blame may also be attributed as an activity of ideological orientation. Thus, good acts will usually be attributed to Us and bad acts to Them. The idea that the psychopath has killed more than one victim (*'killing another victim'*) implies that there is some justification in retaliation – following the principle derived from militarist doctrines: We must fight against someone who tries to harm Us[3]. Thus, as the vulnerable have been shown to be incapable of protecting themselves against those who wish them harm, our desire to defend is triggered and our location vis-à-vis the psychopath is defined: psychopaths are Our enemy.

Hierarchy of illness

In the Us versus Them section, the focus is on how the media articulate ideological oppositionality. This section concentrates on the hierarchy of illness established through media reporting as a continuation of the ideological structure. In this case, the hierarchy of illness within the media reproduces different versions of mental illness that are measured according to their presumed distance from what the media implicitly constitute as 'normal'. It becomes apparent that, while Us versus Them is an important polarising feature of media discourse, other strategies are at work which have particular implications for how mental illness is conflated with criminality. More specifically, 'mental illness' is presented in a number of ways – three of which are identified in this research – that all work together to bring certain kinds of meanings around the association of criminality with mental illness.

Mentally Ill Criminal portrayal
An article printed by the *Globe and Mail* on 23 August 1990 reveals the constitutive framework for the Mentally Ill Criminal depiction:

Example 2.0
15 per cent of prisoners need mental help
A confidential Ontario government study has found that 15 per cent of the prisoners in provincial correctional institutions have mental problems and that many of them deliberately commit crimes so they will not have to live on the streets.

The study confirms complaints by front-line correctional staff that 'mentally ill people are overcrowding the jails,' said a spokesman for the Ontario Public Service Employees Union, which obtained the study under the provincial freedom of Information Act.

The guards union said the provincial government has been cutting the number of psychiatric beds as part of its program of getting the mentally ill out of institutions and into community help programs.

But Paul Bilodeau, an OPSEU spokesman, said the community programs are so under financed that individual social workers are struggling with caseloads of 300 or more people.

The result is that 'increasing numbers of mentally ill people are ending up in correctional institutions, posing a danger to guards and other prisoners', he said.

'The correctional officers don't want to deal with unpredictable, violent, psychotic people,' Mr. Bilodeau said.

(Galt, V. (1990) 15 per cent of prisoners need mental help, *Globe and Mail*, August 23, A7).

Textual analysts have discovered that introductory sentences usually represent what could be understood as the major event of an article (van Dijk 1998). In this case, fronting the idea that a government study has been released achieves two goals. First, it detracts from the fact that the main event of the article is *not* about findings from the study but rather about the apparent problem of '*mentally ill people overcrowding jails*'. Second, and perhaps more importantly, the distraction offered by fronting the study affords the rest of the article legitimacy, even despite the fact that statements made in the news report are unsubstantiated by evidence from said study. In this way, explicitly ideological opinions and comments are reformulated as facts consistent with the study's findings. This is important as, had the article focused on the problem of overcrowding in the introductory sentence, the comments could have been perceived as discriminatory and unsupported.

Ideology is most often achieved when the exercise of power goes unrecognised (Hall 1997). One of the ways in which news stories achieve ideological representations is to present stories that appear unbiased and comprehensive, while subtly emphasising that some features of the narrative are more important than others. For instance, in Example 2.0, two key proposals are presented as to the cause of the problem in the corrections system. In the first proposal, mentally ill people are established as the problem as they are '*deliberately*' entering prisons. In the second, the problem has been caused because '*the government has been cutting the number of beds as part of its program of getting the mentally ill out of institutions and in to community help programs*'. While these proposals do not necessarily contradict one another, the article implicitly leans toward suggesting that the principal complaint is with the mentally ill.

This is achieved in a number of ways. The first two sentences are clear in highlighting that despite the apparent limitations of '*living on the streets*', the mentally ill have agency, as readers are told that entry into the prison system is 'deliberate' and that '*the mentally ill are overcrowding the jails*'. By proposing an image of mentally ill people as active, discursive weight is placed on depicting 'what the mentally ill are doing' ('*are overcrowding jails*'), as opposed to 'what is happening/being done to them' (being forced into jails due to cuts). Such an emphasis would have been avoided if the article had read something like: '. . . prisoners in the provincial correctional system have mental problems and many of them are being pressured to commit crimes so they will not have to live on the streets'. Or, for the second sentence in the article, rather than reporting that '*mentally ill people are overcrowding jails*', it could read 'mentally ill people are being crowded into jails'. In both of these revisions, the focus is taken off of the mentally ill as the 'problem' and redirected towards seeing some other agentive force (the provincial government) as the principle cause of disruption in the correctional system.

However, the theme of mentally ill people as agents runs throughout the article. The final two sentences of Example 2.0 report that the mentally ill are '*posing a danger*' and are '*unpredictable, violent psychotic people*'. Accordingly, the emphasis is less on the numbers of prisoners in the jail as a result of cutbacks, and more on how the mentally ill prisoners are behaving ('*posing a danger*'). So, while the article does demonstrate a critique of cuts to social spending, this is a secondary emphasis couched in with a sharper focus on mentally ill behaviour. Thus, Our bad actions (not providing adequate services) are under-emphasised/ignored while Their bad actions (violent, psychotic) are highlighted.

The portrayal of mentally ill people as dangerous to Us takes on a unique expression, particularly when contrasted with other forms of deviance. As van Dijk (1998) suggests, contrast is sometimes utilised to emphasise similarities between two enemies in order to magnify the negative characteristics attributed to both (1998: 59). In other cases, opposing the negative actions of one person or group with the good actions of others enhances the negative characterisations of the deviant group. In Example 2.0, the comparison is implicit, as the only clearly identified group is the mentally ill. However, those who are mentally ill are juxtaposed not only against Us, the 'good' people, but also against other 'bad' people, namely, other 'regular' prisoners. In the later case, the mentally ill are '*posing a threat to guards and other prisoners*' to such an extent that '*the correctional officers don't want to deal with unpredictable, violent, psychotic people*'. Thus, mentally ill people are constituted as more dangerous than other deviant groups, including regular prisoners. Further, the term 'people' works to homogenise the mentally ill as a group for whom '*unpredictability and violence*' is considered standard. The ideological framework therefore, not only supports that They are not Us, but that They exist at the extreme end of a deviant continuum.

In another instance, the article makes a clear association between homelessness ('*living on the streets*'), prisoner populations ('*overcrowding jails*'), mental illness ('*psychotic*') and violence. Each of the lexical items builds on the presupposition that violent behaviour is inherent in the homeless and prisoners: each social type informs the other. The intersection of these various deviant types suggests that mental illness is constituted as the layering of homelessness, criminality, and psychosis at the same time. Thus, the kind of violence that this particular group is capable of is presented as unique and distinct from the violence usually attributed to the homeless or to the regular prison population. There is little if any specific information, however, about what kinds of violence mentally ill people have actually committed. What is suggested is simply that '*many of them deliberately commit crimes*', they are '*posing a danger*' and are '*unpredictable, violent psychotic people*'. Thus, the emphasis is not on what they have done but on how they have done it ('*deliberately*' and therefore with intent). The term deliberate, in particular, suggests that mentally ill people are conscious of their actions and therefore understand the difference between right and wrong. Like Example 1.0, the current depiction is able to sustain both the depiction of mental illness as giving rise to rational, ('*deliberately*') as well as irrational, behaviour ('*unpredictable and psychotic*'), without the appearance of contradiction. Although consciousness is generally seen as inimical to being mentally ill, the textual representation of mentally ill people as responsible agents is central to their ideological portrayal as having intent to harm Us. Thus, the juridical and medical criteria that mark the conceptual difference between who is considered mentally ill and who is criminal, falls away. What is achieved is the possibility of seeing mentally ill people as medically irrational, legally responsible and consequently, socially immoral. Taken in concert, it is understood that They are a danger to Us.

Passive Patient Portrayal
While depictions of the Mentally Ill Criminal represent a key discursive site for the association of mental illness with criminality, other formulations of mental illness have an impact on maintaining such associations. For instance, the Passive Patient portrayal is often presented as a non-violent alternative to the Mentally Ill Criminal depiction – the Passive Patient represents how a mentally ill person 'should' and 'can' behave. This has specific implications for seeing mentally ill people as able to control their behaviour, which has consequences for those portrayed as violent and dangerous. Framed by the depiction of the Passive Patient, the Mentally Ill Criminal becomes viewed as cognizant of the implications of his/her criminal actions. Therefore, the determination that the actor is mentally ill becomes a moral category as opposed to a legal differentiation between those with and without intent.

The Passive Patient representation is found in articles that represent mentally ill people as helpless, disempowered and child-like so that the emphasis is not focused on Their behaviour as much as it is on Their attitude and Our evaluations of that attitude. The text is often highly moralistic and value-laden. Yet, as in all portrayals, the underlying message continues to be that it is desirable to be in Our group and undesirable to be in Theirs. In Example 2.1 for instance, one of the ways that polarisation takes place is through the implied attribution of child-like qualities to the members of

'*Club Freedom*'. An assessment of the headline ('*Learning to Fly*') gives a clear indication that the subject of the article is 'like a little bird', perhaps is 'naïve' or 'inexperienced' and is 'learning'. The language of the by-line reads as follows:

Example 2.1
By-line: Learning to Fly
For the members of Club Freedom, learning responsibility and independence skills is one of the paths to mental health.

(Munro, A. (1996) Learning to Fly, *Toronto Star*, 11 January, F5).

The lexical items used in the by-line suggest that one aspect of mental health is being independent and responsible. The by-line thereby infers that those who are mentally ill do not value self-sufficiency and self-reliance – an assertion that denies the material privilege that is required in order to be self-sufficient and self-reliant. This is problematic, particularly in a society that makes distinctions between adulthood and childhood as well as the resources provided to each, based on such markers.

Example 2.2
Learning to Fly
It's more than the common experience of mental health problems that draws members of Belleville's Club Freedom together. It's a common desire for friendship, self-determination and hope. 'We don't discuss mental illness, we discuss mental health', says club member Jackie.
  'Members can provide inspiration to others with mental health problems', says Susan Scott, program co-ordinator. 'Members get to take the bow for their own healing', says Scott. 'To make people responsible for deciding what they need is not something most clinical models make as a priority', says Scott.
  The Belleville club, with up to 20 active members, is one of 16 in Ontario and hundreds worldwide operating with names like Club Freedom, The Friendship Club and Par or Progress Place. But while the names may change, the clubhouse philosophy remains the same to provide a supportive and non-judgmental environment where members can help one another, improve job skills and take on daily responsibilities.

(Munro, A. (1996) Learning to Fly, *Toronto Star*, January 11, F5).

Example 2.2 represents the rest of the body of the article. In it, we can see that the story is not focused on a main event; rather, it concentrates on the attitude of the Passive Patient ('*perseverance, hope and determination*'). The lexical items '*friendship*', '*self-determination*', '*inspiration*' and '*responsibilities*' all indicate that the Passive Patient has a good and positive attitude. Indeed, the article cites a club member who says that '*We don't discuss mental illness, we discuss mental health*'. Unlike other reporting methods focusing on sensationalist topics such as the crimes committed by the violently mentally ill, the Passive Patient story is about the battle to be 'normal'. Thus, the contrast between Us and Them is reconfigured to be determined by a narrative history solely defined by Their internal/psychical struggle to be like Us.

As indicated earlier, my approach to mental illness is to view it not as a form of illness per se, but as suffering caused by poor social, economic and political circumstances. Approaching Example 2.2 from this perspective shows us that the focus of the article is solely on individual healing which serves to decontextualise mental illness, establishing it as a personal problem. Talk about '*encouraging one another*', '*self-determination*' and '*inspiration*' presents mental illness as an individually-based health problem as opposed to a broader social issue. The narrative of the story reveals that individual involvement in self-healing is, indeed, what is being promoted as exemplary. Thus, mentally ill people are represented as 'good' when they try to heal themselves, which also supports the concept that We are not responsible for Their healing.

Further, the narrative is very clearly about people who have been identified as mentally ill not wanting to be mentally ill any longer. It is framed as a success story, a story of bravery and achievement as indicated by the title, '*Learning to Fly*'. Indeed, this story is about the mentally ill person who is attempting to transcend mental illness. Despite the positive tone that this article has been given, we can see that the point is to organise mental illness as something to be championed. This assertion, along with statements about the '*need to overcome*' is presented as commonsensical and serves to reinforce the idea that mental illness is something over which people have control. It follows that those who are not seen as exercising control are bad people. An example of this resonates from previous analyses where badness ('*hunt*', '*killing another victim*', '*deliberately commit crimes*', '*posing a danger to guards*', '*violent psychotic people*') translates into Our repugnance and hatred for the mentally ill. That is, while constructions of various versions of mental illness are simultaneously being formed throughout the article, they are always in reference to an unspoken normative ideal. Their badness reasserts Our goodness.

Furthermore, given that mental illness is represented as something to be championed, it is constituted as a negative attribute. While it is not considered a form of evil, as may be the case for the Mentally Ill Criminal depiction, in this context it is considered undesirable. In fact, the article provides evidence of a mentally ill 'spokesperson' willing to attest to the need to distance oneself from mental illness ('*We don't discuss mental illness, we discuss mental health*'). We know, however, that mental illness is not always experienced in this negative way (Breggin 1991) and it need not be theorised as a purely negative or regretful feature of one's life. This is not the same as saying that insanity is subversive, as argued by a number of feminist academics (see Caminero-Santangelo 1998), nor does it suggest that mental illness is desirable. But certainly mental illness and the variety of experiences it entails are more complex than appreciated in most news articles. Indeed, of the 195 articles used in this research, there was not one indication where mental illness was considered anything but a negative characteristic.

When mental illness is approached in this highly simplified way, the *actual* manifestations of mental illness become inconsequential. What is understood is simply that it is 'bad' and needs to be overcome. Even though Example 2.2 provides no evidence of negative psychical experiences, it is assumed that it would benefit the subjects of the narrative not to be mentally ill (*'common desire'*, *'take a bow for their own healing'*). Where there is no information provided about the particular experiences of the club members when mentally ill, and where we are told the members are *'made responsible'*, it is implied that the values of *'self-determination'*, *'responsibility'* and 'job skills' are Our own. Thus, what the article produces is a script for establishing the legitimacy of Our values for socially acceptable behaviour while simultaneously evidencing that They have none. Consequently, despite the humanitarian tone wherein We appear to be concerned for Their wellbeing (*'members can take a bow'*, *'supportive and non-judgemental'*), it is confirmed that, 'getting better' is less about managing health problems, and more about Them adopting Our value system. This framework services Our own interests by importing evidence of Our superiority over Them: We have values and They do not.

That the Passive Patient portrayal links mental illness with characterisations of dependency and irresponsibility is not surprising as it demonstrates the same kinds of assumptions made about mental illness in general. Recall Example 2.0 in which an association is made between homelessness and mental illness. When such relationships are made successively, mental illness becomes read as a moral category where it is presumed that there is a direct link between being irresponsible, not working (being poor) and mental illness.

This kind of conflation was seen regularly throughout the 23 articles that portrayed the Passive Patient depiction. In fact, 17 of those 23, or 74 per cent of the articles, made references to a need for the mentally ill subject(s) to take 'responsibility', 'be productive', 'start being accountable' and/or 'get a job'. It is not being argued that responsibility or having a job is inherently problematic. Yet, the consistent portrayal of mentally ill people as irresponsible and unproductive, accompanied by suggestions that mental illness is something people choose to have, suggests that a feature of mental illness is laziness. Mental illness then, is an affront to Our Protestant work ethic. Thus, what people must achieve to become 'healed' is steeped in Our values around market participation and independence. Both of these features are more about mechanisms of Western capitalism and less about biomedical notions of brain disease.

Class Based Illness portrayal
The following example provides an illustration of the class dynamics at work in media talk around mental illness. The piece focuses on a speech given to the Canadian Psychiatric Awareness Committee by former cabinet minister, Michael Wilson, regarding the depression and suicide of his son.

Example 2.3
  Speak-Out on Mental Illness: Wilson
  Former cabinet minister tells of family tragedy
  Get over the stigma and speak out about mental illness, Michael Wilson told members of the Canadian Psychiatric Awareness Committee yesterday.
     Speaking personally, the former federal cabinet minister told the crowd he wished he had been more vocal about mental illness. Wilson's son Cameron suffered from depression and killed himself almost exactly one year ago.
     'His depression just became too hard for him to bear. That's why I'm here with you today,' said Wilson, who has held several cabinet posts, including minister of finance. He now heads his own consulting firm and is vice-chairman of RCB Dominion Securities.
     . . .
     Before his son was diagnosed, Wilson said he became aware of the difficulties faced by those affected by mental illness when a friend was trying to raise funds.
     'There is reason for hope, but we have a long way to go.'

(Mahoney, J. (1996) Speak-Out on Mental Illness: Wilson, *Toronto Star*, 9 May, A2).

The excerpt signifies what I have called a Class Based Illness in that the narrative illustrates how representations of mental illness are influenced by references to certain class sensibilities. That is, how we understand different kinds of mental illness relates to the ways in which the popular press associates certain diagnoses and behaviours with class affiliations. For instance, Example 2.3 utilises a number of reporting strategies to illustrate the particular kinds of characteristics of mental illness when it is associated with/ affects members of the middle class.

One of the ways in which this is achieved is through relative inattention paid to the behaviour of the middle class, mentally ill subject. Looking at the corpus, 58 articles significantly index class, in which 22 talk about middle class subjects, including references to particular prestigious occupations, affiliations with notable and/or influential families and relative socio-economic privilege. Of the 22 stories that primarily produce meaning around the middle class, only three (14 per cent) report details of the behaviour of the mentally ill subject. The relative disinterest in reporting the behaviour of middle class subjects stands in stark contrast to the considerable attention usually demonstrated by the media in documenting the behaviour of the mentally ill who are shown to be poor. Indeed, 36 of the 58 (62 per cent) articles drawn from the corpus that significantly index class emphasised being poor as an important narrative feature relating to mental illness. Of these 36 articles, 32 (89 per cent) went into detail describing the behaviour of the mentally ill subject with particular interest in highlighting incidents of criminality, violence and dangerousness while also focusing on such things as homelessness, panhandling, use of a soup kitchen or other explicit markers of poverty. The concentration on representing the behaviour of poor people as a feature of mental illness contrasts significantly with the reporting strategies employed when talking about the behaviour of mentally ill people who are not depicted as poor. These usual ways of representing mental illness may leave some to assume that there exists a direct link between violence, criminality and poverty, yet no such link is indicated when referencing middle class subjects.

If there is relatively little talk about the behaviour of the middle class mentally ill subject, there is an emphasis placed on describing how they feel. It has already been established that most reports about middle class subjects refrain from talking about their behaviour (19 of 22). However, it is worth mentioning that of those 22 articles, 17, or 77 per cent, demonstrate significant interest in reporting how the subjects felt or their emotional status. By emphasising what poor people 'do' (behaviour) versus what middle class people 'feel' (emotions) we can see that there are different emphases in media reports along class lines. Where mentally ill poor people have a tendency to be presented in ways which see them as active and physically engaged in the world, they are imbued with a sense of agency unattributed to middle class subjects. Thus, it may be argued that when questions of responsibility are being raised, poor people may be read as 'more responsible' than middle class subjects simply because of the ways in which the media see one group as active, and the other, when mentally ill, as passive.

In the case of portrayals that conflate mental illness with criminality there is a second order assumption that violence is linked to being poor. This assumption is supported by the relative absence of violence and criminality evidenced in reports about middle class, mentally ill people. The ability of the press to portray these class-based distinctions is contingent upon the regular association of class backgrounds with certain diagnostic labels. Example 2.3, for instance, tells us that the mentally ill subject had been diagnosed with depression. In fact, in 17 of the 22 (77 per cent) articles that highlighted a middle class subject, the diagnosis was depression. The discourse around depression as a marker of a middle class illness is significantly different from a classification such as schizophrenia, which is more commonly associated with poor people (48 per cent). Depression, for instance, is presented as imposing itself on the 'ill' person ('*His depression just became too hard for him to bear*'). In contrast, illness associated with poverty (homelessness, for instance) is generally portrayed as imposing itself in the form of a 'body' (a monster, a psychopath) on society (see Examples 1.0 and 2.0). Further, as Example 2.3 illustrates, other narrative features support the idea that the middle class are non-violent by constructing representations of the mentally ill subject as socially connected, involved in the community, or as a member of some other socially relevant institution.

Wahl and Roth (1982) as well as Day and Page (1986) have noted that mentally ill people are most often portrayed as having no social identity other than being mentally ill. However, the middle class subject in the Class Based Illness portrayal is linked in some meaningful way to others who share a mutual concern for his/her wellbeing. In Example 2.3, the link is operationalised in calling the subject's death a '*family tragedy*', which implies that the mentally ill person was loved, and therefore was not a physical threat. This framing mechanism establishes a context in which the mentally ill person can be seen as engaged in a usual human relationship with people like Us and therefore limits Our ability to imagine Them as violent.

In the establishment of class markers in media depictions, it is apparent that current relations of power are reinscribed. For instance, privileged spokespeople are permitted to address at length their experiences with mental illness. Such is the case in Example 2.3 where Michael Wilson talks about his son's depression. It is notable that Wilson is reported as having '*held several cabinet posts, including minister of finance*' and '*now heads his own consulting firm and is vice-chairman of RCB Dominion Securities*'. It can be assumed, from the declaration of Wilson's credentials, that he is permitted to speak because of those qualifications.

The Class Based Illness category is useful in illustrating the privilege afforded to certain people to speak about mental illness in the media. An assessment of the corpus shows that of the 195 articles, only 51 speakers are identified as mentally ill. On the other hand, there are 192 speakers who are identified as a psychiatrist or doctor (103 references), lawyers, judges or coroners (77 references), and police or jail guards (12). Furthermore, by focusing only on the 58 of 195 articles in the corpus that meaningfully index class, it becomes apparent that very few poor people identified as mentally ill get to speak in media text. In fact, of the 58 articles, 33 (57 per cent) did not present talk from any mentally ill speakers, whereas 18 of 58 (31 per cent) were middle class mentally ill speakers, while only seven (12 per cent) were explicitly identified as poor. These data suggest that there exists an inequality in access to the press on the basis of class. It may, however, be useful to assess this further. There are 25 of 58 articles that index class and provide a mentally ill speaker. If we examine those 25 stories, we find that in 72 per cent, a middle class speaker is identified, whereas only 28 per cent are represented as poor. Such disparity in reporting indicates that the social status of mentally ill subjects is an important reporting feature that has a direct bearing upon Our evaluation of Their (lack of) moral character. What becomes amply clear is that media depictions rely upon the repeated representation of class interests in reports about mental illness. These depictions are achieved both explicitly and implicitly and uphold the message that there is a relationship between poverty, violence and mental illness.

Conclusion

This research has demonstrated that newspaper text is replete with formulations of mental illness that consistently associate it with criminality. This association has been produced in the media through the repeated use of a dichotomous framework upholding the ideological oppositionality of Us versus Them. Accomplished through a number of textual techniques, one of the primary findings has been that the conflation of mental illness and criminality has much to do with notions of individual agency and responsibility.

Although the Mentally Ill Criminal portrayal focuses primarily on the apparent irrational and delusional behaviour of mentally ill people, mental illness is constituted as something over which the mentally ill subjects have control. Likewise, the Passive Patient depiction demonstrates that certain mentally ill people do not behave in irrational, violent and unpredictable ways thereby establishing that 'bad' mentally ill behaviour occurs as a matter of individual choice. However, when we begin to examine the Class-based Illness portrayal, it becomes evident that degrees of responsibility for personal behaviour are established, based on particular class affiliations. It was found that responsibility/agency was emphasised for mentally ill subjects indexed as poor, whereas those from middle class backgrounds were represented as agentless. These data suggest that elaborate social descriptions about mental illness in the press are about the distribution and authorisation of social blame on the basis of certain contingent features of identity. Responsibility has been found to be a characteristic of certain versions of mental illness that promote Our relational superiority – a position repeatedly confirmed by specific typologies that verify the basic distinction between normal and abnormal, good and bad, responsible and irresponsible.

This research has been concerned with representations of mental illness and not with the very important question of how audiences interpret those representations. However, despite the absence of empirical research on media reception, we can be critical of the negative and inaccurate ways in which mental illness is represented on the grounds that media discourse is a social fact informed by and existing as a dimension of modern political and popular culture. The cultural significance of representations activates certain forms of social power (Foucault 1972, 1980) not only to define what is manifestly 'different', but to influence the broader production of a discourse on mental illness that includes but ultimately exceeds media representations.

Notes

1 The *Globe and Mail* reports an audited circulation of 335,090 for 1999. The Total Average Circulation of the *Toronto Star* for the 12 months ending 30 September, 1999 was: Monday-Friday 467,498; Saturday 698,261; Sunday 481,172.
2 I have borrowed from Nurith Gertz's assessment of the humanitarian ethos apparent in newspaper coverage of the war in Lebanon (see Gertz (1995) Text and Subtext: Newspaper Coverage of the War in Lebanon, *Social Discourse 7*, 1–2, 121–33).
3 This notion of the militarist maxim is drawn from Gertz (1995).

References

Breggin, P. (1991) *Toxic Psychiatry: why Therapy, Empathy and Love must Replace the Drugs, Electroshock and Biochemical Theories of the 'New Psychiatry'*. New York: St. Martin's Press.

Caminero-Santangelo, M. (1998) *The Madwoman Can't Speak: or Why Insanity is not Subversive*. Ithaca: Cornell University Press.

Colombo, A. (1997) *Understanding Mentally Disordered Offenders*. Aldershot: Ashgate.

Davis, H. (1985) Discourse and Media Influence. In van Dijk, T. (ed) *Discourse and Communication*. New York: Walter de Gruyter.

Day, D. and Page, S. (1986) Portrayal of mental illness in Canadian newspapers, *Canadian Journal of Psychiatry*, 31, 813–16.

Deber, R. (2000) Getting what we pay for: myths and realities about financing Canada's health care system, Prepared for the *National Dialogue on Health Reform: Sustaining Confidence in Canada's Health Care System*, University of Toronto, April.

Durkheim, E. (1964) *Suicide: a Study in Sociology*. London: Routledge and Kegan and Paul.

Fleming, M. and Manvell, R. (1985) *Images of Madness*. Toronto: Associated University Press.

Foucault, M. (1972) *The Archaeology of Knowledge and the Discourse on Language*. New York: Pantheon Press.

Foucault, M. (1980) *Power/Knowledge*. Brighton: Harvester.

Fruth, L. and Padderud, A. (1985) Portrayals of mental illness in daytime television serials, *Journalism Quarterly*, 62, 384–7.

Galt, V. (1990) 15 per cent of prisoners need mental help, *Globe and Mail*, 23 August, A7.

Gertz, N. (1995) Text and subtext: newspaper coverage of the war in Lebanon, *Social Discourse 7*, 1–2, 121–33.

Gilman, S. L. (1988) *Disease and Representation: Images of Illness from Madness to AIDS*. Ithaca, NY: Cornell University Press.

Hall, S. (1997) *Representation: Cultural Representations and Signifying Practices*. London: Sage.

Howlett, M. (1998) *Medication, Non-compliance and Mentally Disordered Offenders: the Role of Non-compliance in Homicide by People with Mental Illness and Proposals for Future Policy*. London: The Zito Trust.

Kitzinger, J. (1994) Visible and invisible women in AIDS discourse, In Doyal, L., Naidoo, J. and Wilson, T. (eds) *AIDS: Setting a Feminist Agenda*. London: Taylor and Francis.

Kitzinger, J. (1998) A sociology of media power: key issues in audience reception research, In Philo, G. (ed) *Message Received*. New York: Addison Wesley Longman Limited.

Lull, J. (1988) *World Families Watch Television*. Newbury: Sage.

Mahoney, J. (1996) Speak-out on mental illness: Wilson, *Toronto Star*, 9 May, A2.

Mathieu, A. (1993) The medicalization of homelessness and the theatre of repression, *Medical Anthropology Quarterly*, 7, 2, 170–84.

Miller, D. and Philo, G. (1998) The effective media, In Philo, G. (ed) *Message Received*. New York: Addison Wesley Longman Limited.

Morley, D. (1986) *Family Television*. London: Comedia/Routledge.

Morrall, P. (2000) *Madness and Murder*. London: Whurr Publishers Ltd.

Munro, A. (1996) Learning to fly, *Toronto Star*, 11 January, F5.

Nunnally, J. (1961) *Popular Conceptions of Mental Health*. New York: Holt, Rinehart and Winston.

Philo, G. (1996) The Media and public belief. In Philo, G. (ed) *Media and Mental Distress*. New York: Addison Wesley Longman Limited.

Philo, G. (1998) Conclusions on media audiences and message reception, In Philo, G. (ed) *Message Received*. New York: Addison Wesley Longman Limited.

Pron, N. (1992) Psychopaths hunt the available, vulnerable, *Toronto Star*, 3 April, A4.

Scheff, T. (1966) *Being Mentally Ill: a Sociological Theory*. Chicago: Aldine.

Szasz, T. (1973) *The Manufacture of Madness*. St. Albans: Granada.

van Dijk, T. (1998) *Ideology: a Multidisciplinary Approach*. London: Sage Publishers.

Wahl, O. (1992) Media Images of mental illness: a review of the literature, *Journal of Community Psychology*, 20, 343–52.

Wahl, O. (1995) *Media Madness: Public Images of Mental Health*, New Brunswick: Rutgers University Press.

Wahl, O. and Roth, R. (1982) Television images of mental illness: results of a metropolitan media watch, *Journal of Broadcasting*, 26, 599–605.

Chapter 7

Actor networks, policy networks and personality disorder

Nick Manning

Introduction

Personality disorder is a relatively recent category to have appeared within psychiatric classification, claiming its own special axis in the American Diagnostic and Statistical Manual (DSM) from 1980. This separate axis II, set alongside axis I in which all other mental disorder is classified, attests to both the importance of personality disorder, and to its difference from the run of the mill of other psychiatric classifications. The history of this development and the circumstances that gave rise to it are detailed elsewhere (Manning 2000). A particular feature of the personality disorders is that in contrast to mental illness, they are mostly detected through behaviours rather than through independent biological or psychological signs, which makes the separate classification of criminal and psychiatric acts very difficult.

Over the last 10 years there has been a surge of interest in the treatment/ management of personality disorder in the UK from within both the psychiatric profession and government ministries, and particularly those personality disorders deemed to be severe or dangerous. This has resulted in the development of a new psychiatric classification, the 'dangerous and severe personality disorder' (DSPD), and the funding and development of a new service to deal with it at a cost of £126 million. Major new mental health legislation has been set in train to provide legal backing for the pre-emptive detention of patients with such a diagnosis, despite widespread uncertainty over its status, reliability or predictive capability.

In this chapter the story of this development, together with an analysis of its constituent elements, will be laid out using two models drawn from unrelated and distant parts of social science. The first is the sociological study of actor-networks, originating in the sub-field of science and technology studies. The second is the political science study of policy networks, originating in the sub-field of public administration. In the course of this analysis, some comparisons between these two models will be explored.

Dangerous and severe personality disorder

In 1999 the UK Departments of Health and Home Office issued a joint consultation paper on the management of dangerous people with SPD (HO/

DoH 1999), and in 2000 a White Paper (cmnd 5016 – I) outlining the shape of the proposed new Mental Health Act appeared. The latter is divided into two parts, the second part being devoted to 'High Risk Patients'. In the Foreword to the White Paper the Ministers of Health and the Home Office (Milburn and Straw) jointly state:

> Public confidence in care in the community has been undermined by failures in services and failures in the law. Too often, severely ill patients have been allowed to drift out of contact with mental health services. They have been able to refuse treatment. Sometimes, as the tragic toll of homicides and suicides involving such patients makes clear, lives have been put at risk. In particular, existing legislation has also failed to provide adequate public protection from those whose risk to others arises from a severe personality disorder. We are determined to remedy this (2000: 3).

The 1999 DSPD proposals are radical. They outline new principles for mental health services in the UK, and they advocate the expensive development of an entirely new set of services. The new principles are marked by the elevation of risk to a central place as one of the key organising ideas for service development:

> At present individuals in this group *(DSPD)* may, broadly speaking, be detained in prison as *punishment* following conviction for an act they have committed, or in hospital to receive *treatment* designed to bring about an improvement in diagnosed mental disorder. The approach the government has developed to managing dangerous severely personality disordered people involves the idea of detention based on the *serious risk* such people present to the public. These three concepts – punishment, treatment, and risk – overlap in many respects (HO/DoH: 6).

Why is a new act required? Under existing legislation patients cannot be compelled to accept treatment unless they are admitted to hospital. Most psychiatrists do not regard personality disorder as treatable, and therefore do not want to compel people with these diagnoses to enter hospital. In practice many are in prison, following offences, but on release they return to the community – and are increasingly seen as a threat to the public. The government wants to use the new and central principle of potential risk, even without any offence, to detain DSPD patients. To place them in prison, however, in advance of any offence, would contravene the European Convention on Human Rights, unless the detention were to be in some kind of hospital for the purposes of some kind of treatment. The solution has been to develop a new service with new treatments for DSPD patients, involving building new institutions in both prisons and special hospitals, and due to take patients from 2004.

This story, however, contains a number of uncertainties which have not as yet been settled in connection with DSPD patients. They include diagnosis, prevalence, treatability, professional opinion, evidence base, and the assessment and prevalence of risk. In all of these areas there is academic, professional and policy uncertainty. The question here is how we can understand the way in which a sufficiently stable understanding of the issue has been constructed on which government policy and substantial expenditure has been based.

At the heart of the story is the development of a new psychiatric category and potential treatments for it (see also Manning 2000), combined with a number of closely related concerns, such as professional ambitions and public anxieties.

DSPD is most closely related to the term psychopathic disorder, which was identified as a specific legal category in the 1959 Mental Health Act. Its inclusion there was heavily, possibly solely, influenced by Dr. Maxwell Jones (Whiteley 1980: 46) who from 1947 had almost single-handedly acted as a charismatic innovator to pioneer a specific treatment, the therapeutic community, for patients of this type. The 1975 Butler report recommended the replacement of the term psychopath by the term personality disorder. In 1980 the separate axis II category appeared in the DSM system. Dolan and Coid (1993) observe in their extensive review of 'psychopathic and antisocial personality disorders' commissioned for a UK government review of the treatment and management of mentally disordered offenders (Reed Report – DoH/HO 1992), that there is no agreed system for measuring the severity of personality disordered patients. Nevertheless, Norton and Hinshelwood (1996) employ the term severe personality disorder (SPD) as an organising category for a review of inpatient psychotherapy units. It is important to note that Norton holds Maxwell Jones's old post as medical director of the Henderson Hospital, and Hinshelwood had the same position at the Cassel Hospital – the other key centre in which this treatment type originated in the 1940s (Manning 1989). Indeed the fortunes of the therapeutic community and the category of personality disorder have been inextricably linked. It merely remained for the qualifier 'dangerous' to be added to SPD when the new government set to work in 1997 for the current category to become stabilised as a new entity worthy of a major service development.

Nevertheless, diagnostic reliability is very weak. A major review of the diagnosis and assessment capability of the forensic professions was commissioned in 1997 by the UK government-sponsored Virtual Institute for Severe Personality Disorder (VISPED). In a key collection of papers (Meux 2000), there was one aspect that all experts agreed upon: the diagnosis and assessment of personality disorder was in disarray. The following quotes from two of the most eminent and respected professors in the field are typical:

Reliable assessment of diagnostic categories has not resolved the issue of validity. Studies of concurrent validity, i.e. how far different measures of the same disorder produce the same diagnoses, indicate that questionnaires agree reasonably well with other questionnaires, but less clearly with interviews, while interviews agree only moderately with other interviews. Overall agreement on the diagnosis of specific categories is poor. Reviewing studies in which two or more assessment procedures had been compared, Perry (1992) noted a median kappa across categories of 0.25. This means that 75 per cent of the variance in assessment is due to factors other than patients' personality dysfunction, and as Perry observes, 'this is not a scientifically acceptable state of affairs' (Blackburn 2000: s14).

Whether those involved in the treatment of personality disorders welcome it or not, the notion of 'severe personality disorder' (Home Office and Department of Health 1999) is probably here to stay, and not only the Home Secretary of the British government will be using it frequently in the future. I personally feel that this is a useful concept in personality measurement although it has far to go before it can be refined and defined satisfactorily. At present one can only paraphrase Marx in developing new approaches to the measurement of personality disorder and exhort: 'forensic psychiatrists of the world unite, you have nothing to lose but an outdated and useless classification of personality disorder, you have a dimension of rich description to win' (Tyrer 2000: s62).

Despite these observations, there is an operational problem for staff in the clinical setting where they nevertheless have to make decisions about treatment. Interviews with staff involved with developing the DSPD service reveal that in practice they frequently use the Hare psychopathy checklist (Hare 1991) as a shorthand and summary judgement about patients, sometimes actually tagged as 'Hare psychopaths'. The checklist was developed out of the qualitative work presented by Cleckley in *The Mask of Sanity* (1941/1976). It has settled down after a period of development to a 20-item scale, giving a score between 0 and 40, with 30 now widely accepted as the threshold for indicating psychopathy (note the retention of this historical descriptor in a central part of this field). Within the research community it has also become the most common measure in a wide and contested field of measures (Blackburn 2000: s10, Dolan and Coid 1993: 19–20).

Moreover, treatment interventions are not clear cut. In their comprehensive review Dolan and Coid state that:

The conclusion must be that there is no evidence for the efficacy of a specific treatment. This should not be taken to mean that the treatment itself is ineffective, but rather that efficacy cannot be demonstrated from the available evidence (1993: 261).

Nevertheless, they found that studies of the therapeutic community showed the most promising results of any modality (1993: 264). The therapeutic community almost disappeared in the 1980s under the twin influence of the decline in residential care, for which it claimed to have a special relevance, and the almost wilful neglect by its practitioners to develop the evidence for its effectiveness that has come increasingly to dominate health policy. However, since the 1990s there has been a reversal of its fortunes. Partly this has been that, in the manner of a solution looking for a problem, it benefited from a track record of coping with personality disordered patients when few others wanted to, and in the face of almost no alternative treatment possibilities (see Dolan and Coid 1993 for a detailed technical review). It has also benefited from the rise in residential numbers in prison, and the evidence that this population includes very high numbers of personality disordered inmates (Social Survey Division, ONS 1998). With the attention of criminologists rather than psychiatrists to the evidence base, especially at the five communities making up Grendon Underwood prison, the therapeutic community has begun to flourish under new investment by the Home Office. A recent systematic review and meta-analysis (Lees *et al.* 1999) has established, after some 50 years of practice, that the therapeutic community does indeed have strong evidence for its effectiveness with PD patients.

Several additional factors are pertinent. A number of high-profile homicides by mentally disordered people, and corresponding reactions, such as the work of the Zito Trust, have led the UK government to be concerned about public protection from a perceived rise in risk. Indeed, as I quoted earlier, Health and Home Office Ministers have elevated the management of risk to rank as a matter of principle alongside treatment and punishment as one of the three major rationales for service development. This in itself resonates with a wider discussion about the nature and perception of risk in late modern societies, which in part has an insecure evidence base (Dingwall 1999, Furedi 1997). This is also the case for homicide rates, where the rate for those associated with mental disorder has actually been steadily falling since the middle of the 20th century (Taylor and Gunn 1999). Nevertheless, the UK government thinks that the public is concerned about risk and protection.

In fact the prevalence of DSPD people has been estimated to be around 2,400, of whom 1,400 are in prison, 400 in the secure psychiatric hospitals, and up to 600 at large in the community (DoH/HO 1999: 9). The latter group may well have been in prison, but completed their sentences, and this is a part of the risk concern. The other type of risk assessment, that is, of individual people, has to a certain extent, as with the Hare checklist, been manualised into the system recommended by the Royal College of Psychiatrists, the Violent Risk Appraisal Guide (VRAG). Nevertheless, the assessment of risk remains very uncertain (Moore and Hogue 2000). This is illustrated by the general unpopularity of this group with social and medical staff.

Even psychiatrists themselves have strong reservations about many of these issues. Haddock *et al.* (2001) report from a survey of 153 forensic psychiatrists that 65 per cent felt that severe personality disorder was not identifiably different from personality disorder, that 82 per cent felt that available risk assessment procedures were inadequate to reliably identify potentially dangerous individuals, and that 75 per cent objected to the indeterminate detention of unconvicted cases. A wider survey of 1,000 general psychiatrists reported by Crawford *et al.* (2001) also reported that 80 per cent did not support the DSPD proposals. Psychologists are also expressing concern that they will be pressured into taking responsibility for some of the assessment decisions where it is clear that there is professional doubt about the clarity and reliability of the instruments that can be used (Cooke *et al.* 2002).

Such scientific and professional uncertainty begs the question of where the thrust for this development has come from. The answer is that the government has taken the lead. It is also clear, however, that the government has been mindful that there should be an evidence base to this development, that it can help to develop this, and that until this has been built, the assessment of risk, diagnosis, and treatment will remain contested.

Accordingly, the DSPD development, and the £126 million earmarked for it, has been presented as a 'pilot' programme (Sedgwick 2001). Underlying this pilot was the foundation of the Virtual Institute of Severe Personality Disorder (VISPED) in 1997 by the High Security Psychiatric Commissioning Board (which managed the secure psychiatric hospitals at that time). This network of 11 largely university-based academic units and members was designed to encourage and support a research and evaluation programme. Six million pounds has been earmarked for research into the DSPD area (Sedgwick 2001).

What questions does this story raise? How does this development get started and continue in the face of such flimsy evidence? There are two distinct research questions that stand out. The first concerns the nature of psychiatric knowledge, from diagnosis to treatment. How does it develop? Under what circumstances, and through what actions does this knowledge come to stabilise sufficiently for new and costly service developments to be undertaken? These are issues of both medical science and medical technology.

The second question centres on government action. Who sets the priorities for government intervention? How are perceived public concerns used to justify new policies, and how are the relevant professional groups involved and persuaded to support and deliver new services?

These two questions, about knowledge and government action, would conventionally be theorised and tackled through the sociology of science and public policy, respectively: two sub-fields of social science that appear to be entirely separate and unconnected. Yet both have recently spawned theoretical innovations, centred on the notion of the 'network', that, it will be argued, are particularly appropriate to this case study. These innovations have in both cases been developed to overcome prior theoretical difficulties, outlined below, such that the conventional analysis of particular interests or historical developments have proved inadequate. In the course of outlining these network approaches, and applying them to this case, a third set of questions arises about the possible similarities and contrasts between them.

The approaches focus on slightly different aspects of the story, and provide different ways of understanding it. The social-studies-of-science tradition, and particularly 'actor-network theory', would raise the question of how the development of DSPD is being performed or sustained, and what the heterogeneous elements, human and non-human, are that are being brought together into a coherent strategy. A particular focus would be the key elements that are sedimented or crystallised repositories of meaning and action. On the basis of these, various interests and elements are translated into a coherent strategy for action, for example the diagnostic categories of PD, SPD and finally DSPD, or the Hare checklist, or the therapeutic community, or the Virtual Institute.

The second approach is concerned with the question of how the policy was developed, and implemented. The social studies of policy and public administration, and particularly the use of the 'policy network model', would consider why the government is pushing this development, and who is involved in the policy-making process. A particular focus would be on what the prior connections between the policy-making participants has been, what ideologies and resources they bring to the process, how coherent a group or policy community they have become, and in particular what they hope to gain by engaging in the process.

Actor-network theory

This approach had its origins in science and technology studies in the early 1980s. The sociology of science had by that time moved from a sociology of error to a fully social constuctivist approach, exemplified in the landmark study of laboratory work in Latour and Woolgar (1979) – see Manning (2000) for a fuller review. In relation to this position, the identification of interests, what and whose they were and how they might impinge on the science process, was a critical and unresolved problem. How could one know what such interests were, whether they were effective, and to what extent they were constrained by the material world with which science worked? Clearly, not anything could be socially constructed. An analogy with economics might see this as the difficulty of identifying preferences in the context of a constraining market. The answer in the latter case is to look at what people actually buy and sell, and at what prices.

The equivalent solution in science and technology studies was to think about the way in which people acted on their interests, and the processes by which they brought elements of the material world together in pursuit of a strategy or goal. In other words the focus was on the process involved, rather than on the starting points. In particular, this included the notion of the way in which material, technical or information systems were constituted out of the embedded labour or social relations from previous rounds of scientific or technological development (we are all familiar with the qwerty layout of the keyboard as the embedded solution to the separation of mechanical keys on the early typewriter).

Originating in France this was presented as a sociology of 'translation', in which the key focus was on the way in which social action and material and technical elements were brought together, or translated, into a coherent network out of which certain achievements were attained. In particular, all elements were seen as capable of 'action', not merely the human actors in the network: thus in two well known studies, scallops, in relation to French fishermen and restaurants (Callon 1986), and boats, in relation to Portuguese maritime exploration (Law 1987), were as important as the human actors in the story.

There are a number of other key aspects of what has come to be known as actor-network theory (ANT) – itself now the condensed repository of 20 years of social science development, or translation. First is the principle of heterogeneity. This asserts that any elements, human, animal, or technical, can be enrolled or translated into the network, without any prior assumptions as to which are the significant actors at any one point – this is to be revealed in empirical observation and analysis. Second is the idea of action at a distance, through which networks can be seen to extend across space and time. The telephone or the scientific paper are good examples of such effects. Third is the related observation that past networks, in which actors have brought together, or translated, a network into the achievement of some strategy, can get simplified. It can become 'punctualised' into a shorthand, taken-for-granted, and often-forgotten, package or routine, such as the Microsoft machine code embedded into much of the software we use today. Fourth, and bringing these ideas together, there is the idea of strategies and centres (even 'machines') of translation, through which networks are rendered capable of having effects. These effects include the exercise of power, and the creation of social structures – themselves highly complex and durable punctualised networks. Finally, and following from this last point, ANT emphasises the way in which social relations are performed, rather than perceived, arguing that some of the traditional dichotomies in social science between actors and structures, or between micro and macro levels, dissolve when approached from this perspective (Law 1992).

This approach furnishes a distinct set of researchable questions, many of which can be considered in thinking about the DSPD development. Law (1992) lists some possibilities as follows:

What are the kind of heterogeneous bits and pieces created or mobilised and juxtaposed to generate organisational effects? How are resistances overcome? How it is (if at all) that the material durability and transportability necessary to the organisational patterning of social relations are achieved? What are the strategies being performed

throughout the networks of the social as a part of this? How far do
they spread? How widely are they performed? How do they interact?
How is it (if at all) that organisational calculation is attempted? How
(if at all) are the results of that calculation translated into action?
How is it (if at all) that the heterogeneous bits and pieces that make
up organisation generate an asymmetrical relationship between periphery
and centre? How is it, in other words, that a centre may come to speak for
and profit from, the efforts of what has been turned into a periphery?
(1992: 390).

Policy networks

This approach had its origins in the studies of British government structures
and dynamics, also in the early 1980s. By that time the study of the central
institutions of Whitehall, and the idealistic model of the British central executive control of the state, had come under attack through studies such as
Heclo and Wildavsky's 1974 account of the Whitehall 'village' in which the
treasury dominated the other Whitehall ministries through a tight and closed
culture. In particular, Richardson and Jordan's *Governing under Pressure:
the Policy Process in a Post-Parliamentary Democracy* (1979) showed that a
focus on parliament and political parties missed out another, and possibly
more important, world of policy networks and communities. A critical issue
that emerged was the question of what the nature of these policy worlds was
– who was in them, and particularly the way they operated. What interests
were pursued? What mechanisms connected the actors? To what extent were
these varied in relation to the nature of the policy areas under consideration,
for example industrial policy, or health policy, or defence policy?

The attack of the Conservative government after 1979 on a whole array
of traditional institutions, including the way in which central government
related to local government, and the way in which central government deliv-
ered services through government agencies, accelerated the question about
the way policies were actually generated and implemented. The solution was
to reconceptualise the Whitehall model in terms of a 'differentiated polity'
(Rhodes 1997: 7) in which the state is seen as a complex mixture of inter-
governmental relations, and where the different parts are in a complex relation of 'power-dependence' which bargain, coerce or ally with or against
each other. In particular, the approach focused on the resources the different
parts either wanted or possessed, and which influenced their strategies in the
political game.

Particularly in the work of Marsh and Rhodes (1992), this alternative
model of the British state was developed through the idea of policy networks
(PN) as an 'organising perspective' for undertaking a series of case studies
of the way in which the 'differentiated polity' engaged with different areas of
policy. Rhodes sets up a typology of PNs, ranging from at one end tightly-knit

policy communities with a shared culture in which the key players interact frequently, the boundaries are fairly tight, and there are distinct advantages to those on the inside; at the other end of this continuum are loosely-integrated issue networks where the actors come together for the pursuit of specific gains, but in which there are few long-term and regular interactions or a shared culture. Between these there are varieties of PNs, more or less integrated, which are strongly shaped by the issues and materials that are the focus of the network's concerns – for example health policy, or engineering standards, or European agricultural support. Rhodes suggests then that the substantive concerns of the network have a significant and possibly determinate influence on the type of PN that develops, and the policy outputs that it generates.

There are a number of key aspects of the PN perspective. First, networks are situated within real-world constraints – the substance of their concerns affects the way they work. For example, where professional interests, such as in health care, are concerned, the patterns of shared cultures and resource dependencies will be different. Second, networks develop and are sustained because of mutual dependencies between individuals and networks, for example in the general relations between central and local government, or ministries and local agencies such as hospitals. The relative power between the individuals or networks will both shape their interaction and, as relations develop, reproduce or change these power relations. Third, the effects or outputs from networks varies between four types: economic resources, ideologies, knowledge, or institutional changes. Much of the time there are multiple outputs of several of these factors. Fourth, the government has become much more aware of the networked nature of its work, and indeed has in some respects promoted it through the differentiation between policy, steering and service delivery in many parts of government (for example the purchaser-provider split in health care). This has intensified the government's own involvement in the resultant proliferation of networks, in many ways shifting its attention from 'rowing' to 'steering' (Osborne and Gaebler 1992). The rise of 'political spin' is one consequence of this. Fifth, the coordination of networks is based on trust and co-operation, in contrast to the price mechanism in markets, or the command structure of hierarchies. They are thus necessarily and pervasively social constructs, and offer a means of integrating micro-level analyses (individual political actors) and emerging stable political and social structures, for example the dominance of the treasury in the British government system.

This approach also furnishes a distinct set of researchable questions, drawn in part from Rhodes (1997: ch. 9) and Marsh and Smith (2001: 537): what are the interests, expectations and values of participants? What is the cultural context of organisational and inter-organisational bargaining? What are the relative strengths of group cohesion and the rules for action in the group/network? To what extent are sustainable strategies developed and implemented from within the network? Where are they developed, and how far do they spread? What are the means by which the network judges itself, or defines progress or success? Is there a core and periphery within the network? What are the relations between these? How do members join or leave the network?

Application to DSPD

These theoretical approaches suggest partly similar and partly contrasting answers to the two key questions set earlier, about knowledge and government action.

Who are the key actors in the DSPD story? What heterogeneous elements have been enrolled into the network? Law (1992: 386–7) asks: 'How is the work of all the networks that make up the punctualised actor *(here, the DSPD policy/service)* borrowed, bent, displaced, distorted, rebuilt, reshaped, stolen, profited from and/or misrepresented to generate the effects of agency, organisation and power?'.

The ANT approach is to look to see how all the elements, human and non-human, fit together, which of them either does the work of enrolling or organising the strategy of the network, and which of them contains punctualised or condensed sets of prior networks that themselves were organised around some kind of strategy.

The key non-human actors here appear to be the category of DSPD itself, assessment techniques for identifying the DSPD and its associated risks, and the treatments available for DSPD. The category PD is typically reduced to two types in the literature and in professional usage, one of which, the borderline type, emerged in the late 1960s, sponsored in two places – American academic psychiatry and psychoanalytic practice. The other has a much longer history as moral insanity and, more recently, psychopathy. Each of these types is itself closely associated with networks of interests – indeed in ANT terms they represent punctualised networks, subsuming all the debates, professional practices, academic papers and patients that gave rise to their stabilisation as psychiatric categories in the 1980 DSM (Manning 2000). As I have suggested, the qualifier – severe – was added to PD sporadically from the 1970s, and systematically from the mid-1990s, and appeared to have been sponsored by senior figures in hospitals that could be characterised as offering a treatment solution in search of a problem. The final stage was the government sponsorship of the further qualifier – dangerous – to produce the new category of DSPD, for which it decided to organise a new service.

The stabilisation of DSPD, however, was/is not a foregone conclusion. Law notes that ANT is interested in analysing the ways in which actor networks perform to produce and stabilise the networks and strategies they create. In particular this requires attention to the struggles and difficulties that continually threaten stabilisation:

Any particular effort at ordering encounters its limits. Another way of saying this is to note that the bits and pieces assembled *pro tem* into an order are constantly liable to break down, or make off on their own. Thus, analysis of ordering struggle is central to actor-network theory (Law 1992: 386).

In this case the identification, assessment and treatment of DSPD are extremely problematic, with significant sections of the professional and academic communities threatening to 'make off' and, at best, disagreeing with the techniques for solving these problems, or, at worst, actively opposing them. In opposition to this tendency are specialist teams and individuals concerned to stabilise routine techniques for dealing with these issues in such a way that their development becomes stabilised and punctualised. This is so that the uncertain assumptions beneath them disappear into an apparently pre-ordained and invisibly supported taken-for-granted activity. Thus, there are disputes about whether the use of assessment schedules, or interviews, or observations are the best way to assess patients. As I have noted the Hare psychopathy checklist (1991) has recently made a strong running as the punctualised technique for the identification of the DSPD, whereas the means of assessing the risk of dangerousness is still very uncertain, and subject to further development. The process by which this takes place and the outcome in terms of a stable and punctualised risk assessment technique will be interesting to observe in the near future.

Possibly the most material expression of the DSPD network is the development of several large, multi-million pound purpose-built units, which have now been modelled in detail and have reached a detailed planning stage, and will take material form in 2002/3. This is literally a stable punctualisation of the knowledge and practices that are debated and reviewed in the DSPD network. The author was able to undertake ethnographic fieldwork in 2001 with the national leaders for the development of the assessment and treatment strategies for the national DSPD programme, the architects, the security leads and the unit managers as they visited similar units in the Netherlands and Germany, and discussed the principles and practices that had to be expressed and encapsulated in the new buildings. Many issues of uncertainty – the daily regime, the treatments, the security systems – were discussed back and forth with their European colleagues. Nevertheless, and perhaps surprisingly, the nature of this new service is, in the opinion of other specialists interviewed, no different from existing secure treatment regimens.

Another key part of the DSPD actor network is of course the government. Indeed in many ways this actor is the key player in the whole ensemble. Not only does it have the legal and financial means to secure particular outcomes for the whole DSPD project, but also it is directly involved in managing the agencies that deliver the service aspect to the network, that is the prisons and secure hospitals. This perhaps is the routine nature of government influence. A much less common element is the sponsoring of a particular scientific network to underpin the evidence base. This is epitomised in the Virtual Institute of Severe Personality Disorder (VISPED).

Created self-consciously as a small actor network in its own right, VISPED includes a roll call of the great and the good in British forensic and criminological academic centres of excellence. It was founded on a series of conferences and academic reviews of the issues involved in developing the severe personality disorder concept, not all of which made comfortable reading for those working to pull the DSPD strategy together – some of the parts, as Law observed, were tending to make off on their own (see the earlier quotes in this paper from Blackburn and Tyrer). It is interesting to note that the editor of VISPED's newsletter, *Dialogue*, is based at the Henderson hospital, one of the key parts of this network with much to gain from the stabilisation of the network. Indeed, in a related but separate development from the new DSPD service, the government has already invested in two new hospitals and a substantial research programme to reproduce the Henderson hospital's therapeutic community approach to the treatment of SPDs.

The government's key concern is to tackle the issue of public unease about risk and dangerousness head on. To do this entails the detention of those thought to be dangerous, even though they have committed no offence, in addition to those already in gaol or secure hospital who have already committed offences. In the view of numbers of psychiatrists, many people who are alleged to have (D)SPD should not be detained and indeed are not seen as treatable either. Yet they can only be detained on such grounds under current legislation, and because of this, new powers will be set in place for their detention. This will have to be on the grounds that new treatments will be applied. This points to the government's desire to sponsor academic and clinical research that will make the case for this detention, for these are the only grounds that circumvent the European Convention on Human Rights – another actor in the network. Indeed, the government has self-consciously developed the new DSPD service as a 'pilot', by which it appears to mean that it is part-research tool, and part-development trial, so that it might have the grounds for handling the manifest uncertainties in the network.

The human actors involved are of course a vital element. The key groups acting as organised agents include general academic and professional organisations, specialist interest groups, the patients and potential patients, and key individuals. The professions have different views. Forensic psychiatrists have something to gain from the DSPD development in two respects. Forensic psychiatry is regarded within the wider psychiatric profession as being somewhat out of the main stream, so that the prospects of new research money, and a new service with a new and stable diagnostic category in place will help to enhance their status and standing within the profession. However, the profession as a whole is apprehensive about the government's removal of treatability as the criterion for the detention of 'patients'. Psychologists are also quite apprehensive that they will be given the task of diagnosis and assessment where the tools and techniques are highly contested (Cooke *et al.* 2002).

For some individuals this will also mean career opportunities and pay enhancement where NHS trusts and prisons compete for the services of the relatively few consultants available. Some of the more manualised treatments being trialled by the DSPD network, such as cognitive behaviour therapy (a relatively simple system that can be operated independently by psychologists or nurses), will also offer career opportunities.

What of the public and the patients? The real risk to the public is low and falling; but the perceived risk may be high and rising. The British Crime Survey regularly finds that public fear of crime is exaggerated (Hale 1996). The government may therefore be wise politically. But the cost to those 2,400 people who are being targeted is as yet unclear.

Turning explicitly to a consideration of the policy networks involved in the DSPD story, how integrated are they? What resources do they hold or seek to hold? What are their beliefs? The PN perspective is built around the methodology of the case study. This involves observation, interviewing and the collection of network tracers such as personnel profiles, memoranda, policy statements, and other documents. Marsh and Smith argue in a development and restatement of the PN perspective that:

We identify three dialectical relationships that those who study networks need to examine, between: structure and agency; network and context; and network and outcome (2001: 537).

The key interests in this story are, at the most general level, public perceptions of the risk of violence from DSPD people, reflected in media attention and the activities of lobbying groups such as the Zito Trust. The government feels a responsibility to respond to this perception. It could of course undertake a public education campaign to proselytise the evidence that objective levels of risk are very low and falling. However, where for example there have been attempts to relocate paedophiles in community settings there has indeed been a sharp public reaction. It is known from research (Dear and Taylor 1982) that this can be assuaged. Indeed, during the fieldwork for this paper, Dutch colleagues gave examples of the entirely successful management of such public concerns where new facilities were being sited in the Netherlands. Nevertheless, the government has adopted the alternative approach which is to bring in new legislation and to develop an expensive new service. Thus they appear to be doing something to minimise the threat that the public perceives. This is commensurate with a long-term commitment of successive Home Secretaries to play tough on such issues, and vividly illustrates the ability of a key player in the network to set an agenda and a cultural tone.

This approach to the DSPD problem has been directed by the government towards a forensic professional community which is split over its own interests and values on the issue. A core of those with special interests in this category support the government line, and indeed have a number of potential benefits to gain. They will gain resources from active involvement in the network, and they hope to be laying the evidence base for a new branch of psychiatry. The rest, along with the large body of general psychiatrists and clinical psychologists, are distinctly cool, concerned that they might be trading in their autonomy under the new legislation. On the other hand, there is widespread dislike of the personality-disordered patient, sometimes referred to as the 'heart sink' case, because of the trail of chaos and upset that they leave in their wake, both in their families and in their frequent and demanding contact with health and social services. The prospect of taking these patients out of the hair of other professional groups is a considerable external benefit outside the immediate network.

The network around personality-disordered patients is not simple. At the core for this study is the DSPD network. This has several circuits. One is the academic circuit collected together in VISPED. However, many of these clinical academics are interested in PD generally, as well as the smaller group of DSPD; those, for instance, who deal with DSPDs in existing prisons and secure hospitals – they will also, at least a number of them, be supplying the staff for the new service under construction. Another can be found in the central government ministry sections that deal with security issues and legal issues at the Home Office, and those more generally responsible for commissioning existing secure services in both the health and prison sectors. Another is the network of therapeutic communities that claim to have a viable treatment for PDs, but who are regarded by many general psychiatrists as slightly idealistic and radical (this is the stable they came from in their early years of the 1950s and 1960s). Another is the Royal College of Psychiatrists, where support or opposition to these different networks is closely affected by the formal position that different key members of the college hold, particularly the presidency. The salience and leverage that these different networks have in relation to an issue depends both on their status, and on the rules of engagement for the issue. For example, there is no doubt that evidence, preferably generated by the meta-analysis of a set of randomised controlled trials, is the key resource for winning arguments about treatment and service development. The only network to have produced this level of evidence is the therapeutic community network (Lees *et al.* 1999), yet because of the network's slightly outsider status, the core of the professional groups and government agencies involved are reluctant and sceptical, preferring to look elsewhere for treatments.

Despite the variegated pattern of these networks, their members are well known to each other and frequently criss-crossed by the normal traffic of academic and clinical work. This traffic includes referring grant proposals or academic papers, referring patients, sitting on working parties and strategy groups, and undertaking management responsibilities for universities, trusts and ministries. Biography and history intersect in a delicate and labyrinthine dance, but one which appears not to be undertaken on a level ballroom floor – not only is there a slope in favour of some networks or network members, but there are all kinds of hidden depressions and hillocks and screens around and over which the participants have to manoeuvre.

Each of the networks has to operate within a context – a significant part of which will be the effects of other networks in the whole ensemble. From the PN perspective, a crucial area of interaction will be the trading between networks for resources and the accumulation of power that this may enable over time – power not only to act, but crucially to shape agendas both in terms of highlighting issues that should be addressed, but also in terms of suppressing issues that should be hidden. A striking example is the issue of security. Those who already work in secure settings are actively concerned about – one might even venture, obsessed by – security issues. This, they say, is in response to such priorities being set by the Home Office. The fieldwork trip to mainland Europe in 2001 was heavily dominated by such considerations, and elaborate comparisons made between European and British systems and designs for security. However, while this was displaced onto central government by way of explanation, and treated as a constraint, there is also a great deal of investment being made by the government in new security systems. This expenditure is the quid pro quo for this inter-network exchange. In other words, the network has some incentive to go along with the security agenda set outside.

A contrasting issue is provided by the European discussions about the internal regimes to be set up once the new units are built. This is not to be dominated by central government concerns, but 'left to the professionals'. The Dutch system used the term 'social therapy' in several units to describe the therapeutic management of the daily lives of the patients, outside specialist treatment sessions that they might receive. This has sometimes been referred to as the 'other 23 hours' in the literature to mean that specialist treatment is relatively infrequent during the day, and that the interactions that govern the routine of daily life merit attention as a therapeutic input in their own right. That element of the Dutch model was steadily ignored by the British visitors, and in subsequent discussions the only key participant to raise it was the architect – hardly qualified in this particular aspect of treatment! One possible reason is that this element of the patient's daily life is at the very heart of the therapeutic community model which, as I have suggested, has a relatively outsider status on this network.

How do these policy networks judge a successful outcome? Clearly some of the issues at stake are zero sum conflicts in which no amount of trading can produce benefits on all sides. The legal framework for detaining DSPD people without trial or treatment cannot be fudged, and for many psychiatrists there can be no compromise on this issue. Since the government will in all likelihood undertake this step, then this will be a permanent loss for that network. By contrast, as illustrated in the quote from Tyrer earlier in this chapter, other networks can trade to mutual advantage. The government wants an evidence base to reinforce the DSPD category, its assessment, treatment and management. The clinical academic network wants research-grant money and the satisfaction of inventing, refining and working with the new category. Mutual trade here, in the form of VISPED and various strategic working groups, and research initiatives are already benefiting both sides. This may not hold – it depends on the evidence:

> Psychiatrists, as any human beings, will grasp at straws. With the introduction of insulin shock therapy, reports of 90–95 per cent cures appeared, and we were carried away with enthusiasm. Thousands of papers were written on the subject, physiological explanations for its effectiveness were propounded. Yet, where is insulin therapy today? Who can report such cures now? (Gralnick 1969: 90).

Where the evidence base is insecure or disputed, as is undoubtedly the case for DSPD, then the power base of different networks is driven more by culture, pre-existing links and past commitments.

Actor networks, policy networks and personality disorder

The questions raised about the DSPD development were two: the nature and development of psychiatric knowledge, and the bases for government action. In turn, the further question was raised as to the complementary or different analyses and answers that might be provided by deploying two unrelated sub-fields from distant parts of social science theory.

What have these analyses helped us to understand about the DSPD service, and how might they furnish predictions as to the way developments will unfold? The critical lesson from ANT is an explanation about the nature of knowledge-in-construction. While the government is well aware that there is as yet an insecure basis for the treatment and legislative innovation it has set in motion, it has taken a number of steps to create that knowledge, even if the outcome is highly contested. This has involved the creation of VISPED, and the enrolment of the key players within forensic psychiatry, and others in the academic medical and criminological centres of excellence, together with the resources to generate both research capacity (attracting younger people into the field through PhD, post doctoral and other research fellowships) and actual research projects. The characterisation of the new service as a 'pilot' when it actually looks like the final development is designed both to acknowledge the difficulties of a thin evidence base and, at the same time, to ward off criticism and bring the wider professional groups on board.

The research capacity and activity has been put in place to furnish the technical capability of DSPD diagnosis, assessment and treatment, in the classic manner of the sociology of 'translation' whereby the network has enrolled or disarmed the key elements, technical and human, and stabilised the development and production of new knowledge. To the extent that the research falters in this quest, then the government may not be able to hold the network together against the sceptics, and the 'translation' will unravel. ANT has few examples of this, but newer work, for example on cervical screening (Hetherington and Law 2000), has highlighted the uncertainties and ambiguities in much applied medical knowledge. The future in this case may be an uneasy mixture of limited legitimate knowledge production, together with repeated cycles of government innovation in the management of 'risk', together with public reaction and disaffection.

The PN perspective is far less focused on the nature of the knowledge or evidence base for the policies generated in these overlapping networks. The key focus is on the tightness of the network structures, the trading for resources that goes on within and between the relevant networks, and the room for manoeuvre that unfolds in the sequential rounds of action and structure that characterise the networks. Some of the networks are given, for example the relatively small worlds of forensic psychiatry or the technology and management of secure spaces in hospitals and prisons. Others are significantly changing as a result of the resources and opportunities being furnished by government action, for example the similarly small world of therapeutic communities in which the funding of new hospitals and prisons for PD patients has driven splits between the older networks actors, characterised by a strong mutual support ideology, and the newer actors who are more strongly oriented to their new resource rich networks than their older allies.

Those networks that are most tightly integrated retain their cultures and modes of action, for example the forensic psychiatry network. The injection of new resources has not changed the network, but rather, has provided it with a number of new academic and professional recruits, and in that way has strengthened and stabilised it. If the network can deliver the government's objective which is to detain suspected DSPD people, and thereby reduce the public perceptions of risk, then it can continue to expect a good flow of resources. Public concerns about risk, however, are volatile and distorted, as we have noted, and may run well ahead of the capability for the forensic network to deliver demonstrable security.

The relations between the networks involved in this area are less certain. For example, the disquiet that clinical psychologists feel about becoming involved in the diagnosis or assessment of potential DSPD people has not prevented a number of their members from being prepared to use the government's need for their services as a bargaining position through which they can enhance their pay and status – a perennial concern for the clinical psychology network.

Turning to the comparison of ANT and PN, what light does this case study throw on these rather different analytical traditions? The intellectual origins of ANT and PN are remarkably similar, although entirely unrelated. Both arose out of dissatisfaction with a well-established prior theoretical model which had reached its limits and for which a new departure was timely. For ANT, this was the twin problem of how to identify the social interests that were felt to drive scientific work, and the limits of fundamental social constructivism. For PN, it was the evident gap between the traditional model of British government that focused on Whitehall, and the reality of local and regional government experience revealed in empirical case studies. Furthermore, it was the actual disintegration of that model in reality under the twin impacts of the Thatcher government and growth of the European Union. In Kuhn's (1970) terms there was such an accumulation of anomalies within the prior paradigms that the time was ripe for a fundamental paradigm shift. A similar story can be seen in the emergence of American structural functionalism and exchange theories out of the failure of Pareto's scheme for developing a scientific sociology (Mulkay 1971).

Both ANT and PN rose to prominence in their original form in the early 1980s, and key statements of their mature formulations appeared in the same year (Law 1992, Marsh and Rhodes 1992). Since then they have both stimulated a steady and growing set of case studies in their own traditions, but also a growing critical antithesis, in the time-honoured manner. For both, this has been reflexively acknowledged by the key protagonists as legitimate under the impact of post-modernist intellectual currents (Law and Hassard 1999, Rhodes 1997), yet there is little evidence yet of the accumulation of anomalies that might presage a further paradigm shift – indeed it may be that the post-modern celebration of knowledge as relativist means the end not only of the grand narrative, but of the 'grand paradigm', too.

Both approaches recognise explicitly that the human actors involved are limited by material and systems elements that at least act as constraints and may act in their own right. Both approaches understand that there is a complex interweaving of networks as structures and networks as action, and that over time action gives rise to or shapes the structures within which further rounds of action will take place. Both approaches are interested in the way in which power is exercised or achieved within the networks. The two theoretical traditions, which undoubtedly they are (with a recognisable pattern of innovative development, application, extension, defence, and revision), share some common antecedents. They both acknowledge their resonance with Giddens's structuration theory. They both cite Granovetter's (1973) pathbreaking work on network ties and the embeddedness of social relations.

There are, however, differences. Law (Hetherington and Law 2000, Law and Hassard 1999) acknowledges that ANT has not ventured much beyond science and technology studies: a little into medical practice, organisations and economic networks – but as yet ANT has not been applied to political networks and the achievements of formal or substantive power. PN, on the other hand, is almost entirely confined to the substantive political system, perhaps not surprisingly since its principal authors are all in political science. PN has not been applied to the wider world of organisations, science and professional work, markets and so on. ANT claims, or at least some of its proponents have claimed, it to be a developed social theory, drawing on and elaborating insights from such theorists as Foucault and Bourdieu (it was after all born in Paris, too). PN does not – it is only an 'organising perspective'.

A particular contrast between the two approaches concerns the nature of power and the political process. Despite its origins in the criticism of conventional political science, and the recent claims by some of its adherents to embrace a sociological approach to politics (Marsh and Smith 2001), the PN approach makes the assumption that power and its expression are externalised as a given in the political system. Indeed, its adherents have always stopped short of claiming that it is a theory, and reserved for it the more modest claim that it is merely an 'organising perspective' – such modesty providing the basis for a sustained attack by methodological individualists (Dowding 1995, 2001). From this point of view the analysis of DSPD is a culturally informed, but conventional, identification of 'who rules'. ANT on the other hand has made much larger claims, presenting itself as an alternative social theory that offers a basis for resolving some of the major difficulties of Western social theory, particularly the tension between action-oriented and structural accounts. From this perspective, power is brought within the analysis as something to be analysed and explained as a social accomplishment, and as a property generated in the course of social and technical interaction. The latter view offers an analysis that can incorporate the creation of power through the technical development of diagnostic and treatment methods as a solution to the popular fear of risk, in part created and in part resolved by government-sponsored innovation.

There have been strong criticisms mounted. ANT has been castigated for its managerialist focus on achievement – it has, rather like publication bias in the reporting of medical research, tended to go for success stories rather than those of failure. Studies of the marginal and the weak have been thin on the ground, as feminist theorists have in particular noted (Hetherington and Law 2000). A related weakness is that it has offered studies in which ambiguity and uncertainty have been overcome, so that the final result of the network has been the elimination of conflict or alternative voices and viewpoints. PN in turn has been excoriated for its inability really to explain how and why individuals act, and for its naïvety about the space for negotiation in political networks, when the larger structures set the agenda well away from the network in view. However, if the amount and intensity of these reactions, often of an impossibly fundamentalist nature (Dowding 1995, 2001), is any guide to the power of the model itself, then this may suggest that it is indeed providing a useful and effective organising perspective.

Does this case study in any way help us to develop, refine or reject these two analytical stances? Certainly they have been helpful in highlighting and making sense of the DSPD story. But there is little in the case study as understood to date that would repudiate or provide anomalies for the two approaches – although the subsequent unfolding of this story over the next few years may do so.

Acknowledgements

I would like to acknowledge the critical responses that have helped me to shape this paper: Steffan Davis, Ian Forbes, Dave Harper, various members of the London Medsoc meeting at which it was first outlined in October 2001, and the anonymous reviewers.

References

Blackburn, R. (2000) Classification and assessment of personality disorders in mentally disordered offenders: a psychological perspective, *Criminal Behaviour and Mental Health* 10, s8–s33.
Butler, R.A.B. (1975) *Report of Committee on Mentally Disordered Offenders*, Cmnd 6244. London: HMSO.
Callon, M. (1986) Some elements of a sociology of translation: domestication of the scallops and the fishermen of St Brieuc Bay. In Law, J. (ed) *Power, Action and Belief: a New Sociology of Knowledge?* London: Routledge and Kegan Paul.
Cleckley, H. (1941/1976) *The Mask of Sanity*, 1st/5th Edition. St. Louis: C.V. Mosby Co.
Cooke, A., Harper, D. and Kinderman, P. (2002) Government proposals for reform of mental health legislation: implications for psychologists, *Forensic Update*, 68, 6–16.
Crawford, M.J., Hopkins, W., Thomas, P., Moncrieff, J., Bindman, J. and Gray, J.A. (2001) Most psychiatrists oppose plans for new mental health act, *British Medical Journal*, 322, 72–90.
Dear, M.J. and Taylor, S.M. (1982) *Not on our Street.* London: Pion Limited.
Department of Health/Home Office (DoH/HO) (1992) *Review of Health and Social Services for Mentally Disordered Offenders and Others Requiring Similar Services*, (Reed Report), Cmd 2088, London: HMSO.
Dingwall, R. (1999) Risk Society: the cult of theory and the millennium, *Social Policy and Administration*, 33, 474–91.
Dolan, B. and Coid, J. (1993) *Psychopaths and Antisocial Personality Disorders, Treatment and Research Issues.* London: Gaskell.
Dowding, K. (1995) Model or metaphor? A critical review of the policy network approach, *Political Studies*, 45, 136–58.
Dowding, K. (2001) There must be end to confusion: policy networks, intellectual fatigue, and the need for political science methods courses in British universities, *Political Studies*, 49, 89–105.
Furedi, F. (1997) *Culture of Fear: Risk-taking and the Morality of Low Expectation.* London: Cassell.
Gralnick, A. (1969) *The Psychiatric Hospital as a Therapeutic Instrument.* New York: Brunner/Mazel.

Granovetter, M. (1973) The strength of weak ties, *American Journal of Sociology*, 78, 1360–80.

Haddock, A.W., Snowden, P.R., Dolan, M., Parker, J. and Rees, H. (2001) Managing dangerous people with severe personality disorder: a survey of forensic psychiatrists' opinions, *Psychiatric Bulletin*, 25, 293–96.

Hale, C. (1996) Fear of crime, *International Review of Victimology*, 4, 79–150.

Hare, R. (1991) *The Hare Psychopathy Checklist – Revised*. Toronto: Multi Health Systems.

Heclo, H. and Wildavsky, A. (1974) *The Private Government of Public Money*. London: Macmillan.

Hetherington, K. and Law, J. (2000) After networks, *Society and Space*, 18, 127–32.

Home Office/Department of Health (HO/DoH) (1999) *Managing Dangerous People with Severe Personality Disorder*. London: Department of Health.

Kuhn, T. (1970) *The Structure of Scientific Revolutions*. Chicago: Chicago University Press.

Latour, B. and Woolgar, S. (1979) *Laboratory Life, the Social Construction of Scientific Facts*, London: Sage.

Law, J. (1987) Technology and heterogeneous engineering: the case of Portuguese expansion. In Bijker, W.E., Hughes, T.P. and Pinch, T.J. (eds) *The Social Construction of Technological Systems, New Directions in the Sociology and History of Technology*. London: MIT Press.

Law, J. (1992) Notes on the theory of the actor-network: ordering, strategy, and heterogeneity, *Systems Practice*, 5, 379–93.

Law, J. and Hassard, J. (eds) *Actor Network Theory and After*. Oxford: Blackwell Publishers.

Lees, J., Manning, N. and Rawlings, B. (1999) *Therapeutic Community Effectiveness. A Systematic International Review of Therapeutic Community Treatment for People with Personality Disorders and Mentally Disordered Offenders*, CRD Report 17. University of York: Centre for Reviews and Dissemination.

Manning, N. (1989) *The Therapeutic Community Movement: Charisma and Routinization*, London: Routledge.

Manning, N. (2000) Psychiatric diagnosis under conditions of uncertainty: personality disorder, science and professional legitimacy, *Sociology of Health and Illness*, 22, 621–39.

Marsh, D. and Rhodes, R.A.W. (1992) *Policy Networks in British Government*. Oxford: Oxford University Press.

Marsh, D. and Smith, M.J. (2001) There is more than one way to do political science: on different ways to study policy networks, *Political Studies*, 49, 528–41.

Meux, C. (2000) Editorial: exploring the assessment of personality disorder, *Criminal Behaviour and Mental Health*, 10, s1–s7.

Moore, E. and Hogue, T. (2000) Assessment of personality disorder for individuals with offending history, *Criminal Behaviour and Mental Health*, 10, s34–s49.

Mulkay, M. (1971) *Functionalism, Exchange and Theoretical Strategy*, London: Routledge and Kegan Paul.

Norton, K. and Hinshelwood, R. (1996) Severe personality disorder. Treatment issues and selection for in-patient psychotherapy, *British Journal of Psychiatry*, 168, 723–31.

Osborne, D. and Gaebler, T. (1992) *Reinventing Government*. Reading, MA: Addison-Wesley.

Perry, J.C. (1992) Problems and considerations in the valid assessment of personality disorders, *American Journal of Psychiatry*, 149, 1643–45.

Rhodes, R.A.W. (1997) *Understanding Governance, Policy Networks, Governance, Reflexivity and Accountability*. Buckingham: Open University Press.

Richardson, J.J. and Jordan, G. (1979) *Governing Under Pressure: the Policy Process in a Post-Parliamentary Democracy*. Oxford: Martin Robertson.

Sedgwick, J. (2001) *DSPD Programme, Progress Report* (November). London: Department of Health, Home Office, Prison Service.

Social Survey Division, ONS (1998) *Psychiatric Morbidity amongst Prisoners in England and Wales*. London: The Stationery Office.

Taylor, P.J. and Gunn, J. (1999) Homicides by people with mental illness: myth and reality, *British Journal of Psychiatry*, 174, 9–14.

Tyrer, P. (2000) Improving the assessment of personality disorders, *Criminal Behaviour and Mental Health*, 10, s51–s65.

White Paper, (2000) *Reforming the Mental Health Act*, cmnd 5016-I.

Whiteley, J.S. (1980) The Henderson Hospital, a community study, *International Journal of Therapeutic Communities*, 1, 38–58.

Chapter 8

Temporarily insane: pathologising cultural difference in American criminal courts

Sita Reddy

Introduction

Writing about 'other' cultures and criminal law acquires poignant significance in the aftermath of the September 11 tragedy. At a time when cultural difference marks Arab-American and Asian-American immigrants as actual or potential targets of 'ethnically motivated' violence, it may be less urgent but nonetheless important to describe the reverse process in American criminal courts: those instances when cultural difference is used by immigrant *defendants* to diminish responsibility for their crimes. This chapter focuses on what is known as the 'culture defence strategy': the argument, most frequently invoked in criminal proceedings, that the defendant's cultural background should excuse crime, mitigate responsibility, or substantially reduce the penalty because of a lack of requisite criminal intent.

Over the last fifteen years, American criminal courts have heard a string of diverse cases that relied on the culture defence strategy: there have been Laotians who claim they were engaged in traditional bride capture (*zij po niam*) but have been charged with rape (*People v. Moua* 1985b); a Japanese woman whose practice of parent-child suicide (*oyaku-shinju*) was charged with murder (*People v. Kimura* 1985); an Eritrean who claimed he shot a woman to defend himself against her witchcraft (Oliver 1988); and Chinese and Hmong men whose murder of their adulterous wives was excused as a culturally legitimate response (*People v. Chen* 1989, *People v. Moua* 1985b).

While these are not the first attempts to bring culture into the civil (Winkelman 1996) or the criminal (*People v. Poddar* 1972) courtroom, it is only in the last fifteen years that culture defence has emerged as a methodically formulated argument and one of the primary defence strategies considered by recent Asian immigrants in certain types of cases such as honour killings, bride capture, sexual assault, and spousal murder because of adultery (Winkelman 1996; Magnarella 1991). If in the past, US courts repeatedly rejected cultural background as defence for native-born minorities (*People v. Rhines* 1982, *People v. Klein* 1922), they have been far more tolerant of culture defence for foreign-born 'aliens' with markedly different cultural practices from those in America (Magnarella 1991).

In this chapter I argue that the rise of culture defence rests on a paradox. As criminal courts increasingly allow cultural evidence, the success of this strategy relies on a tendency to reduce alien cultural practices to individual disorders. Thus culture – which has to do with *group* identity and webs of social meaning – gets distorted in the courts to pathology which resides essentially in individuals. In many of these cases, cultural differences are converted into psychological aberrations or emotional conditions, or in some cases 'instinctual regressions'. In the process culture itself gets portrayed in medicalised rather than moralistic terms, as something that new immigrants, in particular, 'suffer from' or 'have to recover from' as they strive to assimilate. If, as Adele Clarke (1998) states, 'late capitalism has fallen in love with cultural difference' (1998: 6), American criminal courts encourage a view of cultural difference as pathology.

By focusing on this 'medicalisation of culture', this chapter departs from previous studies of culture defence in two ways. First, while most analyses – legal and anthropological – tend to view this new legal strategy as an index of cultural conflicts in multicultural arenas, I argue that it reflects the more widespread cultural ethic that Philip Rieff (1966) termed 'the triumph of the therapeutic'. Multiculturalism alone explains neither the initial emergence of culture defence in the courts nor the medicalisation that lies at the heart of this strategy in practice, both of which in fact predate the multicultural debates of the 1990s over individualised respect for all cultures in the law[1]. Moreover, while recently immigrated foreign-born Asian defendants have been the most successful users of this strategy, they are by no means the only ones eligible to use culture defence in the courts. Contrary to popular conception, the culture defence is open to anyone who can invoke the 'culture contrast argument' (Torry 1999: 131), a list that includes Native Americans, African Americans, and 'bonafide ethnic groups' (Renteln 1993: 497) but excludes other subcultural groups, such as gangs, for whom a class-based 'rotten social background defense' is claimed the more suitable (1993: 497).

Instead of multiculturalism, I analyse the culture defence strategy as an example of how another dominant code of moral and cultural understanding – the therapeutic ethic – takes on concrete institutionalised form within the criminal justice system. If medicalisation can be defined as the process by which lifestyles, conditions and life events come increasingly under the medical gaze (Foucault 1973) and medical professional authority (Conrad and Schneider 1994) – what Fox (1977) terms the 'annexation of not-illness into illness' – the therapeutic ethos describes a more widespread cultural impulse that encompasses medicalisation and influences social institutions far beyond those connected with the medical world[2]. In his summary drawn from the sociological literature on the therapeutic perspective (Kittrie 1971, Gross 1978, Sykes 1992, Lasch 1978, Bellah et al. 1985), Nolan (1998) characterises the therapeutic ethic through the following core defining features: (1) a pronounced cultural preoccupation with the individual self; (2) a concern with the place of emotions in making sense of the social world; (3) the emergence of a new class of therapeutic experts to guide the emotion-laden self through modern social life; (4) the 'medical' reinterpretation of a growing number of behaviours through the disease model or pathological definitions of addiction and disorder; and (5) the cultural emphasis on the language of victimhood.

As a significant cultural sensibility, the therapeutic ethic has been shown to have a significant impact on a number of society's institutional structures and realms of the American state (Kittrie 1971) including education (Kramer 1991), the military (Herman 1995) and civil law (Nolan 1998). Following recent work on therapeutic justice and criminal adjudication (Nolan and Westervelt 2000), this chapter examines culture defence as the most recent in a line of criminal defence strategies that rely heavily on the therapeutic ethic. Culture defence can thus be seen not only against changes within criminal law, such as the general rise in legal excuses (Winkelman 1996, Horowitz 1986), but also as an instance of how other cultures and their crimes are 'therapeutised' in the legal domain. As a legal strategy that combines cultural difference and criminal culpability with illness exemptions, it opens up new intersections for sociological literatures on criminology and medical sociology. The rise of culture defence complicates simple linear 'medicalisation of deviance' trajectories from 'sin to crime to sickness' (Conrad and Schneider 1994) – in this case the medicalisation of cultural difference may go hand in hand with the criminalisation of 'culturally motivated' behaviour.

Second, this chapter also departs from standard criminological assumptions about the culture-criminal law nexus. By viewing the culture defence strategy as the legal last resort for multicultural conflicts, previous studies tend to focus on only one half of the dialectical relationship between culture and criminal law. This tendency to view culture defence as a legal solution for cultural conflicts or as an instrument for future cultural change, falls more in line with orthodox legal scholars who believe in the relative autonomy of the criminal law (Dressler 1987, Friedman 1994). Instead, I rely here on long-held sociological tenets, since Durkheim and Erikson, that criminal law reflects and creates societal cohesion and moral boundaries. Following Nolan and Westervelt (2000), this paper thus takes the counter view: that criminal law not only influences culture (in this case immigration patterns and assimilation) but is in turn fundamentally influenced by it. In this view, changes in criminal legal processes – such as the rise of the culture defence strategy – can be seen as indicative of larger cultural changes in moral understanding.

Through an empirical analysis of culture defence cases in the criminal courtroom, this chapter examines the extent to which this new legal strategy, as an increasingly popular argument used by immigrant defendants, relies for its success on the core features of the therapeutic ethic. I begin with a description of the medicalisation of cultural difference in practice; go on briefly to outline the development of the culture defence strategy; and finally examine how the five core features of the therapeutic ethic are embodied in this emerging legal defence.

Medicalising culture

Few immigrant culture defence cases have so intrigued law review analysts as the murder trials of Fumiko Kimura, Tou Moua, Dong Lu Chen, and

Moussa Hanoukai. In the earliest of these cases – *People v. Kimura* (1985) – Fumiko Kimura, a Japanese immigrant to America, was charged with murder and two counts of felony child endangerment when she tried to drown herself and her two children after learning of her husband's infidelity. Both children died and the mother pleaded that the practice of parent-child suicide (*oyaku-shinju*) was the proper response for a traditional Japanese woman under such circumstances. The court admitted this cultural evidence covertly and distorted the nature of this Japanese cultural practice by reducing it to a psychological problem for which counsellors and psychiatrists were the only proper solution (Woo 1989: 418). Based on the defence's plea of insanity, the court reduced her charge to voluntary manslaughter, deemed her temporarily insane at the time of the crime, and sent her for psychiatric assistance during a suspended sentence.

Later that same year, in *People v. Moua*, the bias remained psychological, even when cultural evidence was more overtly allowed. Tou Moua, a Hmong man, was charged with second-degree murder when he shot his wife to death in a 'blind rage' after she admitted to an extramarital affair. A culture defence was entered into the proceedings at the charging, evidentiary and sentencing stages of the trial. Expert anthropological testimony claimed that in Hmong prescripts a wife's adultery was punishable by death with the husband as executioner. The defence argued that Moua's actions were the result of the culturally legitimated rage felt by any Hmong man faced with infidelity, and that led to a state of 'temporary insanity' which diminished responsibility for Moua's criminal actions. The judge accepted this argument, reduced the charge to voluntary manslaughter and handed down a reduced sentence of eight years.

Almost four years later, in the widely publicised case of *People v. Chen* (1989), culture was the precipitating, if not causal, factor in a mental breakdown. Dong Lu Chen, a Chinese immigrant who bludgeoned his adulterous wife to death with a claw hammer was placed on probation after being charged with murder. The defence offered anthropological testimony that Chen's violent attack was *necessitated* by the shame felt by any 'reasonable' Chinese person in his place, and occurred in the absence of a cultural support group that would normally have intervened to stop the full fury of his response. The judge accepted Chen's action as culturally compelled and stated, 'I was convinced that at the time he had become temporarily, totally deranged. He had no intent, he was just the product of his culture, it was something that made him crack more easily. It was the cracking factor' (Woo 1989: 422). Chen was found guilty of the reduced charge of manslaughter in the second degree and placed on probation for five years.

More recently, in the 1994 case of *People v. Hanoukai*, culture moved from being the cause to clearly becoming the 'problem'. In a murder trial of an Iranian Jew who killed his wife after years of 'psychological abuse' the defence attorney went so far as to argue, 'Why did he do it? He was in a dissociative state. But why wouldn't he fight back? Being a Persian Jew determined his personality. *Culture* is what he was suffering from. It was almost like an illness'.

If these four cases provide a historical narrative, it is the progressive medicalisation – even psychologisation – of culture in the criminal courts. Over time, they show how cultural difference is increasingly problematised so that it slides more easily into psychological disorder. 'Other' cultures are gradually made more accessible to American criminal courts because they are introduced as personal features, like mental state, or as individual pathologies, like addiction or dysfunction.

Taken together, the cases also tell a story about the common elements of a successful culture defence strategy, which can be broken down into the following five essential components:

1. The defence emphasises the cultural background and identity of the defendant rather than the immediate behaviour at the actual time of the crime (*actus rea*), and then distinguishes between 'American' and 'ethnic Asian' identities on the premise that non-American cultures should not be judged by American standards.
2. The defence seeks to establish a pattern of cultural compulsion faced not just by the defendant but by any 'reasonable' member of that community.
3. The defence presents expert testimony either by anthropologists – on 'normal' cultural behaviour – or transcultural psychiatrists – on the psychological impact of the defendant's cultural background on her state of mind (*mens rea*).
4. Since cultural defence usually turns on psychological compulsion (Torry 2000), the defendant is often diagnosed as suffering from some syndrome or disorder directly resulting from this cultural pressure. This stage often involves collapsing the particular psychological history of the defendant into the category 'normal' ethnic Asian.
5. The defence actively shifts blame for an unlawful act from the defendant to her/his cultural community, and reconstructs the defendant's identity from deviant rule breaker to subcultural rule adherent. Thus, immigrant defendants who blame culture for their crimes must do so as its 'sick' or passive 'victims', if their charges are to be excused or their sentences reduced.

As I will attempt to show through a systematic empirical analysis of cases, these components of the culture defence strategy map almost perfectly onto the core features of the therapeutic ethic. In multicultural legal arenas, the therapeutic ethic may *become* the culture defence for foreign-born immigrant defendants in certain cases. Since there is little research on the development of this legal strategy with empirical data, such an examination will also contribute to the small critical anthropological literature that has begun to focus on actual cases in the culture defence archive (Rosen 1977, Torry 1999, 2000, Magnarella 1991, Winkelman 1996). This chapter will be among the early sociological analyses of the archive to examine legal briefs and their coverage in law reviews and the popular press. In the next section, I turn to a brief description of the culture defence strategy in practice before analysing the influence of the therapeutic ethic on this new form of jurisprudential defence.

Culture defence strategy: development and history

Culture defence does not in itself constitute a recognisable formal defence in any American jurisdiction or statute. In practice, however, a growing number of attorneys and judges have used their discretion to introduce cultural evidence at all stages of criminal trials (Volpp 1994). Courts have permitted the incorporation of cultural factors into existing, legally recognised defences, especially that category of defences known as 'excuses' – which regard the act itself as wrongful but forgive the actor because she lacks the requisite culpability (Winkelman 1996). Thus, defence attorneys have introduced culture defence covertly through *de jure* excuses such as provocation (*People v. King Moua*), mistake of fact (*People v. Moua*), diminished responsibility (*People v. Chen*) or even insanity (*People v. Kimura*). If the growing number of cases using the culture defence strategy since the 1980s is any indication, this approach is fast becoming a new method of argument used by defence attorneys to reduce charges and sentences faced by immigrant defendants[3].

Although authorities disagree on the precise applicability of culture defence strategy in legal excuses (Winkelman 1996, Coleman 1996), most agree that in practice it is largely in establishing the *mens rea* (state of mind) required for criminal guilt. Cultural evidence is used primarily to make the defendant's state of mind more comprehensible, and the argument tends to rest on culturally motivated 'psychological compulsion' (Torry 2000) – a process that converts cultural difference into psychological and emotional disturbance that reduces culpability for the crime, or turns it into 'irresistible impulses' that dictate particular behaviours (Winkelman 1996). This emphasis on the personal state of mind in culture defence cases may be related to the general rise of excuses in criminal law that speak to the inner state of the person – for instance, the battered wife defence, the victimisation defence, the post-traumatic stress defence – compared to 'justifications' that focus on the blameworthiness of the criminal act (Horowitz 1986).

It is worth noting, however, that this emphasis on personal state of mind in culture defence has been criticised both by legal scholars (Coleman 1996), and by commentators on multicultural jurisprudence (Woo 1989). Coleman has argued that instead of an appropriate use of cultural evidence to show provocation or mistake of fact, culture defence tends to be used *inappropriately* to reduce the defendant's specific *intent* that is required for a murder charge through the *mens rea* requirement (Coleman 1996). In a different argument, Woo (1989) argues that the emphasis on personal state of mind in culture defence may reduce the penalty for the criminal act but ends up negating the very meaning of cultural practices such as *oyaku-shinju* – in other words, the psychiatric orientation simply becomes a 'western cultural defense' (1989: 418).

To examine this trend in the culture defence archive, I relied on a number of data sources. The primary source was trial court decisions that form the core of culture defence jurisprudence supplemented, where possible, with the appellate decisions that make 'state law' (Nolan 1998). Since culture defence has only rarely appeared at the appellate level (Volpp 1994), the methodological focus of the study was a *textual* analysis of trial opinions rather than a doctrinal analysis of precedential appellate cases. Because culture defence jurisprudence is a sprawling, disjointed body of literature (Torry 2000), secondary source material, such as law review articles and legal memoranda, were also used to find applicable cases or to understand their legal arguments. Finally, I relied on popular print media articles both to gauge the extent of public reaction to selected cases, as well as to highlight popular conceptions of particular immigrant trials.

When examining court cases, I searched for cases in which the defence successfully incorporated the five essential components of a culture defence strategy: namely, an emphasis on cultural background of the defendant; evidence of a pattern of cultural compulsion for a reasonable member of that community; anthropological expert testimony about the psychological impact of this cultural background on the defendant; the 'medical' definition of a cultural defendant's specific mental problems that could be collapsed into the normal person from that culture; and the reconstruction of the defendant as a cultural victim. In this paper I present detailed analysis of eleven trial court opinions, and three appellate decisions, all of which successfully used the culture defence. These cases were then coded for the following: the cultural identity of the defendant and victim, the legal arguments used by both sides, the final case disposition, the source of that cultural pressure and the excuse that was claimed.

In trial court cases, analysis reveals that the culture defence strategy was first used in two types of representative cases – what Volpp (1994) has called the 'two factual patterns' in culture defence cases involving Asian-Americans. The first type resembled that of Tou Moua – cases involving family honour and marital infidelity in which immigrant men sought a cultural defence for murder or violence, arguing that traditional values explained their actions and excused them from full responsibility. Many of these cases included 'traditional' cultural practices, such as Hmong bride capture (*zij po niam*) that led to rape and kidnapping charges. In *Moua*, the defence focused on the defendant's Hmong cultural background rather than on the events immediately surrounding the act in question, and provided evidence that any reasonable Hmong person would experience the blind rage induced by spousal infidelity. Expert anthropological testimony was offered to show

how this cultural predisposition led to a diagnosable 'dissociative state' that preceded the actions. And finally, throughout the trial, the defence shifted the blame from Moua himself to Hmong culture, arguing that the defendant was no deviant but an 'exceptionally good Hmong person'. Thus, all five components of the culture defence strategy were used to explain why the defendant's cultural background should explain and justify his present actions.

The second type of cultural defence case resembled that of Fumiko Kimura – cases in which *female* defendants sought to admit cultural factors to explain mental states when attempting to commit parent-child suicides or honour suicides (Volpp 1994). Seeking the cultural defence for these practices involved the same five components of the therapeutic ethic, but with slightly different emphases. In these cases, the defence reduced blame and criminal culpability by proving cultural 'dictation' or cultural coercion because of internalised norms. However, if anger and rage were the precipitating emotions in the first type of case, shame and humiliation predominated in the second. In Kimura's case, an appeal to universal 'maternal' or 'wifely' motives complicated the relativistic argument outlining a Japanese woman's response. Expert testimony, moreover, concentrated on culturally relevant psychological pressure that made these traditional practices seem like reasonable solutions. In the process, however, the courts reduced these practices to psychological problems, a process that ultimately deprived them of meaning, and reframed the defendant as an immigrant 'victim' – a passive and naïve product of a static, monolithic culture, further isolated by language and custom from the cultural assimilation that would have acted as internal and external deterrent to the crime.

The first state appellate acceptance of the culture defence strategy as a new legal argument was in 1986 in *People v. Aphaylath*. Here the defence had attempted to introduce cultural evidence in a murder trial to support a claim of diminished responsibility. At trial, several elements of the culture defence strategy, including expert testimony, were rejected as irrelevant. On appeal, the New York Appeals court ruled that the trial court had erred in excluding cultural evidence, and reversed and remanded the trial court's findings indicating that the *entire* culture defence strategy should be permitted. In a second successful appellate case in 1989 – *People v. Wu* – a Chinese woman in California was accused of filicide when she had attempted parent-child suicide. The appellate court overturned a trial court ruling rejecting cultural evidence as irrelevant to her mental state, and permitted Wu the use of experts to fathom her perspective on what had happened (Volpp 1994). Wu relied on a battery of transcultural psychologists who opened up lines of cross-communication by which the court could see itself in her position and clarify her 'Chinese values' and 'maternal' motives. She was given a reduced charge of manslaughter and a mitigated sentence (Torry 2000).

Although appellate courts in the remaining states have not had to rule on the issue, and legislative statutes show no full-fledged institutionalisation of the strategy, they indicate some initial acceptance of the *premise* behind culture defence. At least a few states have passed statutes that cultural factors may affect the ability of a person to form the intent necessary for criminal culpability or to control his actions in an acceptable fashion (US Court of Appeals, D.C. Circuit, 1967: 453). Thus despite the fact that some legal opinion has repeatedly rejected such a defence (Magnarella 1991), culture defence strategy is nevertheless emerging as part of the legal landscape.

Moreover, the applicability of cultural factors in formulating a defence varies not only by offence and by jurisdiction, but also by criminal codes (Dressler 1987). In the Model Penal Code, a legal compendium of recodified criminal law with broad applicability, there is no explicit reference to culture defence, but its formulations are specific enough to include cultural evidence on the actor's state of mind in order to define whether or not a crime occurred, or in differentiating between the various degrees of a crime (Sheybani 1987). The fact that the Model Penal Code has been adopted in whole or part by thirteen states (Winkelman 1996), indicates some degree of acceptance in criminal law of the culture defence strategy.

Thus, since the mid-1980s and through the 1990s, the culture defence strategy has developed into an increasingly popular legal argument in practice when linked with other existing defences. This is not to say that all immigrant defendants accused of murder, infanticide and rape use this strategy, but that many of them can now avail themselves of a powerful new argument in the courtroom that was unavailable to them fifteen years ago.

Illness and the culture defence archive

While courts commonly hear cultural evidence in trials where plaintiffs seek to augment cultural group rights that are under dispute, culture defence cases are unique in their focus on the cultural identity of the *defendant*, and on diminishing individual *responsibility* for the criminal act (Torry 1999). As Torry (2000) argues, the culture defence archive provides an unparalleled research resource within which to examine intersections between changing notions of culture and legal responsibility in multicultural arenas.

This focus on individual responsibility becomes particularly relevant in criminal defence because of the relationship between the 'disease' model of behaviour and criminal culpability. While the legal system dictates that individuals are held responsible for behaviour that is freely chosen, *i.e.* a result of free will (Dressler 1987), sickness and disease are seen as states over which people have no control. Actions resulting from illness are attributed to the power of the illness, as a result of which the individual is not held accountable for behaviours beyond her/his control (Torry 2000). Interpreting behaviour from within the disease model can thus directly affect an individual's level of criminal accountability, as seen by its successful use within the context of many criminal defence strategies. As with the 'guilty but mentally ill' verdicts that combine notions of criminality with exemptions because of illness, culture defence strategy is a legal expression of the general ambivalence in American society surrounding rights and responsibility, exemptions and control.

For the most part, this ambivalence is ignored in legal scholarship on the culture defence archive, which turns on the *normative* debate over the standardisation of criminal law versus the elaboration of different defences based on different cultural backgrounds. Thus, proponents for a formalised culture defence, who find support in liberal notions of individualised justice for criminal defendants on a flexible case-sensitive basis (Note 1986), are pitted against critics who argue that a formalised culture defence conflicts with an American jurisprudential tradition that favours equal treatment and procedural consistency (Sams 1986). Since a disproportionate number of cases involve physical violence of male defendants against typically female and child victims, another critique of culture defence is that it justifies violence against women and results in a 'liberal's dilemma' (Coleman 1996) between multiculturalism and feminism. In this argument, progressive ideals of individualised justice for defendants are pitted against personal security interests of the immigrant victims of their crimes, often violent crimes driven by patriarchal values of their cultures of origin[4].

But this broadly political question of formal standardisation is not the only one posed by the culture defence archive. A more important issue deals with the operationalisation of culture in criminal courts. Recent law review studies have begun to interrogate what culture really means in criminal adjudication by exposing flawed conceptions of culture inherent in culture defence, such as the ethnocentric notion that recent immigrants have a culture while US law does not (Volpp 1994), or the cultural determinism that one's behaviour is completely defined by one's identity (Woo 1989). The analytic focus in these studies, however, has been on *gender* as the missing component in the culture defence archive. Here, I identify *illness* as an equally powerful theme in the practice of culture defence. Among other questions, I ask whether the therapeutic lens forces a view of culture as a personal feature, like mental state, or one that can be easily converted into an aspect of psychodynamics? Does the *pathologisation* of cultural difference commit us to particular views of cultures – as monoliths – or to fictional views that permit certain jurisprudential results? The next section attempts to answer these questions through an empirical analysis of cases in the courtroom.

Therapeutic ethic as culture defence

Following analyses of the impact of therapeutic ethic on criminal justice (Nolan and Westervelt 2000), I suggest that the therapeutic ethic can be added to cultural pluralism as a powerful influence on the emergence of this new legal defence strategy. Using actual legal cases as points of illustration, I show here how the culture defence strategy embodies to a greater or lesser extent each of the five features defined previously as the core features of the therapeutic ethic.

The therapeutic self

First, as mentioned earlier, the therapeutic ethic takes the self as the centre of moral authority and as ultimate arbiter of values and behaviour. But compared with the rugged individualist isolated self of the previous century, in which externally-derived standards were used to judge action (Bellah *et al.* 1985), the contemporary therapeutic self is seen as more vulnerable, inward-looking and outwardly expressive (Nolan and Westervelt 2000). The culture defence strategy takes this therapeutic self as its primary reference point. As expressed in court, the goal of this strategy is to counter labels placed on the defendant from the outside, such as offender or murderer, and instead tell the defendant's story from her/his subjective, culturally-relative perspective. The hope is that the defendant's actions will be found reasonable, or at least excusable, when understood and judged from her/his point of view, rather than from some universalistic standard insensitive to cultural nuance.

At the centre of this subjectification is an attempt to shift the emphasis from the defendant's criminal acts to her/his *cultural identity*, and to distinguish between Asian and American identities. Thus, in *People v. Moua*, for example, the defence claimed that the key to understanding Moua's action lay in understanding his 'Hmong mindset' within which spousal infidelity was particularly humiliating and punishable by murder. Similarly, in *People v. Kimura*, the defence presented evidence that Japanese standards needed to be applied because it was 'the roots of Kimura's Japanese culture, not her American personality, that directed her to act'.

Interestingly, this strategy seems to be successful in the courts when cultural background is introduced not as a minority view, but as a personal feature or subjective state that is both private and internal. In practice, this is usually argued through the legal excuse of diminished capacity where the focus is primarily on the defendant's state of mind (*mens rea*). Thus, defence lawyers in *People v. Chen* argued that cultural pressures had provoked Chen into a mental state of diminished capacity, rendering him incapable of forming the requisite intent for premeditated murder. While explaining that a ruling based solely on cultural background would be wrong, the judge claimed that Chen's unique culture defence, based on his Chinese identity, was similar to other mitigating circumstances such as behavioural problems caused by pre-menstrual syndrome or post-traumatic stress suffered by Vietnam veterans.

When cultural evidence was not permitted, as in *People v. Kimura*, the defence relied on the insanity excuse to prove that the defendant was mentally incapable of the premeditated murder of her children. But, in doing so, the court also nullifed the cultural reality of *oyaku-shinju* (parent child suicide) – which Kimura claimed to have practised – by reducing it entirely to psychological pathology. Summarising Kimura's situation, the defence claimed 'Culture caused Kimura's actions, but they are only cultural in direction. In origin they are psychological. Perhaps she even *regressed back* (emphasis mine) to earlier instincts learned in Japan that forced her to see her children as extensions of herself' (Sherman 1986). The prosecutor concurred, stating that the important thing was to take into account, 'Mrs. Kimura's Japanese cultural background in considering her *mental illness* at the time of the crime' (Sherman 1985).

The emotivist ethic

Closely related to the centrality of the self is the second core feature of the therapeutic ethic – the emphasis on the emotivist self or 'the ethic of emotivism' (Macintye 1984). Within the therapeutic culture, the dominant form of communication and self-understanding is the expression of feelings through the subjectivised understandings of truth and social life based on emotions rather than on reason or logic.

The culture defence strategy includes this element as one of its pivotal features. The defence reconstructs the defendant from offender to cultural victim by focusing on feelings of shame, rage, dishonour, and humiliation that are experienced in specific cultural scripts of displacement or immigration. As one defence attorney stated, the judge and the jury must understand 'the specific feelings of rage and shame that these Asian defendants are particularly prone to, given the provocations that they faced' (Sheybani 1987).

This step also involves the differentiation of 'average' Asian and American reactions to the precipitating events of a crime. Thus in the case of Dong Lu Chen, the defence claimed that the emotional response for an average Chinese man to his wife's adultery would be debilitating shame over his pariah status in the community, and the rage he would be expected to show in response. Whereas spousal adultery in the US 'was taken normally in the course of an event', it was considered the worst 'emotional stain' upon a Chinese man and indicated a loss of 'the most minimal standard of control' over his wife.

A very different emotional argument emerges, however, in cases where *female* cultural defendants were charged with filicide. Here alien cultural practices are not merely psychologised, but linked with universal maternal emotional motives that any reasonable traditional woman in any culture is thought to share. Thus, other legitimate excuses such as self-defence (for *e.g.*: battered wife defence) are often invoked in an attempt to straddle the difficult line between the culturally strange and the emotionally or psychologically familiar. In *People v. Kimura*, expert psychiatric testimony for the defence claimed that Kimura suffered from 'guilt, frustration, sense of failure, poor self-image, and stress disorders'. The motivating emotion was the traditional Japanese woman's shame and guilt over being a bad wife and mother once she learnt of her husband's adultery. Interestingly, the excessive maternal feelings attributed to Japanese culture were viewed as both emotionally 'regressive' and psychologically deviant – expert testimony focused on the 'psychological concept of introjection' which prevented Kimura from distinguishing her own life from those of her children.

In *People v. Wu*, the emphasis in the initial trial by both prosecution and defence was on whether Helen Wu was a 'traditional Chinese woman' with 'motherly feelings' towards the son she killed. On appeal, however, the defence offered new testimony that Helen Wu's mental and *emotional* state was intertwined with her cultural background. Unlike the Chen case, where the defendant's mental breakdown was seen as typical for an average Chinese man, the defence for Wu claimed that her criminal actions stemmed from the guilt and love of an average mother. As one of the expert psychiatrists argued, 'it is a mother's altruism, benevolence. Ultimately this is something all mothers will instinctively understand. In Helen Wu's mind it was better to do this than to leave him behind in what she thought a cruel world'. One of the most interesting aspects of this case was the use of transcultural psychiatric testimony on 'parent-child suicides by American mothers in 1920s Chicago'. Rather than creating distinctions between cultural identities, this involved collapsing differences between American and Chinese cultures in an attempt to clarify Wu's true maternal motives for the court (Volpp 1994). Thus, gender was clearly a complicating factor in what was considered reasonable from the point of view of traditional culture.

Expert testimony

A third element of the therapeutic ethic is the increasing importance of psychologists and psychiatrists both in American society and in the criminal courtroom. These professionals enjoy expert status as those most able to understand human actions in the complex modern world, and thus to offer expert testimony on culpability.

In culture defence cases, although expert testimony can be provided both by psychiatrists on the state of mind as well as by anthropologists on cultural background, the role of the former tends to outweigh the latter. Thus, even when cultural evidence is allowed in courts, psychological expert testimony offers evidence that cultural pressures produce particular psychological compulsions (*People v. Aphaylath*) or result in certain sorts of mental breakdown (*People v. Moua, People v. Chen*). When cultural evidence is not allowed, expert psychiatric testimony transforms cultural practices into psychological aberrations. In *Kimura*, for instance, the court not only relied on the expert testimony of nine psychiatrists – only two of whom were familiar with Japanese culture – but also suggested psychological counselling as the only solution for her temporary insanity.

The role of *anthropological* experts, on the other hand, has been less consistent in cultural defence cases. Anthropologists may contribute to pre-trial, guilt and penalty phases of trials but their involvement is most likely in cases of 'murder with special circumstances' where the Model Penal Code states that defendants may receive court funds for expert defence presentation (Winkelman 1996). As Rosen (1977) claims, anthropological testimony on the cultural *background* of defendants has often been denied in the courts, despite the fact that there had been early recognition by some courts of cultural evidence as relevant to criminal intent. For instance, in *People v. Poddar* (1972), the court refused anthropological testimony on the cultural background of an Indian 'ex-untouchable' charged with the murder of a woman who had insulted him. Similarly, in *Chase v. United States* (1972), the court refused anthropological testimony on the cultural relativism of insanity for a group of antiwar protestors who destroyed draft files on a defence of 'cultural insanity'.

More often, anthropological expert testimony has been used successfully not to establish cultural background per se, but how this may affect psychological states of mind (*People v. Moua, People v. Chen*). Because of this culture-psyche link, such testimony often ends up reifying a form of cultural determinism – cultures in these depictions emerge as monolithic, overly controlling, and unnecessarily static. Occasionally, it also results in causal links not only between culture and mental state, but in the reverse argument linking defendant's mental state back to her/his culture. In *People v. Chen*, for instance, the defence differentiated between Chinese and American identities by collapsing the defendant's particular mental history with that of a normal person from mainland China. This 'erroneous causal leap' is what needs to be avoided in deliberate uses of culture in the courtroom (Volpp 1994).

This emphasis on culturally compelled states of mind has seen the emerging role of yet another expert: the transcultural psychiatrist. An increasing number of recent culture defence cases have relied on these cross-cultural experts in court testimonies (*People v. Moua, People v. Hanoukai*). In their most successful appellate use – *People v. Wu* – transcultural psychiatrists testified that Helen Wu's cultural background explained her mental and emotional state. Unlike *Chen*, however, where anthropological experts focused first on 'the Chinese' in order to fit the defendant into that generalisation, the psychiatric experts in *Wu* focused their testimony first on the individual defendant, and then analysed how this behaviour fitted into conceptions of traditional culture. With their combined emphases on psyche and culture, the rise of the transcultural psychiatric experts may well be the clearest embodiment of the therapeutic ethos in courts.

Pathologising behaviour
The fourth characteristic feature of the therapeutic ethic is the growing American tendency to pathologise behaviours so that they fall within the medical model, usually in the form of identifiable diagnoses of syndromes or addictions. If medical doctors assume expertise over biological disorders and interpret behaviour within that framework, psychologists and psychiatrists assume expertise over psychological disorders and interpret behaviour within that framework. Not surprisingly then, their view of behaviour has also gained increasing influence both in society and in the courts.

This disease model of social behaviour is a central feature of the culture defence strategy, and expert testimony often takes the form of a diagnosis. According to the Model Penal Code, 'A person is not responsible for criminal conduct if at the time of such conduct as a result of mental disease or defect he lacks substantial capacity either to appreciate the criminality (wrongfulness) of his conduct or to conform his conduct to the requirements of the law' (Sec. 4.01). Thus experts can explain that culture defence rests on insanity, although critics claim that this strains the definition of mental illness to a point where it is unlikely to be accepted by the courts (Note 1986, Kadish 1987). In the only successful case so far to rely on legal insanity – *People v. Kimura* – the defence presented the prosecution with nine psychiatric reports, two by psychiatrists familiar with Japanese culture, to testify that Kimura was mentally disturbed. These experts presented testimony on how Japanese cultural beliefs made Kimura particularly vulnerable to the psychological pressures of her domestic life, and that this culturally-induced mental instability was evident prior to the criminal acts.

For the most part, however, culture defence tends to rely on diminished responsibility, in which defendants are diagnosed not as legally insane but as 'suffering from an abnormal mental condition at the time of the crime' (Sams 1986: 341). In these cases the defence attorney argues that, although the defendant is not legally insane, she should be found guilty of a lesser, included crime because her mental capacity at the time of the criminal act was diminished due to some condition, such as depression or anxiety. In *People v. Chen*, the defence sought to offer expert testimony that he was not insane but had suffered from a temporary derangement and dementia just prior to the criminal act. Similarly, in *People v. Hanoukai*, a psychologist testified that the Iranian defendant who murdered his wife had been the victim of 'psychological abuse', and was in an advanced 'dissociative state' preceding his violent actions.

In some cases, these defences are introduced covertly through the 'concept of irresistible impulse' (Winkelman 1996) which indicates the inability of the defendant to control conduct. Renteln (1993) calls this the 'volitional insanity defense' that can be illustrated in cases like *People v. Metallides*, a Greek immigrant who killed his best friend who had raped the defendant's daughter. The judge ruled that he was 'not guilty by reason of temporary insanity', based on the recognition of the cultural concept of honour, since '. . . a proportional response depends on the cultural background of the person making the assessment' (1993: 452).

Cultural victims
Finally, the fifth feature of the therapeutic ethic, the notion of victimisation, is central to the culture defence strategy. Each of the other elements – the focus on cultural background, emotions, the use of expert testimony to explain the cultural impact on the defendant's psyche, the pathologisation of behaviour – shifts the blame from the defendant to her/his culture, and establishes the status of the defendant as a cultural victim of displacement, compulsion and isolation. One of the underlying goals of the culture defence strategy is thus to reconstruct the defendant from offender in terms

of mainstream values, to victim in terms of immigrant cultural values. Thus, Fumiko Kimura's defence team stated that it was essential to establish and clarify for the court 'who was the real victim'. The defence, in its claims of 'her culture made her do it' blamed not only her Japanese traditions but also the social isolation that she faced as a Japanese immigrant in America.

In *People v. Chen*, anthropological testimony established Chen as a victim of American culture who was not responsible for his actions. The cultural compulsion from Chinese society with 'strong social control' combined with social isolation because of his lack of assimilation in the US made him doubly vulnerable to the news of his wife's adultery. Similarly, the defence in *People v. Hanoukai* presented evidence showing that the Iranian American defendant was a mild-mannered man driven to breaking point by an abusive wife. He was the 'true victim' of his Iranian culture of origin, which made his subjugation particularly hard to bear for a traditional man, and made divorce an unacceptable option.

By using the culture defence strategy, the defendant tells a story of cultural victimisation, a story that is sometimes shared by many immigrants engaged in cultural misunderstandings and translations with a dominant culture. Redefining the defendant as a cultural victim not only implies innocence but maintains that individuals are neither fully responsible for the causes or consequences of their criminal actions. It thus allows the defence a new argument to challenge the defendant's criminal culpability.

Concluding thoughts

As the preceding cases attempt to show, the culture defence strategy – when successful – incorporates core features of the therapeutic ethic, demonstrating the influence of this cultural perspective on one aspect of the criminal law. Given the increasing popularity of culture defence for certain types of immigrant cases, particularly at the appellate level (*People v. Aphaylath, People v. Wu*), and the medicalisation of culture that underlies this strategy in practice, this only foreshadows the increasing impact of the therapeutic ethic on criminal justice for the 'cultural' defendant.

Changes in criminal law are significant far beyond the courtroom, particularly when they introduce new ways in which illness mediates criminal responsibility. As sociologists have argued, criminal law both reflects and determines community standards regarding acceptable behaviour, and conditions under which individuals are held accountable for unacceptable behaviour. In multicultural jurisprudence, changing these conditions of responsibility – particularly for culturally different immigrants – has practical and symbolic importance both inside and outside the courtroom.

The *de facto* acceptance of the culture defence strategy by American courts adds 'cultural difference' to the list of conditions that have been used to excuse criminal behaviours. Defendants can mitigate responsibility by introducing cultural evidence and transforming it into a psychopathology to make it accessible to the courts. Much like excuses that centre on battered-woman's syndrome, post-traumatic stress disorders, or war-induced trauma, culture defence diminishes responsibility by appealing to a set of factors that can be medicalised into an identifiable disorder, psychological state, or most often, a temporary insanity.

But if these cases show that cultural difference is increasingly medicalised in the courtroom, they also indicate that criminal acts themselves are increasingly 'culturalised'. Viewed against the historical construction of criminality since the nineteenth century, this may simply indicate a new way of socialising crime between the two main poles of the criminal (*homo criminalis*) and society. As Foucault argued, the nineteenth century 'positivist' school of criminal anthropology was the first to take account of the 'social dangerousness' of individual offenders (Foucault 1978). If this school of thought replaced the classical typology of crimes with a typology of criminals, culture defence in contemporary America – with the incorporation of the *cultural* background of criminal offenders – might signal a shift toward a typology of cultures.

One consequence of such a typology of cultures in the criminal courtroom may be a 'hierarchy of sickness' at the procedural level. Culture defence is in fact not equally available to all immigrants, and the existing cases point to some of the prominent cultural stereotypes. Since a disproportionate number of these cases involve physical abuse of women by men, feminist critics have characterised culture defence as the use of anthropological expertise to legitimate abuse or reinscribe patriarchal traditions within the family (Sams 1986). Others have argued that the most frequent use of culture defence is for immigrant women accused of child abuse who avoid prosecution because the punishments were customary in their culture (Winkelman 1996). But if feminism can be aligned against multiculturalism as one axis in this hierarchy of cultures, so can Orientalism: particular cultures can in fact be seen as 'sicker' than others in the law, the greater their imagined cultural distance. Immigrants using the culture defence are disproportionately drawn from Asia or the Middle East, and their legal briefs reflect the nostalgia toward these cultures in the American imagination. As Magnarella (1991) has noted, defendants from Western Europe and Eastern Europe rarely enjoy the culture defence. Regardless of who uses the culture defence, this raises the question of whether it becomes a right for immigrant defendants that could be lost the longer they live in the US or that encourages a case by case determination in terms of degree of 'enculturation'. Ultimately, the real subtext in the culture defence archive may be how the metaphor of illness is expressed through the language of assimilation for new immigrants. In the end, guilt or innocence for cultural defendants in criminal courts may be unintended adjudicators not only of cultural identity but also of mental health in multicultural America.

Acknowledgements

I am grateful to Charles Bosk, Jacqueline Hart, Vijayendra Rao, Gayatri Reddy and two anonymous referees for valuable comments on this paper as it took shape.

Notes

1 The persistence of the multicultural lens in culture defence scholarship is particularly striking when compared to scholarship on 'race' in the criminal justice
   system. As an anonymous referee of this paper notes, Critical Race Theory has
   been applied to black people in the criminal justice system to provide a far-
   reaching structuralist critique of the criminal justice system that is focused not
   simply on multicultural diversity but on anti-racism (Crenshaw *et al.* 1995).
   Until a truly critical cultural studies interrogates the use of culture in criminal
   adjudication there may a point of difference that is worth noting in practice: while
   plaintiffs bring race-related difference as complaints that need to be redressed,
   cultural defendants assemble and highlight cultural difference in order to mitigate
   criminal responsibility. By contrast defendants relying on race as a mitigating
   factor are both rare and less successful in practice.
2 While the therapeutic ethos and the therapeutic ethic have often been used inter-
   changeably, I rely on the sociological meaning of an ethic to refer specifically to
   the concrete, motivated ways in which a widespread ethos can be institutionalised
   to broadly affect social and individual action.
3 The exception to this view is Torry (1999) who claims that culture defence in
   practice does not necessarily lean on *de jure* defences but can often go ahead in
   courts on their own steam.
4 For the counter view, see Volpp (1996) who opposes Coleman's views as 'backlash
   politics'.

References

Bellah, R., Madsen, R., Sullivan, W.M., Swidler, A. and Tipton, S.M. (1985) *Habits of the Heart: Individualism and Commitment in American Life*. Berkeley: University of California Press.

Chase v. United States (1972) United States Court of Appeals, Seventh Circuit, Federal Reporter, Second Series, 499: 113–15.

Clarke, A. (1985) Modernity, postmodernity and human reproductive processes c. 1890–1990. In Gray, H.C., Figuero-Sorrero, and Mentor, S. (eds). *The Cyborg Handbook*. New York: Roulledge.

Coleman, D.L. (1996) Individualizing justice through multiculturalism: the liberals' dilemma, *Columbia Law Review*, 96, 1093.

Conrad, P. and Schneider, J.W. (1994) *Deviance and Medicalisation: from Badness to Sickness*. Philadelphia: Temple University Press.

Crenshaw, K., Gotanda, N., Peller, G., Thomas, K. (eds) (1995) *Critical Race Theory – Key Writings that Formed the Movement*. New York: New Press.

Dressler, J. (1987) *Understanding Criminal Law*. Oakland, CA: Matthew Bender and Co.

Foucault, M. (1973) *Birth of the Clinic*. New York: Pantheon Books.

Foucault, M. (1978) About the concept of the dangerous individual in 19th century legal psychiatry, *International Journal of Law and Psychiatry*, 1, 1–18.

Fox, R.C. (1977) The medicalization and demedicalization of American society. In Knowles, J.H. (ed) *Doing Better and Feeling Worse*. New York: W.W.Norton and Company.

Friedman, L.H. (1994) *Total Justice*. New York: Russell Sage Foundation.

Gross, M. (1978) *The Psychological Society*. New York: Random House.

Herman, E. (1995) *The Romance of American Psychology: Political Culture in the Age of Experts*. Berkeley: University of California Press.

Horowitz, D.L. (1986) Justification and excuse in the program of the criminal law, *Law and Contemporary problems*, v. 49, 3, 109–26.

Kadish, S. (1987) Excusing crime. *California Law Review*, 75, 1, 257–89.

Kittrie, N.N. (1971) *The Right to be Different: Deviance and Enforced Therapy*. Baltimore: JHU Press.

Kramer, R. (1991) *Ed School Follies*. New York: The Free Press.

Lasch, C. (1978) *The Culture of Narcissism*. New York: W.W. Norton.

Macintyre, A. (1984) *After Virtue: a Study in Moral Theory*. Notre Dame: University of Notre Dame Press.

Magnarella, P.J. (1991) Justice in a culturally pluralistic society: the cultural defense on trial, *The Journal of Ethnic Studies*, 19, 3, 65–84.

Model Penal Code (1985) The American Law Institute. Philadelphia, PA.

Nolan, J.L., Jr. and Westervelt, S.D. (2000) Justifying justice: therapeutic law and the victimization defense strategy, *Sociological Forum*, 15, 4, 617–46.

Nolan, J.L. Jr. (1998) *The Therapeutic State: Justifying Government at Century's End*. New York: New York University Press.

Note (1986) The culture defense in the criminal law, *Harvard Law Review, v.* 99, 6, 1293–311.

Oliver, M. (1988) Immigrant crimes: culture defence – a legal tactic, *Los Angeles Times*, 15 July, Part I: 1.

People v. Klein (1922) 137 N.E. 145, Ill.

People v. Poddar (1972) 103 Cal. Reporter 84, CA Court of Appeals, First District, Dirision 4.

People v. Rhines (1982) 182 Cal. Reporter 478, CA Court of Appeals.

People v. Kimura (1985) No. A-091133, L.A. Super. Ct.

People v. King Moua (1985a) No. 315972-0, Fresno Super. Ct.

People v. Moua (1985b) No. 328106-0, Fresno Super. Ct.

People v. Chen (1989) No. 87-7774, N.Y. Super. Ct.

People v. Aphaylath (1986) 502 N.E. 2d 998, N.Y. Court of Appeals.

People v. Helen Wu (1991) 286 Cal. Reporter 868, CA Court of Appeals.

People v. Hanoukai (1994) No. 56-4533, Van Nuys Super. Ct.

Polsky, A.J. (1991) *The Rise of the Therapeutic State*. Princeton: Princeton University Press.

Poulter, S. (1975) Foreign customs and English criminal law, *International and Comparative Law Quarterly*, 24, 136–40.

Renteln, A.D. (1993) A justification of culture as partial excuse. *Southern California Review of Law and Women's Studies*, 2, 437.

Rieff, P. (1966) *The Triumph of the Therapeutic*. Chicago: University of Chicago Press.

Rosen, L. (1977) The anthropologist as expert witness, *American Anthropologist*, 79, 3, 555–78.

Sams, J. (1986) The availability of the 'cultural defence' as an excuse for criminal behaviour, *Georgia Journal of International and Comparative Law*, v. 16, 2, 335–54.

Sherman, S. (1986) When cultures collide, *California Lawyer*, 6, 1, 32.

Sheybani, M.-M. (1987) Cultural defense: one person's culture in another's crime, *Loyola of Los Angeles International and Comparative Law Journal*, 9, 3, 751–83.

Sykes, C.J. (1992) *A Nation of Victims: the Decay of an American Character*. New York: St. Martin's Press.

Torry, W. (1999) Multicultural jurisprudence and the culture defence, *Journal of Legal Pluralism*, 44: 127–61.

Torry, W. (2000) Culture and individual responsibility: touchstones of the culture defence, *Human Organization*, 59, 1, 58–71.

United States Court of Appeals, District of Columbia Circuit (1967) *Washington v. United States*, Federal Reporter, Second Series 390: 444–62.

Volpp, L. (1994) (Mis)identifying culture: Asian women and the 'cultural defence', *Harvard Women's Law Journal*, 57, 284.

Volpp, L. (1996) Talking 'culture': gender, race, nation and the politics of multiculturalism, *Columbia Law Review*, 96, 1573.

Winkelman, M. (1996) Cultural factors in criminal defence proceedings, *Human Organization*, 55, 2, 154–9.

Woo, D. (1989) The people v. Fumiko Kimura: but which people? *International Journal of the Sociology of Law*, v. 17, 403–28.

Index